VIRTUAL FAITH

VIRTUAL FAITH

The Irreverent Spiritual Quest of Generation X

Tom Beaudoin

○

Foreword by

Harvey Cox

Jossey-Bass Publishers
San Francisco

Substantial discounts on bulk quantities of Jossey-Bass books are available to corporations, professional associations, and other organizations. For details and discount information, contact the special sales department at Jossey-Bass Inc., Publishers (415) 433–1740; Fax (800) 605–2665.

Jossey-Bass Web address: http://www.josseybass.com

 Manufactured in the United States of America on Lyons Falls Turin Book. This paper is acid-free and 100 percent totally chlorine-free.

Credits are on page 211.

Library of Congress Cataloging-in-Publication Data
Beaudoin, Tom.
    Virtual faith : the irreverent spiritual quest of generation x / Tom Beaudoin : foreword by Harvey Cox.—1st ed.
        p. cm.
    Includes bibliographical references and index.
    ISBN 0-7879-3882-3
    1. Generation X–Religious life.   2. Popular culture.
3. Generation X–Conduct of life.   I. title.
BV4529.2.B43   1998
261–DC21   97-33912

FIRST EDITION

HB Printing 10 9 8 7 6 5 4 3 2

CONTENTS

FOREWORD

SUPERFICIAL, EASILY DISTRACTED, ROOTLESS, INSCRUTABLE, self-centered, unfocused, pathetic, plucky, merely confused: all these labels—and many more—have been pinned on the cohort of twenty- and thirty-somethings that some market analyst has dubbed "Generation X." The term refers to the young adults, born in the 1960s and 1970s, who are currently pushing their life cycle predecessors—the overstudied and overanalyzed "baby boomers"—off center stage. The name Generation X seems anomalous but is oddly appropriate. "X" is, after all, the unknown quantity, and this generation has so far slyly eluded categorization. It is not Gertrude Stein's "Lost Generation" of the 1920s. It is not the mixture of dropouts and political activists of the late, lamented, and still-celebrated 1960s. It is, so far, just that—Generation X—and it is useless, by definition, to try to say anything much about them.

It is even riskier to try to say anything about the spiritual life of Generation X. If their ever-shifting tastes in consumer commodities—Patagonia jackets, Macs and PCs, Tevas, rock music on compact discs, and movies about aliens—have been well charted, at least for the moment, their religious proclivities have remained a mystery almost as inscrutable as that of the Holy Trinity. Here is a generation that stays away from most churches in droves but loves songs about God and Jesus, a generation that would score very low on any standard piety scale but at times seems almost obsessed with saints, visions, and icons in all shapes and sizes. These are the young people who, styrofoam cups of cappuccino in hand, crowd around the shelves of New Age spirituality titles in the local book market and post thousands of religious and quasi-religious notes on the bulletin boards in cyberspace. And remember, it was this puzzling and allegedly secular generation that turned out a million of its representatives to welcome Pope John Paul II to that most secular of cities, Paris, France, in the waning weeks of summer 1997. No wonder the classifiers simply throw up their hands in defeat. Like the God envisioned by the mystics of the via negativa, it seems that whatever one says about Generation X, one must immediately say just the opposite in the next breath. Are they the eruption into history of the classical "coincidentia oppositorum"? Or are they merely conspiring to bamboozle anyone who tries to put them in a pigeonhole?

For three decades now I have been teaching courses on religion at Harvard. I have seen generations come and go, change, modulate, and reverse fields. I have always found it hard to characterize a particular student generation or to read its spiritual temperature, but Generation X tops them all in sheer elusiveness. Still, I remain curious, as any teacher ought to be, about who these young people are, where they are coming from, and how I might best teach them. Tom Beaudoin to the rescue. A few years ago, there appeared in one of my classes a young man with bright red hair, a ready smile, and a voracious intellectual appetite who not only was a certified member of Generation X but also seemed to understand his cohort with astonishing clarity. He seemed to be the first to accomplish the difficult feat of self-analysis since Freud himself allegedly pulled off his own self-shrinkage in that musty parlor in Vienna. Beaudoin wrote a couple of excellent papers for me, then went on to graduate school and returned— at my request—to give a guest lecture. His thesis was, and is, that rather than being a horde of scoffers and skeptics, his contemporaries were in fact engaged in a serious spiritual quest. Admittedly, they were often sick of conventional religious institutions and prepackaged pieties. Indeed, they were often hostile to them. But he saw their anger and their rejection as signs of something deeper, a fitfulness that St. Augustine put his finger on many centuries ago when he wrote, "Our hearts are restless until they find their rest in Thee." The only difference is that when these young people find what they are looking for, they still seem restless. But maybe at some level, the bishop of Hippo never found total stability either.

The reason Beaudoin seemed able to plumb the depths, or at least to get under the seeming superficiality, of Generation X is that he used a point of access virtually unavailable to me. He drank in their songs, watched their MTV, and accompanied them around the Internet. He got into their inner space by following them into cyberspace. He uncovered the reverence behind their irreverence and the seriousness under their silliness. In this absorbing book, Beaudoin engaged in a "close reading" of the message Generation Xers send and receive on their favored means of communication. He allows us to step momentarily into the cosmos of ideas and feelings they share and to see their world as they see it. Like some ingenious cryptographer, he sneaks into the signals and codes so that we can all pick up some hint of what is being said.

But is he right? Since roughly three decades gape between my place in the life cycle and theirs, I am hardly the person to make that judgment. All I can say is that not all of his contemporaries in the same cohort perceive things the way he does. When he gave some of the material in this book as an illustrated guest lecture in one of my courses, his presentation started the row of the semester. Some of the students said he hit it right on the head. Others insisted he got it all wrong. But all were fascinated, and just to hold their undivided attention for as long as he did was something of a feat. Whatever other qualities they have, a long attention span is not something often attributed to this generation.

God may be eternal. But Generation X is a moving target. Pieties may be permanent qualities in human life. But the shape they take changes through the years. The Catholic Church and other Churches often officially opposed or discouraged devotional practices that arose among the faithful, only to embrace them eventually and then to prescribe and nurture them. This rocky road to success marked the history, for example, of devotion to the Sacred Heart. Much Marian devotion has gone through the same tortuous cycle. Apparitions at Lourdes and Fatima were viewed at first with considerable disapproval by Rome and the local religious authorities. When reverence for our Lady of Guadalupe first appeared in Mexico in the sixteenth century, it was forbidden by the hierarchy. Later, though, the Guadalupe was accepted, then became the patroness of Mexico. Now whenever the pope visits Mexico, her shrine is his first stop. It is hard to imagine today that Madonna's "Like a Prayer" will one day be accepted by any church as an appropriate devotion. But stranger things have happened.

Has Tom Beaudoin caught a new wave of spirituality at its birthing? Maybe he has. In any case, he enables the reader to peer into a reality that is both religious and secular, both outrageous and touching, both postmodern and—in its own odd way—very traditional. If he is wrong, he is fascinatingly and brilliantly wrong, and no reader will regret taking this trip through the various layers of our contemporary divine comedy with him as their Virgil.

Cambridge, Massachusetts   HARVEY COX
March 1998

To *my parents, Ross and Nata,*

to my sister and brothers,
Ann, Stephen, and John,

and to my partner, Jennifer

For more love than an irreverent soul
could ever have merited

"... he fell on his face and did reverence ..."
—2 Samuel 9:6

"... he fell on his face and laughed ..."
—Genesis 17:17

PREFACE

MY MOST RECENT RELIGIOUS EXPERIENCE happened in the fourth row at the closing performance of *Rent*. On May 25, 1997, the Shubert Theater in Boston was packed with twenty- and thirty-somethings who resonated with the themes of this quintessential GenX musical. Having played in Boston for six months, the cast had established an intimate relationship with the audience, many of whom had attended dozens of shows (I myself went four times). At various moments during the performance, tears streaked the faces of the cast members. At times I would look up through my own damp eyes to see the entire section around me weeping.

During some songs, people raised their hands in the air as if at an evangelical revival. They seemed to acknowledge that the drama—the liturgy—was *about* us and yet *beyond* us, giving meaning to our lives, and life to our fragmented existence. Still, I was astonished to hear a woman spontaneously utter a quiet "amen" after a song. During most of the show, like Teresa of Avila (who had levitational experiences during Communion), I was everywhere but in my seat. I found myself deeply within the liturgy on stage, inside the ritual. (It *was* sacred ritual for my fourth time there, with the script, songs, and movements all established. The ritual was inflected differently each time, though, under the influence of something seemingly beyond the cast.) Like those around me, I heard a religious message in this drama.

There is, of course, a terrific impropriety about all of this. Some will be offended that I call such a scene religious, but impropriety has been a theme of my life and of the life of Generation X, pointing the way to its unique religious style.

GenX, Popular Culture, and Theology

This is a book about impropriety and irreverence, beginning with my fundamental claim that Generation X is—despite and even because of appearances—strikingly religious. I hope to clarify the ways in which we are religious through a theological interpretation of Generation X's popular culture. It will become clear that my interpretation is filtered through two lenses: my own religious journey and my understanding of Generation X.

It may seem odd to examine popular culture to learn about religion, but for Xers, popular culture is a major meaning-making system. Thus, religious statements about the generation must take pop culture into account. For a long time, experiences such as the one with *Rent* have led me to think that many of life's most religious experiences happen outside religious institutions and "official" worship services. As I began to reflect on the history of Generation X, I realized that there are special reasons that this is true for us. Many of us are at arm's length from religious institutions (even those of us who attend services regularly). At the same time, we are nurtured by the amniotic fluid of popular culture with the media as a primary source of meaning. This generation has inherited from its elders many blessings and freedoms, from an adulthood of relative economic prosperity to religious freedom to a lively popular culture. Our generation has also borne the weight of the dysfunctions, mistakes, and failed promises of our elders, so it is unsurprising that hardship and suffering—for which religion provides answers—would be common. A generation on such intimate terms with popular culture is bound to practice religion at least partly in and through this medium. We express our religious interests, dreams, fears, hopes, and desires through popular culture.

In this book, I try to divine what I call a "GenX theology," or a way of thinking religiously about Generation X. I sketch the beginnings of a theology *by, for,* and *about* Generation X, and I attempt to do so in an understandable manner. Theology has an array of arcane jargon and secret handshakes, and I give the reader as much access to its fruits as possible while steering clear of needless academic theology. Although I have sometimes sacrificed nuance, I have tried to compensate by supplying provocative and clear theological interpretations of GenX pop culture.

As far as I am aware, this book is the first sustained attempt to develop a theology about, by, and for Generation X by attending to popular culture. There are currently a few books about GenX and religion and a small mountain of books about fashion, music video, and cyberspace. But there has been very little thinking about the relationship between the lifeblood of the generation—popular culture—and the lifeblood of the human spirit—religion.

As I explore this relationship as a western pioneer (a popular metaphor for explorers in cyberspace), I hope readers will point out where my wagon wheels are slipping off track. The cultural landscape appears again as new, and I have only begun to measure the terrain. The territory of pop culture may prove to be divinely fecund for the pioneer studying religion, not least because a sacred cavalcade first charted the terrain. God's "wagon tracks," writes the biblical Psalmist, "overflow with richness" (Psalm 65:11). Given its potential richness, there is much more work to be done on GenX, pop culture, and religion.

Audience

This book is meant for the faithful, as well as those who consider themselves unfaithful. For those not familiar with theology, I hope this book will provide a meaningful introduction to ways of thinking about culture in a theological context.

For Generation Xers, my intention is to start a conversation that is not yet happening on a popular level. Ideally, the book will inspire Xers to begin thinking about religion in a new way. By commenting on the extent to which the generation is already irreverently religious, I am offering Xers an opportunity to kickstart their spiritual lives. Xers may find a new theological approach to the popular culture with which they are so familiar and might reflect on the extent to which our pop culture allows us to express our unique way of being religious. I also encourage Xers to reclaim religious traditions without relinquishing the significance or irreverence of religious life in popular culture.

Baby boomers, of course, laid the groundwork for a thriving and image-oriented popular culture, and this book is for them, as well. It is for our many "elders" (baby boomers and older) who seek to understand Generation X, specifically in regard to its cultural or religious character. The media's simplistic caricatures of Generation X have yet to relate something substantial about this generation to its elders, particularly in regard to GenX's unique religiousness. As I have spoken to different groups about the ideas in this book, one of the unexpected fruits has been the intergenerational discussion that has begun about religion and culture between parents, grandparents, children and grandchildren, or even Xer coworkers or coreligionists. Xers and their elders have much to learn from each other in this regard. Boomers will recognize some of their own religiousness in my Xer interpretation, but will also see a growing edge of GenX religiousness.

I write not only as a theologian interested in religion and culture but also as a minister and educator. Because my readers might include ministers and educators, I offer suggestions about GenX ministry. I also highlight what might be learned from GenX religiosity and how to make use of popular culture in ministry. A surprising discovery during my talks with religious groups is that much of what GenX pop culture offers religiously is eminently applicable to ministries outside the generation. Those looking for a way to get Xers into their religious institution should be forewarned, however; I ask my generation to assume a "traditional" religious responsibility but only after taking a fresh look at tradition and taking seriously the religious meanings offered by the popular culture.

Finally, I write for my friends and colleagues in the academy or seminaries who realize how critical it is to understand the relationship between religion and culture. I believe we are at the beginning of an avalanche of books about pop culture and theology, and I look forward to a discussion and clarification of this work in regard to the theological, sociological, cultural, and methodological questions it raises.

I maintain throughout this book that Generation X has something to offer religious institutions and that religious institutions have something to offer the generation. The back-and-forth dynamic is important. The old way in which institutions related to people of faith with a paternalistic, condescending set of assumptions should no longer exist. Religious institutions must learn as well as teach. For the generation, the challenge is the reverse. A continued ironic distance from institutions and religious traditions undercuts an area in which Xers are needed the most and, in truth, insufficiently honors traditions to which Xers owe a great deal. The generation itself must learn as well as teach.

It is often said by (usually much older) pundits that every generation must pass through a time of trial and that the angst, disillusionment, and challenges to religious authority that characterize much of GenX culture are "just a phase." Every cohort of adolescents and young adults, so the argument goes, has to meet the world swinging, wreaking some havoc as a way of defining themselves. Aside from the obvious rhetorical dismissiveness of these claims, the pundits who offer up such opinions often forget one important thing: although it may be true that every youthful generation concocts its own form of rebellion, exactly what *fuels* that questioning, that rebellion, even that revolution, changes from era to era, from culture to culture.

Perhaps what is most interesting theologically about GenX culture is not that the generation is challenging the presuppositions of its religious elders but rather *why* and *how* we are doing so. In the why and the how of this *kairos,* this time of graced opportunity, GenX distinguishes itself from previous generations. In doing so, it offers a unique theological challenge to those who come before and after.

Plan of the Book

All theology is to some extent autobiography, and my readers will likely
soon discern that this book emerges from my love for this generation, my
own spiritual journey, and my passion for theology. It draws on my experience as a member of the generation, my theological and pedagogical
training, and my hands-on work in education and ministry. The generation at large has also been a significant resource. In 1994, when I began
taking notes for this book, I conducted surveys about attitudes toward
pop culture and religion with hundreds of Xers. The past three years have
also produced dozens, perhaps hundreds, of informal conversations with
Xers in coffee shops, concerts, malls, churches, synagogues, convenience
stores, public restrooms (believe it), and street corners. Although I have
incorporated many insights from my interviews and discussions into the
text, this book is emphatically not a formal sociological study. It is a way
of interrogating and interpreting popular culture religiously. (Readers
interested in my method of interpretation should consult the Appendix at
the end of the book.)

I am not simply offering a description and analysis of Generation X
popular culture. Readers interested in formal analyses of popular culture
will find many other books available in sociology or cultural studies. What
I offer in this book is a *theological interpretation* of GenX pop culture. It
is theological because it is concerned with the religiousness of a generation and its culture. Its object is GenX pop culture because that is where
I think Generation X has implicitly displayed its lived theology for at least
the past two decades of its young life. This lived theology is what I am
calling an "irreverent spirituality."

The book opens with a narrative of my own life as a way of illuminating themes that make Generation X distinct. In Chapter One, I focus specifically on the ways in which religion and popular culture have been
ever-present and increasingly intertwined in my life. Chapters Two and
Three investigate the meaning of the term *Generation X* and sketch the
theology that makes my approach to popular culture possible. Chapters
Four through Seven move deeply into my interpretation of pop culture,
each anchored with a primary theme that I find in pop culture: anti-
institutionalism, experience, suffering, and ambiguity. I not only highlight
pop culture evidence for each theme but also cite implications for contemporary religious practice. Chapters Eight and Nine explore the style
and meaning of religious practice in Xers' heavily "virtual" culture, the
challenge for Xers of acknowledging and bearing religious tradition,

and—given the lived GenX theology I distill from popular culture—suggestions for ministering to the generation and for Xers themselves. Chapter Ten attempts to stitch GenX, pop culture, and religion together in a summary of the book's irreverent journey.

Clarity and Conversation

There is no good reason that our generation should continue to avoid talking publicly about religious questions. History tells us that the public square need not be so naked of theological discussion. The great fourth-century theologian Gregory of Nyssa (in modern-day Turkey), a married bishop, reported the extent to which theological questions were discussed on the streets all around him. Those were heady theological times, and one could hardly venture around town, he wrote, without becoming embroiled in a complex theological debate about the "nature" of Christ and Christ's relationship to God. "If in this city [Constantinople] you ask anyone for change, he will discuss with you whether the Son is begotten or unbegotten. If you ask about the quality of bread, you will receive the answer that 'the Father is greater, the Son is less.' If you suggest that a bath is desirable, you will be told that 'there was nothing before the Son was created'" (cited in Frend, 1994, pp. 174–175).

Upon reading such passages, we often laugh dismissively or simply wonder in disbelief at so much popular preoccupation with such a "useless" subject. Yet this popular preoccupation is one of my visions for Generation X. How I would love to walk through Harvard Square, Haight-Ashbury, the clubs of Seattle, the parks of Berkeley, the jazz bars of Kansas City, the coffeehouses and GenX watering holes across America, and hear theological conversation, whether sophisticated or amateur, distant or committed, for the sake of our generation's spiritual edification. My challenge to Generation X is a call to theological clarity. My exhortation is similar to the one that theologian Friedrich Schleiermacher (1996, p. 44) made two centuries ago: "If only you had the religion you could have and only were conscious of what you already do have!"

Like any talk about God or religion, this book is expansive in its intentions and yet limited in what it can finally say with certainty. I am *not* seeking some "original" or "final" meaning in the relationship among GenX, theology, and pop culture. I seek to strike these three areas together and observe the sparks that fly, to be responsible and transgressive at once, and ultimately to show that this generation—my generation—has already been living a practical theology manifest in its popular culture. I try to shine the light of theological reflection onto the shadows where I sense this implicit theology lurking. As in music videos, cyberspace, and fashion, however, I am only able to capture the lived theology of Generation X in transition, to inspect a few stilled frames in a moving reel. I have taken up only one discrete "bit" of GenX data; it awaits correlation with other interpretations. In this way, my project is incomplete, which is the way I can be most faithful to my generation—a generation whose mark, "X," implies an insoluble, elusive quantity.

Much of this book has the flavor of a coffeehouse conversation. This is appropriate, given the genesis of many of its ideas in coffeehouses as I reflected with Xers on religion and pop culture in Boston, Kansas City, Santa Cruz, Palo Alto, New York, and in on-line interactions around the country. These discussions bore out the biblical proverb "As iron sharpens iron, one person sharpens the wits of another" (Proverbs 27:17).

Some generalizations are necessary as I describe Generation X throughout the book. Constant insertion of qualifiers such as "some" or "many" would make reading tedious. The reader can assume that my comments about Xers apply in varying degrees to each member of the generation. Cumulatively, however, I think my interpretation resonates with a substantial part of the generation, even if each particular GenX reference does not meaningfully describe or interpret the experience of each GenXer.

It is important to note that I do not intend to attribute *any* religious motivations to artists or any other producers of popular culture. If I do assign responsibility to particular artists for religious ideas, it is merely as a form of shorthand, to keep from constantly writing "in *my* theological interpretation. . . ." It is also worth noting that most lyrics for the music videos I discuss are absent from this book. Having been denied permission to use them (with the exception of R.E.M.), and respecting the rights of artists to control the use of their work, I have refrained from quoting lyrics. I encourage readers of this book to look up the lyrics for the videos I discuss.

My theological interpretation of popular culture is errant, over interpreted, serious, soulful, outrageous, creative, partial, associative, irreligious, ridiculous, and spiritual—like our culture, like our lives. It is a holy meandering across the ephemeral surfaces and into the surprising depths of pop culture. It is just this irreverence of interpretation that makes mine a GenX work, even a religious work. Like the rabbinic tradition of playful interpretation that produced the Talmud (although with slightly less religious authority), I press the weight of theological imagination hard onto the text and try to read the Spirit's imprint.

Somerville, Massachusetts   TOM BEAUDOIN
February 7, 1998
520ᵗʰ Anniversary of the Birth of Saint Thomas More

THE AUTHOR

TOM BEAUDOIN spends much of his time bridging the worlds of theology, popular culture, and Generation X. Born in 1969, right in the middle of Generation X, he was raised on a diet of video games, MTV, and Catholicism. After an award-winning stint as a public high school teacher (and an ignoble career as an altar boy), he earned his Master of Theological Studies at Harvard University School of Divinity. It is there, working with Harvey Cox and in conversation with fellow Xers, that he began to sift out the religious qualities of his generation's popular culture. He is currently working toward a Ph.D. in Religion and Education at Boston College, concentrating on the uses of postmodernism for Catholic theology and religious education. Holding together GenX concerns, pop culture messages, and theological commitments, he constantly shuttles between the church and the academy. Active in ministry as a religious educator and lay preacher, he refuses to separate theology and ministry. His young life has included volunteering as a soldier in the Israeli Defense Force, surviving Woodstock '94, and a continuing role as bassist in the rock band e(X)-nihilo. He lives with his spouse, Jennifer Watts, in Somerville, Massachusetts, where he continues to write on religion and culture.

ACKNOWLEDGMENTS

I WOULD LIKE TO REVERENCE all those who fed this book's theological irreverence. In the early stages of the project, that included my unforgettable students at Lee's Summit High School, and my "Jesus and MTV" working group at Harvard in fall 1994. I am particularly grateful to Theresa Rusho, whose media savvy was continually helpful. Ross Beaudoin, Harvey Cox, Chris Vogt, Peter Bebergal, Amelia Dunlop, Rick Kohut, and Nick Davis all read early drafts of the manuscript and offered support and helpful criticism. Ongoing conversations with Loye Ashton, Ted Trost, Thomas Groome, Margaret Guider, Kurt Shaw, Robert Ludwig, Nancy Fraley, Tito Cruz, and Paul O'Connor enriched me theologically, musically, pedagogically, and spiritually.

Special thanks for the guidance of Darren Hall and Sarah Polster at Jossey-Bass, who took a chance on an unknown theologian/educator and provided the perfect mix of affirmation and provocation. Don Cutler, my agent, gave me insightful theological direction from a different generational viewpoint and was patient and gracious with this young author.

Thanks to all those whose irreligious character convinced me of God's ability to unsettle every stability, including those Xers I have talked with over the last several years and the dozens at coffee shops who delayed, and inspired, my work (as well as Brad the gothic cab driver). Grateful thanks are also due for inspiration along the way to the Chrisman High School class of 1987; the University of Missouri at Kansas City class of 1992; the Harvard Divinity School class of 1996; my current colleagues and teachers at Boston College; and my Catholic community, the Paulist Center. I would also like to thank John Beavindoodin, Mina, and Daisy for their inspiration. I could not have written without brief rests, and Cybersmith in Cambridge was a daily pilgrimage for several rounds of *Quake*.

My family, who will recognize my autobiographical fingerprints throughout the book, deserves thanks and praise for giving the ideal amount of familyness that I wish everyone could have. Finally, I am grateful to my beloved partner and best friend Jennifer Watts, who has not only read drafts and shared conversations about these ideas for two-and-a-half years but reminds me daily of the meaning of sacramentality and the significance of irreverence.

VIRTUAL FAITH

PART ONE

WHY RELIGION STILL MATTERS

GenX, POP CULTURE, AND THE SEARCH FOR GOD

A GenX Journey

LIVING ON THE BOUNDARY BETWEEN
RELIGION AND CULTURE

"ALL I WANT TO DO IS TO HOLD OUT until I'm thirty," the character Ivan laments in Fyodor Dostoyevsky's *Brothers Karamazov* (1993, p. 302).

I can sympathize.

I wasn't always certain I would live for three decades. Even now, from almost thirty years' distance, I imagine my birth year of 1969 as the eye of a cultural hurricane, surrounded on all sides by turbulence and destruction.

Of the heroes that were exalted during my childhood, almost all were dead before I was in grade school. Icons of model Americans swirled around in this hurricane, heroes and events living on in nostalgia and media memory. In the few years preceding my birth, John F. Kennedy, Martin Luther King, Jr., Robert F. Kennedy, and Malcolm X were murdered. During my early childhood, the Kent State massacre, the Watergate crisis, and the Vietnam War etched themselves not only into the history textbooks but also into the heart of a little boy—and the consciousness of a generation of children. When Neil Armstrong walked on the moon, I was two months old. Later that summer, Woodstock happened and drugs killed Janis Joplin and Jimi Hendrix. All of these "events" were our parents' stories, but our symbols. These symbols were not our own creation; they were strictly media references.

The cultural hurricane that preceded the peaceful year of 1969—at least in my memory—continued to create disarray in the following decades. Three decades later, the late 1960s can be seen as the fulcrum of a historical seesaw, halfway between the rise of the civil rights movement and the decline of affirmative action, the midpoint of the nuclear age, halfway between the emergence and conclusion of the Cold War.

I was born in this still moment, the hurricane's eye, on April 27, 1969. Much later, I discovered that my birth year fell in the middle of what demographers and cultural critics labeled "Generation X."

Entering a Turbulent World: 1960s and 1970s

I grew up not only in a "middling" chronology but within a middle-American geography. In the heart of the United States, in Kansas City, Missouri, I awoke to the world in a fragile urban setting with racial strife literally a stone's throw from my delivery room.

Despite this turmoil, my parents greeted my birth with words of hope. My father carefully inscribed a poem in powder blue ink on white posterboard, framed by dangling blue and yellow crepe paper. When my mother returned home from the hospital, he presented her with the only poem I've known him to write.

A MOTHER AND CHILD

A Son with a smile
Bring new spring flowers and leaves
To a World brought to its knees
By winter and hardness and cold.
Mother. Son.
A world new begun.
Thank you God.

At age eight, I began to fathom the interrelationship between God and the world that was implicit in the poem. Around that time, my father began taking me with him on regular visits to the Kansas City Municipal Correctional Institution, a large local prison. My father, who would soon be ordained a Catholic deacon, had been working in prison ministry for several years. Under moderate surveillance by armed prison guards, my father and I gathered behind bulletproof doors. I watched him read the Bible and distribute Communion to the inmates. From a young age, it seemed natural to me that the "Church" existed not only in the suburban building where we worshiped on weekends but also amid flaking, lime-colored walls and slightly dangerous, intriguing prisoners with names like Mick and Spacey.

Many from my generation had less familial or religious care in their early years than I did in this prison ministry; at a young age, they learned to care for themselves, as did I. With both parents working, I was a latchkey child by third grade. My daily grade school homecoming was a five-part ritual: ride the school bus home, let myself in, lock the door behind me, grab some cookies and milk, and park in front of the television. Every day I baby-sat my sister and two brothers until my parents returned from work, usually exhausted.

The latchkey childhood of my generational peers was central in establishing our deep relationship with popular culture—largely through the media. In loco parentis, television provided daily entertainment for those who had to fill time between the end of the school day and the return of working parents. My generation later reported that we spent more time with the television than with our parents during childhood (Gross and Scott, 1990).

The importance of the latchkey experience in shaping my generation during its most malleable years can hardly be overstated. Massive amounts of unsupervised childhood time enabled our addiction to and indulgence in popular culture, forming habits and tastes that have endured for decades and that may last a lifetime. (It is no wonder that we can effortlessly recite such media trivia as plots and theme songs from television shows; they were seared into our minds during childhood.) This entry into the world of pop culture at such a young age is one reason our generation is unique. Whereas baby boomers also had an intimate relationship with popular and media culture, GenXers found it at an earlier, more critical age and without the familial supervision of previous generations.

Popular culture, particularly music, was omnipresent from my earliest years. This was true in both my public and private worlds. Popular songs were the typical curriculum of my elementary school music classes, and show-and-tell enabled us to share our favorite records. Rainy day indoor recess was an ideal excuse to roll out the vintage 1965, ten-pound record player from the janitor's closet and play popular 45s. Several of my junior high and high school teachers even allowed popular music to be played during classes, while we were supposedly working diligently on assignments.

In fifth grade, I discovered a reel-to-reel tape machine in the dank recesses of an old house into which our family had recently moved. For three full hours one summer afternoon, I crooned "Cat Scratch Fever" by rock star Ted Nugent into the machine, exhausting not only myself but the entire reel of tape. Over dinner that evening, I played five minutes of the performance before my parents mercifully ended my singing career by unplugging the machine. My experience was not unique, however. The accessibility of cheap recording devices made it possible to "privatize" popular culture. Taping one's favorite music (with cassettes, not reel-to-reel tapes) and displaying pop culture expertise became a sort of pop "performance" in itself. It was a way to display commitments, ideals, and politics, however immature and incomplete these were in grade school.

By third grade, my friends were bringing handheld electronic games to school, introducing me to another piece of popular culture that soon competed for allowance money. I was enchanted by tiny glowing green screens containing minuscule, darting blips. The portability of the new technology meant that we could play these games everywhere: on the bus, at assemblies, and between classes. These games encouraged technological literacy (one hallmark of my generation) and gave us greater access to what had been previously considered "diversions," thereby blurring the distinction between work and play.

Access to "diversions" meant that the separation became fuzzy not only between work and play but also between different technologies (foreshadowing what would happen in cyberspace more than a decade later). The sudden accessibility and affordability of handheld calculators in the 1970s shifted their status from luxury purchases to math class requirements—and this while many of my math teachers still hung chalkboard-sized charts on the wall illustrating the proper use of a slide rule. Subverting this technology while exploring its diversionary value (another characteristic of our cohort), my schoolmates and I quickly discovered that we could turn our calculators upside down. Discreetly tapping messages to each other, we read the upside-down numbers as letters. My most cunning friends developed complex algorithms to create short phrases.

When I was in sixth grade, from 1980 to 1981, the calculator morphed into a computer in my own hands. To keep a friend and me from becoming bored (and getting into trouble), our resourceful teacher assigned us the daunting task of building a computer from a do-it-yourself kit. After weeks of stripping wire and slotting sharp metal brackets into odd crevices, we created a computer (a glorified calculator) that could play five different number games. Although the result was anticlimactic, I sensed that something numinous and full of potential lay in front of me, slumbering inside shiny copper intestines and boxy, plastic skin. The technological world was opening before me.

If technological literacy is one hallmark of my generation, tolerance of religious diversity is another, although it is one I did not learn until I went to Catholic school. I began my formal education in public schools and attended Catholic schools from second through fifth grades. Only about half of my classmates at Holy Family Catholic School in Independence, Missouri, were Catholic. The rest hailed from various Protestant traditions scattered around the city. Although we were anything but a group of young theologians engaged in an ecumenical dialogue, the exposure to "otherness" that is so typical of the generation was there for me in the form of religious difference. I was aware that not everyone could participate in our celebrations of the Mass and that some were awkwardly sitting or kneeling at the "wrong" times. A few friends chose to stay back in the classroom, exempting themselves from Communion, which is the most communal demonstration of Christian identity (ironically for Catholics alone, I realized).

Like many families in the late 1970s, my Catholic parents were outpriced by their own local Catholic school. With four children in 1980 they were struggling to keep a grip on the greasy rungs of the socioeconomic ladder—to stay in the middle class, ultimately. My father took second and third jobs, and my mother juggled full or part-time work with raising four children. Although both of my parents worked, we just scraped by from week to week. As was true for many families, the hyperinflation of the decade affected our dinner table. To help my family survive, I enrolled in a federal free lunch program at school and we moved into government-sponsored public housing. (With our generation, and for the first time in American history, poverty was more common among youth than the elderly, as Geoffrey Holtz has noted [1995, pp. 45–50]). By fifth grade, I was wearing generic clothing brands (a minor scandal in my suburban milieu). I struggled to accept that I could not compete with my fashion-conscious peers, who increasingly derived their tastes in bodily adornment from our favorite movies and television shows.

Enduring the Crisis Years: 1980s and 1990s

If I was born into the eye of the hurricane, I increasingly felt its swirling winds in the next decade. Our culture seemed to be limping through crises mirrored by my own unsteady negotiation of adolescence.

A Theme of Absence

From the early 1980s to early 1990s, I (and the majority of our generation) struggled through teenage years. Given that adolescence is such a formative period, the more the 1980s and early 1990s (a period I simply refer to as "the 1980s") are excavated and interpreted, the more that era will yield insight into our generation's relationship with religion and culture. My peers demonstrate their close relationship to the decade by minting the era as a common coin of conversation. Whether for nostalgic or psychotherapeutic reasons, we constantly return to the culture of the decade out of ambivalence about our experience of the 1980s. We have unresolved feelings about the values that characterized the decade, particularly as experienced intimately in our fractured families.

One of the great mysteries of my childhood was why so many of my friends left town every other weekend. My naïveté was dispelled one day when a gentle "room mother" explained divorce informally to our class. I slowly realized that all my friends who went away on weekends were not simply vacationing in the Ozarks; they were visiting their father or mother. By high school, I found myself among a minority of friends with "original" parents at home. "Mom's boyfriend" and "Dad's girlfriend" were common—if awkward—points of reference in our conversations.

The tragic tone for this period was established in the popular 1980 movie *Kramer Versus Kramer*, a sensitive story that Xers did not need to witness in a theater. We knew from "real life" about parents who could no longer live together and about children disoriented by the rending of the household. With about half of all marriages breaking up in the 1980s, Xers not only personally learned about the fragility of commitment but were also forced into a premature—and untutored—adulthood. The ease with which my friends could talk about divorce, sex, and other adult issues astounded me. Their childhood experiences of poverty, latchkey independence, and divorced and "blended" families all hyperaccelerated the maturation process. These influences also led to an immersion in popular culture as both substitute parent and surrogate minister. In fact, as churches ostracized the divorced mothers of many of my friends, these women frequently left their church communities. This situation made many of my peers further alienated from religious institutions.

Our fragile families seemed to be a microcosm of (as my father wrote) a world "brought to its knees." It was a world—or at least a nation—under the spell of *Star Wars,* which was both the title of a blockbuster 1977 science fiction film and the name of President Ronald Reagan's antinuclear missile defense system. My immediate surroundings were ground zero in a nuclear attack; Kansas City, Missouri, and Lawrence, Kansas, were obliterated in the television film *The Day After*. Our generation's nuclear fears were concentrated in this television event. This apocalyptic movie united both aspects of *Star Wars,* the terrifying and the fictional, in a media spectacle that aired on November 20, 1983, to a hundred million viewers. (As evidence that the gap between simulation and reality was rapidly closing, especially in media culture, and as proof of the palpable popular fear of nuclear war, Secretary of State George Schultz appeared on television following *The Day After* to assuage fears about the horrors becoming reality.)

In my high school in Independence, Missouri, and across America, counselors were provided during the days after the movie to ease our generation's anxieties. The anxiety had physical and psychological effects: several of my friends suffered various degrees of depression or feelings of hopelessness during the 1980s as a result of aching apprehension about nuclear warfare and the likely forfeit of their future. At least as troubling, and rarely noted, were the millions of Xers who subtly incorporated the probability of impending annihilation into their ways of living.

Many had long prepared for this generationwide moment of despair and angst by viewing "disaster preparedness" (read: nuclear survival) films in school. In health classes, I watched grainy black-and-white movies displaying proper ways to store food in a fallout shelter and illustrating charts about the number of days before a human could "safely" return outside after a nuclear blast (we memorized charts detailing distances from the theoretical blast site). The degree to which we could calmly assimilate instructions about fallout shelters and radioactivity into our lives was a sobering measure of the degree to which we accepted radical uncertainty about our future.

In the 1980s, the media gave my generation access to the world's fragility and the possibility of disaster. An uncanny concatenation of apocalyptic events—a series of natural and human disasters—etched themselves into our (un)consciousness, contributing to the dubious character of our future. Earthquakes, air travel disasters, AIDS, terrorism, environmental catastrophes, and even a major volcanic eruption on the mainland United States all contributed to an apocalyptic atmosphere during our 1980s adolescence.

Memorable among these events was the explosion of the *Challenger* space shuttle on January 28, 1986. A junior in high school, I arrived to my last class of the day to find fellow students huddled silently around a tiny portable television. For the next fifty minutes, we watched replay after replay of the explosion, each time secretly hoping the outcome would be different, that the tragedy was one more illusion. When the dismissal bell rang, the fifteen hundred students in my high school walked numbly to our buses, a massive funeral procession. During the slow-motion ride home, as some spoke in hushed tones, I sat silently with my forehead against the window, not sure how this could happen and wondering what it meant. Things were slipping; I felt a great unhinging around me.

This great unhinging also seemed to delink people in my generation from one another. The dearth of unifying causes became evident to me in a particular moment at the Woodstock '94 concert, in Saugerties, New York. A speaker from an environmental activist group found it impossible to win the attention of the assembled throng, made up mainly of Xers. Many tried to shout him down. As one member of our generation later put it, it is no longer any use "fantasizing about the revolution, which, if you studied the 1960s, you know will never come" (Roberts, 1996).

We were the first American generation in at least a century to lack a common cause. Previous generations had the Vietnam War, World War II, the Great Depression, and World War I as rallying points. In contrast, Generation X reached adulthood in the absence of a theme, and even with a theme of absence.

This was not made vivid to me until I realized just what our generation was missing. I took a course with Professor Harvey Cox while I was studying at Harvard for a master's degree in theology. Cox lectured one day about Jesus, nonviolence, and Martin Luther King (Cox had participated in the civil rights movement with King). While he played a tape of King's speaking, Cox sat down behind the lectern. With his elbow on the desk and hand on his forehead, he quietly wept, remembering King. The rest of us, born after King's death, listened as his disembodied voice echoed through our classroom. When the tape ended, Cox stood up with some effort and leaned on the lectern. "That's all," he said to no one in particular, staring at the floor. The class was spellbound. In that moment, I realized that my generation would never weep in public for the memory of a great leader or a great movement.

Much of my generation's antipathy to grand social movements comes from opposition to the idealism of the baby boomers in the 1960s. Although the young adults of that era won tremendous gains for many previously excluded members of American society, the decade also failed on many counts to live up to its promises. One generation's gain was another's loss; whereas the previous generation saw huge advances, our generation witnessed many disappointments. Propelled by mighty ideals, the baby boomers undertook organized social actions. In contrast, my generation inherited not free love but AIDS, not peace but nuclear anxiety, not cheap communal lifestyles but crushing costs of living, not free teach-ins but colleges priced for the aristocracy.

The baby boomers cannot be blamed for the unhinging of society, however. The dynamic of admiration for and repugnance at the previous generation is common enough in American history. As Baptist theologian Langdon Gilkey writes, "It is an all-too-familiar experience how each generation inherits from its fathers and mothers a confused, warped world which it tends to detest and repudiate; and then thirty years later it finds itself—to its horror—bequeathing the same sort of mess, in different colors and shapes perhaps, to its own sons and daughters" (1981, p. 50).

We were bequeathed a culture in crisis.

A generation born during Watergate, nourished on the stories of baby boomer protest against "the war," disillusioned by the rollback of civil rights in the 1980s and 1990s, and exposed to the Iran-Contra hearings in the 1980s had little trust left in the possibility of a benevolent government.

By the end of the 1980s, our heads were spinning with the political changes afoot. At the same time, technology enabled us to have solidarity with other young adults around the world. In 1989, I witnessed two epic events: the Tiananmen Square massacre and the fall of the Berlin Wall. Although I was not physically present for either event, something of their historical magnitude and drama pulsed my way over the Internet. I sat in disbelief at my computer as text from friends in China scrolled furiously before me, telling of tanks that rolled past their rooms and of students who were gunned down. I also communicated through e-mail with friends while the Berlin Wall was reduced to souvenir rubble. West German correspondents wrote me with fingers still tingling from taking a sledgehammer to Cold War concrete. As witness to—or vicarious participant in—these events, our generation seems to have had a keen sense of the instability of the political world, but not as much about its hopefulness, its possibilities.

Technologized (Un)Reality

Technology was one key to forming a shared generational culture amid a world of tension and ambiguity. Access to cheap personal computers grew as the generation came of age; for us, computer skills are commonly a second (or third or fourth) language. By the time I was in high school, mastery of computer languages was as important as fluency in French, German, or Spanish.

My affinity—and much of the generation's—for computer technology arose hand-in-joystick with an indulgence in video games. The popularity of video games must be seen in the context of the previously described technological developments. Video gaming was (and still is) largely a matter of reality imitation, of inhabiting a virtual world (hence the popularity of fantasy role-playing games during our adolescence). Comfort in the virtual world characterized our generation from its youngest days.

I was one of the few kids in my neighborhood who did not have cable television early in the decade, so I watched at friends' houses. There I entered the video-music world of MTV, or music television, and experienced the image-rich overflow of twenty-four-hour programming in the mesmerizing medium of hyperquick cuts and odd, ever-varied camera angles.

The remote control that accompanied cable television was a revelatory piece of technology. At first, "remotes" were tethered to the television or cable box by a thin wire. As technology progressed through the 1980s, the cord disappeared and the remote control became more "remote" from what it "controlled." Symbolically, our umbilical cord to reality became decreasingly visible, its location only roughly estimable.

Cable television was only one entry into the fantastic explosion of popular culture, however. On Sunday mornings, I tuned in to the radio show *American Top Forty* to learn which songs were most popular that week. Personal stereos, or "boom boxes," were suddenly omnipresent, supplanting transistor radios and catalyzing this immersion into popular music.

MTV constantly threatened to supplant radio. Although it was merely one cable channel among dozens when it appeared in 1981, it quickly became the generation's medium par excellence. On lazy summer afternoons and after returning from school throughout my junior high and high school years, I (and fellow latchkey alumni) took in music videos. MTV became a source of news and a world of meaning all its own.

But our visual culture was hardly restricted to MTV. Thanks to cable television and a profusion of movie screens in suburban malls, our generation became immersed in the world of popular film. Recycling dialogue from movies and television was a prominent form of humor and communal bonding. Celluloid indulgence was made easier by the affordability of the videocassette recorder (VCR) to middle-class families and young adults.

Television assumed such an important popular cultural role in the 1980s that many educators exhorted parents to restrict children's viewing hours. The prevalence of television fascinated or abhorred my teachers. It seemed that each of them, from grade school through high school, took a survey about television ownership and viewing in our homes. Every year, my teachers found that we had four or five televisions on average and watched about three hours per day.

Our indulgence in popular culture also assumed other incarnations, such as comic books, cartoons, clothing, fantasy gaming, sports, and concerts. This signal element of the 1980s, the omnipresence of popular culture, had at least as profound an impact on GenX as any of the social or political events happening "outside" the popular culture system.

With the ascendance of popular culture, the 1980s gave access to what has been called a culture of simulation. The simulation (or imitation) of reality found in video culture—for example in film, music video, and video games—was of a piece with the rise of lip-synching, the Internet, and virtual reality. These latter media were forms of not-quite-real communication, usually measured against "real" communication. Alongside what we used to think of as exclusively "real," its imitation gained prominence.

Spirituality and Music, Hold the Religion

My increasing immersion in popular culture was coupled with a diminishing religious participation over the course of the 1980s. Televangelists' clanging decline and fall and the mainline Churches' more silent slip into irrelevance hastened my departure. Many members of our generation who belonged to various religious traditions (myself included) waded into pools of agnosticism, apathy, or cynicism as the gap grew between the preaching and practice of religious institutions.

Members of our generation expressed their cynicism about religion by assuming one of two stances: either playfully ironic or completely dismissive. I found these postures appropriate, as Churches seemed laughably out of touch; they had hopelessly droll music, antediluvian technology, retrograde social teaching, and hostile or indifferent attitudes toward popular culture. For my peers, this distancing from religion often wasn't new at all, because their families had treated religion as a disposable accessory. Many baby boomers had kept institutional religion at arm's length until midlife. For their children, GenXers, the step from religion-as-accessory to religion-as-unnecessary was a slight shuffle, not a long leap.

What intrigued me by the late 1980s was the way Xers remained ambivalent or hostile toward "religion" in general but still claimed a sense of "spirituality" in their lives. Wasn't this counter to all we had experienced? These spiritualities, though varied, often consisted of a hodgepodge of theological symbols and traditions. I myself read theology from a variety of sources: the Catholic Hans Küng, the Jewish Martin Buber, and the Protestant Søren Kierkegaard.

I began to notice how the popular culture seemed suffused with religious references. Our popular songs, music videos, and movies were about sin, salvation, and redemption, among other themes. Contrary to common perception, we appeared to have a very theological culture. Perhaps we were even a religious generation. I started to suspect that popular culture increasingly trumped institutional religion in attracting Xers; we dedicated much more time to pop culture, and it had vastly more religious content that was relevant to our generation. Could it be that popular culture was our religious arena?

In sum, by the late 1980s, I was awash in the popular culture and alienated from official religion. Despite all this, I still considered myself unmistakably "spiritual." By this, I meant that I thought about religion, I thought there was more to life than materialism, and I pieced together a set of beliefs from whatever religious traditions I was exposed to at the time. I considered myself a little Jewish, Protestant, and Catholic all at once.

In the late 1980s, I began to reconsider religion, tentatively reentering more organized, "churchy" religion by way of pop culture; during my last year of high school, I played bass guitar in a Christian rock band. Under the sponsorship of an evangelical Christian church, we played Christian songs, trying hard to "sound secular" but equally hard not to "be secular." On a bus trip to one of our biggest shows, a Fellowship of Christian Athletes conference somewhere in the great Midwest, the guitarist and I sat in the back seat listening to secular hard rock bands on our headphones. Something about that music spoke to me more deeply than the Christian artists I was supposed to be emulating. This insight scandalized a few of the church directors of our band, but this was not my first irreverence in this context. During one rehearsal, the guitarist and drummer and I broke into a few bars of the rock classic "Sunshine of Your Love" by Cream when we were supposed to be playing a soft rock contemporary Christian ballad. This transgression was revealing, and it required some discipline to avoid such temptations in the future.

During college in Kansas City, I abandoned Christian bands and played in a secular rock band named "Household Word" (unintentional irony: we were virtual unknowns). My experiences playing rock were usually more religious than I had found in most churches. I discovered a sense of spirituality "in the pocket," playing tightly with a drummer. As a bass guitarist, when I am traversing the deep rhythm, riding the low notes, or stomping through a syncopated rumble, *something happens*. After the band's last concert, a woman approached me and said, "You play the bass like it is part of your body." Later I thought, that is the way good religious ritual, or liturgy, works. We move our bodies and souls in harmony with the music, which is in harmony with the Spirit, with God. The spectacular liturgies of rock are part of my continued affinity for arena or stadium rock bands. I treasure the irreverence of this rock religiosity, considering it just as important to my own sense of spirituality as any commitment to an institutional Church.

Experimentation

During my college career, I experimented with spiritualities in cordial relationships with various synagogues and churches. Over the course of five years and two undergraduate degrees, I regularly attended a reform synagogue, a moderate Southern Baptist church, and a progressive Catholic church. At Sabbath synagogue services, I felt the aching and ancient pulse of Judaism. On mysterious Friday nights, yarmulke constantly slipping off my head, I tasted reverence for the holy in venerable text, tradition, and land. More than anything, I learned about the faithful perseverance of God from the audacious, sheer tenacity of Jewish faith, which overwhelmed me in its radical contrast to my own lack of spiritual resolve.

For a time, I was dating a Jewish woman and reading Hugh Schonfield's *Passover Plot,* a book purporting to expose the inconsistencies in Christian scripture and striving to show what a radical and unfaithful break Christianity made from Judaism. I was not well enough informed to be a critical reader, but the book and the relationship opened my eyes and heart to the spiritual parentage of Christianity. I was introduced to rabbinic tradition, the Talmud, and a religious zeal for the state of Israel (an experience that seemed infinitely more wholesome than suburban churches' misplaced obsession with their wealthy and manicured grounds). Once, the woman I was dating asked me a question that changed the entire course of my religious seeking in an instant: "How can you read the Gospels if you don't know Judaism?" How could I have been a "Christian" for over twenty years and never asked such a question?

After taking courses in Jewish history and theology, I made my first pilgrimage to Israel in 1990. I went as a volunteer soldier in the Israeli Defense Force, so Israel almost entirely paid for my trip, which gave me ample opportunity to travel. (A friend and I sold boxes of "Jerusalem Dirt" to friends back home to help defray other expenses.) On a remote military base in the Golan Heights, near the Syrian border, I was the only Christian (however uncertain) among hundreds of American and Israeli Jewish women and men, some of whom—to my amazement—had spent little time with Christians. The reappraisal of my own faith (which had begun with the question about the Gospels and Judaism) took an unexpected turn one afternoon, as I was sitting outside our stuffy barracks in the 110-degree Middle Eastern sun. A woman I had recently befriended, a Jewish volunteer from New York, asked me so bluntly that I thought she was joking, "So what about Jesus rising from the dead? Do you believe it?"

I was not surprised that my rambling response did not satisfy her, a devout Jew. I was more startled that my answer failed to convince even me.

While I was attending synagogue on a semiregular basis, I was also frequenting a local Southern Baptist church on Sunday mornings. Among a starched but selfless community, I first felt the claim of the Christian scriptures on my life. I had been able to ignore them for twenty years, until I attended this Baptist church and confronted the absurdity of trying to defend some Catholic teachings, such as the Assumption and Immaculate Conception of Mary, with indisputable biblical evidence. I looked and looked, but could not find any such proof. Only later would I understand the Catholic position that the Bible itself is part of a grander stream of a tradition of faith, a stream that does not always flow into or out of Scripture. My focus on the Bible provided a fresh font for religious growth, and I felt called to preach. This was curious, because I could not easily do so as a layman in my native Catholic context. So it was in a Baptist church that I learned how to preach, with the pastor even giving me the pulpit on a few occasions, including a sunrise service on Easter.

The institution to which I felt least responsible was my own local Catholic church, which I attended more sporadically than the synagogue or Baptist church. After Saturday mass one August afternoon, however, a stranger followed me home as I walked. A portly and balding middle-aged man in a tan windbreaker stopped me after three blocks. He said, "You are searching and very troubled. Do you know what *shalom* means? It means peace." Taking my hand, he said, "*Shalom aleichem*, peace be with you." Finding it almost impossible to look him in the eyes, I knew that I should, and forced myself to do so. Through thick glasses, he briefly returned my stare, squeezed my hand, and walked away. Like the end of a poem I had read somewhere, the moment whispered calmly: "You must change your life." This uncanny, anonymous blessing—by an angel following me home from church—caused me to reconsider the possibilities of finding "peace" in my own Catholic Church.

Withdrawing from Pop Culture

I found a decent job after graduating from college in 1992. As a teacher in a largely white suburban high school, I barely made a living wage and feared that I would not be able to pay back college loans, but was using my gifts and doing what I felt called to do. During two years of teaching, I observed many reasons for fear and hope about the youngest wave of my generation. On the one hand, my students (only a few years younger than I) had experienced a withering dissolution of their well-being: broken families, teen pregnancy, unstable sexual identities, physical and emotional abuse, drug addictions, alienation from family, alcoholism, disrespect for authority, short attention spans, and overall bouts of nihilism.

On the other hand, I experienced great joy with and for them. They were generally unafraid of transgressing almost any boundaries (irreverence—whether political, religious, or sexual—was almost a way of life). My students trusted their friendships over all other relationships, playfully ironized and satirized themselves and their culture, were wise about the psychology of "systems" and "institutions" at a young age, and were less snobby about high culture and more open to exploring (and exposing!) artifice than their elders.

Initially, I had serious trouble relating to them. During my first year of teaching, I took a vacation from popular culture. The television I had borrowed from my parents was dead and I could not afford another one. After deciding to try to complete this break from the pop universe, I stopped listening to the radio, buying rock records, reading popular magazines (dropping *Newsweek* in favor of the *Atlantic*), and in general becoming quite conceited about my involvement with high culture. I bragged about this to my high school students. When they asked me about television shows, songs, or movies, I honestly would not know about them. But each time they asked me, I was intrigued. I felt ostracized and out of step, as if my way of understanding myself and the world was incomplete. Sad to say, I didn't quite know how to understand myself without the familiar amniotic fluid of pop culture.

After a year of teaching, I could afford to reenter the (lower) middle class. I could also return to pop culture, and it felt like I was coming home. I needed to establish some sort of control over it, though, and feel as if I had a choice about the entire matter. I could not live without it or outside it, because even outside it I had continually needed to deflect its influence. My antipop experiment had failed, but I was reentering pop culture more on my own terms than when I had left it.

Crossing Boundaries

I next took up graduate studies in religion, for which I had secretly been preparing while teaching high school. Instead of grading papers, I had frequently found myself immersed in theology. Making my way through Hans Küng's *Does God Exist?* (quoting snippets to my students during slow moments in class) convinced me that faith and reason did not have to be enemies and that a religious life and an intellectual life might actually need each other. Reading this book was part of an intellectual and spiritual turning point for me—one that I wanted to embrace, to my surprise.

In graduate school, I studied the crossroads of culture and theology and further discerned the lived theology of my "nonreligious" peers that I had first suspected a few years earlier. This seemed to be a lived theology expressed not in traditional sacred ritual but in and through popular culture. Personally, I continued to experiment religiously while remaining anchored in Catholic churches. For the spring semester in 1995, I went to a Messianic Jewish synagogue, where I worshiped with, argued with, and was captivated by a congregation of Jews who praised Yeshua, or Jesus. As a boundary-crossing Catholic, I felt right at home. I began to wonder if this "scandalous" religious behavior, this boundary crossing, this flouting of religious propriety, gave me a key to understanding my generation and its relationship to pop culture and religion. The more I attended to Xers' insouciant and unorthodox attitudes toward religion as expressed in popular culture, the more *irreverence* seemed an eminently appropriate religious category for us.

I began to scribble notes about these mysteries. Among them, I wrote:

. . . Christmas 1995: The pope goes on-line. The world's largest Christian denomination just got bigger. I rush to the Vatican Web site, which is decked out in lemon-pudding yellow, and find I can send the pope e-mail! For the first time in modern Catholic history, the hierarchy has begun (to establish the illusion of?) asking Catholics around the world to send Rome their thoughts. The Vatican continues to preach a gospel that often pitches unsteadily between the twentieth and sixteenth centuries, and yet more and more "seekers" are congregating in the company of the pope on-line. Nothing has changed, yet *everything* has changed.

. . . "What if God was one of us?" asks pop music star Joan Osborne in 1995. She is the latest in a noteworthy flurry of musicians to ponder the mystery of incarnation—God in human form—and its meaning, if any, for a largely dechurched and hypercynical generation. Religion rules pop culture: Pope John Paul II is popular culture's stern but heart-of-gold Catholic father, and Madonna is his wayward daughter, the Catholic schoolgirl gone bad. While the pope calls for unity and an end to sects, Madonna calls for unity in sacred sex. She triumphally establishes the authority of religious symbols in the midst of the "pagan" world of music video.

. . . Dateline Harvard Square, Cambridge, Massachusetts: Down on one knee I gaze into "the pit," the epicenter of all things "alternative" in this venerable capital of liberalism. For the second day in a row at this popular gathering spot, I see a twenty-something woman clad in a T-shirt honoring John Paul II. Like the previous one, this shirt looks like a rock tour memento. It features the pope's face on the front and says "Boston '79— John Paul II" on the back. The young woman is reading C. S. Lewis to her friend, a longhaired young man with an equally provocative shirt, bearing a cross and skeleton on the front and the slogan Freedom From Religion across the back. How can their attire be so different, and yet have so much in common?

. . . "Acid! Who has acid for me?" When a half million people from Generation X get together at Woodstock '94 in August, at least a dozen of them seem to be following me everywhere, begging bystanders for drugs. Acid is just one of the hallucinogens making the rounds over these three sopping wet days. An orgy of sensations. I can only wonder what this massive self-indulgence means for our generation. Everyone is simultaneously seeking community (through shared alcohol, communal drugs, anonymous sex) and avoiding community (through shared alcohol, communal drugs, anonymous sex). If the five hundred thousand have anything in common, it is that they are collectively a lustful bacchanal seeking "otherness," an experience of something beyond their limits, if only for a moment. Their willingness to engage in behavior and live under conditions that would scandalize mainstream America bespeaks a widespread carelessness mixed with angst, a free fall into the arms of this media event named Woodstock in whose care we live for three days. Camera crews and journalists are omnipresent; we know how to live in a media event, and the way we choose to live it is revealing.

Asking Whether Religion Still Matters

A final anecdote concerns an episode from teaching high school that sums up much of my nearly thirty years of living in religion and pop culture. This particular experience established the question that this book seeks to address.

I had just finished giving what I thought was an incisive lecture on the American emancipation movement in the nineteenth century and its religious origins. After the bell rang, all my students sauntered out, except one. She stood casually in front of my lectern and stated, "I don't understand why people are so caught up in religion." I was about to wiggle my way out by remarking that we had been talking about Americans of a century ago, but she persisted. "Why can't people believe whatever they want to believe and be respected by everyone else? *Does religion really still matter?"* She uttered the words italicized; I merely record them verbatim here.

Perhaps I could have understood the remark as an unexamined truism parroted by an impressionable adolescent. This girl, however, was one of the top students in her graduating class of over seven hundred suburban students.

Does religion really still matter? For a generation, this book is my answer.

FORMED BY POP CULTURE

THE SHARED IMMERSION THAT
MAKES US A GENERATION

ANY THEOLOGY ABOUT GENERATION X must take popular culture seriously. Finding a common starting point in understanding pop culture, theology, and GenX requires some discussion of these terms. Thus, in this chapter I will discuss what I mean by *popular culture, theology,* and *Generation X* and will begin to explore how they are related.

Reared on Popular Culture

Taking the religious pulse of this generation requires a full-bodied plunge into popular culture. As I suggested in Chapter One, the childhood and adolescence of GenX seeded fertile ground for an intimate relationship with popular culture. During our lifetimes, especially during the critical period of the 1980s, pop culture was the amniotic fluid that sustained us. For a generation of kids who had a fragmented or completely broken relationship to "formal" or "institutional" religion, pop culture filled the spiritual gaps.

As a generation of latchkey children, we gained our independence at an early age, taking on a premature adulthood, and exercising our freedom of choice in the world of culture. As surrogate clergy, popular culture usurped the role institutional religion played for previous generations.

This deep immersion in popular culture was enabled by sizable chunks of teenage disposable income, which was the fruit of summer work, part-time jobs during the school year, weekly allowances, or parental generosity. Our parents' absence from the house made cash more available for many Xers, because they had increased responsibility for household chores. Our parents also gave us more spending money as an apology for not "being there" enough. With our personal cash flow, we indulged in movies and music, as well as in fashion trends, which ran the gamut from costly designer jeans to cheap, ripped shirts. Our familiarity with television, electronic products, and games readily transferred to a high degree of comfort with computer technology when it arrived in the mid-1980s. For all of these reasons, many Xers can chart their personal histories with explicit references to popular culture. Our complicity with it was firmly established in childhood and adolescence and remains—however ironically indulged—to the present day.

Between Generation X and popular culture, then, there is a profound symbiosis. GenX cannot be understood apart from popular culture, and much of popular culture cannot be interpreted without attention to Generation X. Whether our generation defines itself with or against the ubiquitous popular culture, we still fundamentally define ourselves in relation to it.

This shared generational experience of popular culture "events" produced an actively and potentially shared constellation of cultural meanings. By *events* I mean a host of different pop culture phenomena, including bodily costuming, music videos, and cyberspace, as well as movies, popular songs, television shows, board games, and countless other popularly engaged "products," "trends," or the like. All of these, for better or worse, have stamped a generation. Pop culture provides the matrix that contains much of what counts as "meaning" for our generation. As Douglas Rushkoff pithily observes, Generation X has an uncanny "ability to derive meaning from the random juxtaposition of TV commercials, candy wrappers, childhood memories, and breakfast treats" (1994a, p. 6).

The extent to which popular culture has meaning for our generation gets at the heart of what makes it a distinct group. In addition to a unique set of social and economic conditions that prevailed for those of us born in the 1960s and 1970s, our generation—tens of millions of us—readily "respond" to (find meaning in) a shared set of cultural referents. These pop culture "events" significantly influenced and continue to shape the meaning systems and values of this generation, both actively and potentially, explicitly and implicitly.

No two GenXers carry around precisely the same popular culture memories or were influenced by the exact same "events," but there is overlap in many of our pop culture memories. The existence of this communal constellation of cultural referents enables the GenX readers of this book to draw something other than a mental, emotional, or spiritual blank when they recall:

Pac Man   *Knight Rider*   The Go Gos   *Flashdance*
Desperately Seeking Susan   Iran-Contra   Duran Duran
Star Wars   Challenger explosion   Atari   Baby on Board
Jesse Jackson   Madonna   parachute pants   Frogger
MTV   Ronald Reagan   AIDS   Kurt Cobain   deconstruction
Jordache   Live Aid   Just Say No   Woodstock '94   Pearl Jam
JFK (the movie)   divorce   2 Live Crew   *Reality Bites*
Slacker   Grenada   Lebanon   *Gilligan's Island*   crack
Schoolhouse Rock   Fat Albert   *The Partridge Family*   Gap
World Wide Web   *Friday Night Videos*   *American Top Forty*
postmodernism   Flock of Seagulls   Hall and Oates   Dukakis
Noriega   the "Operation" game commercial   pine tar
Apple II   *E.T.*   Leif Garrett   *Miami Vice* disco   e-mail
Tori Amos   XTC   political correctness   iced cappuccino
Tipper Gore   *Wired*   Space Invaders   Willie Horton
Swatch   Birkenstock   *Love Boat*   rap   *The Day After*
virtual reality   REO Speedwagon   Vanessa Williams   Prozac
progressive rock   safe sex   Beavis and Butthead   the animé
Beastie Boys   Lollapalooza   friendship bracelets   ponytails
Cabbage Patch dolls   *Three's Company*   "Where's the beef?"
The Cosby Show   Milli Vanilli   *Tron*   Tammye Faye Bakker
Rubik's Cube   valley girl   break dancing   *Ghostbusters*
Moonlighting   Rick Springfield   Run-DMC   *Family Ties*
Boy George   Trivial Pursuit   Dungeons and Dragons   *Dallas*
Footloose   *Pee Wee's Playhouse*   "We Are the World"   Devo
"Who shot J.R.?"   *Mork and Mindy*

These are just a few of the popular culture events that, played in various combinations, make up the soundtrack for a generation. Far from residing in a cultural wasteland devoid of spiritual symbols, Generation X matured in a culture of complex and contradictory signs, some of them religious. Some currents within that GenX pop cultural stream carry more than mere microbes of an inchoate GenX spirituality. They are sufficient to begin funding a new theology by, for, and about a generation.

Whither Religion?

Although many studies of Generation X ignore popular culture's importance in forming the generation, some suggest that a crisis of religious meaning binds us together. According to researcher George Barna (1994, pp. 23, 69), who conducted interviews with hundreds of Xers from 1990 to 1992, only half of Xers defined themselves as "religious." At the same time, more than two-thirds asserted that "absolute truth does not exist." (As I will suggest in Chapter Seven, absolute truth and religious identity do not necessarily cohere in Xer experience; GenX raises the possibility of living religiously amid extreme ambiguities.) Barna also found that the generation had devoted steadily less time to church or "religious involvement" (p. 83). Of those he surveyed, only 1 percent considered "absence of religious faith" to be the "most significant national or international issue" (p. 46). Although data such as this are frequently mentioned in discussions about GenX and religion, it remains uncertain whether such attitudes indicate a lack of religious interest or a reluctance by Xers to make religiousness explicit. It could even mean that Xers associate religiousness with a traditional institution and therefore hesitate to call themselves religious.

In the same vein as Barna, one of the most influential studies of GenX finds religion to be an almost irrelevant topic for this generation. In *Thirteenth Gen,* the demographers Neil Howe and Bill Strauss assert that GenX lacks serious religious or philosophical interests and is drugged in a sluggish "spiritual passivity" (1993, pp. 20, 183). The authors do not consider that the generation's popular culture could be so rich with religious meaning that Xers frequently fail to view religion as a unique category worthy of attention.

In his book on GenX and Catholicism, Catholic theologian Robert Ludwig agrees that the generation is "increasingly alienated from the institutional church," but he suggests that new spiritual opportunities are emerging. Xers "become more and more open to the experiences that lie at the core of [Catholic] tradition," he writes (1995, p. 9). Because Catholicism is so much about experiences, Ludwig argues that an emphasis on core Catholic experiences will open the Catholic Church to Xers while bringing the Church itself back to its roots.

Until Xers have access to these core religious experiences, many will continue to have an intense sense of "aloneness," as William Mahedy and Janet Bernardi point out in *A Generation Alone* (1994). Indeed, Episcopalians William Mahedy (a college chaplain) and Janet Bernardi (a campus minister) find Xers' anxiety about a lack of meaning in their lives to be similar to that of war veterans who suffer post-traumatic stress disorder!

Whereas many GenX books do not allow Xers their own religious voice, Michael Lee Cohen (1993) attempts to remedy this oversight. After interviewing Xers all over the United States, Cohen included a few religious anecdotes in his book *The Twentysomething American Dream*. Cohen discovered some diversity in religious attitudes, but a response typical of many Xers came from "Suzanne," who explained that "one of the reasons I don't go to church like I should [is that] they're just hypocritical" (1993, p. 97). This common attitude affects the value Xers place on "religious" practice and is the most common charge I have heard from Xers about religion. The perception of hypocrisy is one reason religion is not a security blanket but a wet blanket to so many. Howe and Strauss report that "religion ranks behind friends, home, school, music and TV as factors [Xers] believe are having the greatest influence on their generation" (1993, p. 187).

Something more than criticism of hypocrisy is afoot, however. In a different interview in *The Twentysomething American Dream*, "Lavonda" expresses another common GenX attitude: "What the hell's going to church for? These days you've got to take religion in your own hands" (p. 183). Taking religion into their own hands is just what many Xers have done. Aside from living religiously through the popular culture, which the remainder of this book will consider, Xers have taken religion into their own hands in two other ways.

First, they have a widespread regard for paganism—however vaguely defined. Popular books and record store offerings bear witness to this interest, as do the topics of popular young adult education classes and the profusion of Internet information on paganism. Practices or rituals suggestive of paganism even surface in some universities, particularly as an effect of one strand of feminism within the academy.

A second way Xers take religion into their own hands is through a growing enchantment with mysticism. In popular discussion, at bookshops, and in music stores, mysticism abounds. (I see a preponderance of interest in Jewish or Muslim mystical practices. I attribute this to the way people mistakenly associate Christian mysticism with ultraconservative Christianity, though the two are hardly related at all.) As practiced by Xers, mysticism is defined as broadly as paganism and is often expressed as religious eclecticism. Xers take symbols, values, and rituals from various religious traditions and combine them into their personal "spirituality." They see this spirituality as being far removed from "religion," which they frequently equate with a religious institution. As one GenX friend observed, "My spirituality is drawn from Hinduism, Buddhism, Christian and Muslim mysticism, and Native American religions." With these words, she summarized dozens of my religious conversations with Xers.

Mysticism may be more than a fanciful flight from old-time religion; it might be a way of criticizing our wider culture. Catholic theologian David Tracy (1994) argues that popular interest in mysticism is a way of being prophetic, reacting against the "barbaric" excesses of modern Western culture. Perhaps so many GenXers claim to have mystical and pagan practices out of a sense of alienation from these excesses. They may feel that our culture's untrammeled trust in reason is not enough, that grand narratives (about power or patriarchy) swallow our individuality, and that our Western solipsism ignores everyone else on the planet.

Challenging the modern world in such a way puts Xers in what could be called a "postmodern" world. Tracy suggests that "the recovery of mystical readings of the prophetic core of Judaism and Christianity is one of the surest signs of a postmodern sensibility" (1994, p. 114). Xers did not invent this interest in paganism and mysticism; they learned it from their baby boomer elders. Generation Xers, however, are much more immersed now than boomers in experimentation, alienation, and pop-cultured religiousness, because we were steeped in popular culture, and on our own, at an earlier age.

In Cohen's *Twentysomething American Dream,* "Paula" discussed her journey of faith as a GenX Jewish woman and rabbinical student. Paula did not have a traditionally religious upbringing but grew to love working in Jewish camps and campus organizations, digging into her Jewish heritage to find the roots of social activism. By age twenty-seven she had managed a soup kitchen and served as an advocate for the homeless. Although she downplayed the significance of religion in her decision to become a rabbi, she offered an unusual explanation of faith in regard to her work: "I feel commanded by God to feed the homeless." Like some Xers, however, she had difficulties overcoming workaholism. At age twenty-seven, she was already wondering whether she was overcommitted. Paula's story paints a real-life picture of the ways an Xer incorporates religious beliefs into her daily life, even into her social activism (1993, pp. 211–218).

Cohen's discussion of GenX is one of the few to take religious questions seriously. Time and again, feature stories on GenX in popular magazines ignore religious questions. Is this because the journey of faith or the search for religious meaning is relatively unimportant to Generation X? Or is it because—and this is my contention—the right questions have not been asked of Generation X and its popular culture? If we have yet to ask the right sort of questions, then it is appropriate to set out the groundwork for interpreting GenX popular culture theologically so that more appropriate questions can be asked. To consider a GenX theology, one must first have a detailed understanding of the term *Generation X.*

The X Generation

Why *Generation X* and not *Generation Z, B,* or *Q?* Why must there be any label at all?

Those of us who have been lumped under the GenX banner have sound reasons for skepticism about the moniker assigned to us. One reason for such antipathy is the proliferation of perfidious labels for this generation, including "the whiny generation," "a generation of gripers," "a generation adrift," "the tuned-out generation," "slackers," and "the numb generation."

In addition to feeling revulsion at these denigrations, Xers have what might be called a strong "postmodern" skepticism about the descriptive power of universal themes or "big explanations." It is right to resist any categorization of such a diverse cohort of Americans. All attempts to affix one label to millions of people will be insufficient.

I think it is possible to honor the skepticism of many, as well as to account for the generational data (both "statistical" and more broadly "cultural") that exist. The solution lies in creating a definition of GenX that highlights its relationship to popular culture. Such a definition must show how pop culture has served as a maker of meaning for Generation X, indeed "making" the generation itself.

Despite my own conviction that popular culture is key in defining GenX, it is helpful to survey the work of others who have attempted to define what makes Generation X unique. Douglas Coupland's novel *Generation X* (1991) introduced a provocative epithet into popular discussion. Where did Coupland get the "Generation X" moniker? Its origins are murky. It may have been a slogan for corporate advertising strategies aimed at American youth, a 1960s term for British adolescents, or the enigmatic name of a 1970s English punk band. Regardless of the term's origins, Coupland is responsible for associating it with the creative, lonely, and restless middle-class young adults who populate his novels *Generation X, Shampoo Planet* (1992), and *Microserfs* (1995).

Sociologically, *Generation X* has been defined in a variety of ways. In *Thirteenth Gen* (1993), Neil Howe and Bill Strauss say that the United States's "thirteenth generation" was born between 1961 and 1981, a span that includes nearly eighty million Americans (p. 7). They note that 1961 marks the first wave of "babies people took pills not to have." Suggesting that "modern generations stretch across a little over twenty birth years," they place the latter birth year at 1981 (p. 13).

Others have delineated a smaller GenX cohort. George Barna and William Dunn suggest that GenX's birth boundaries mark a "baby bust," a period of relatively low birthrates that followed the great postwar "baby boom." Both Barna and Dunn think the "buster" era began in 1965, although they disagree about when it subsided. Barna claims it ended by 1983, which would make busters seventy million strong (1994, pp. 14–15). Dunn places the marker at 1976; his more conservative estimate means that there are forty-four million busters (1993, p. x). The variety of estimates about exactly when the GenX years begin and end has stymied Generation X studies and encouraged leagues of naysayers who, because of the elusiveness of a firm definition, rail against the very possibility of an identifiable generation.

What is frequently overlooked is that many GenX studies are attempts to corral *chronologically* what is primarily *cultural*: a living generation. The varying estimates of the boundaries of America's thirteenth generation often seek to place artificial fences around a group of Americans who, in my view, respond to similar popular culture events. To the extent that they shared such events, they draw upon a common well of responses and growth experiences that were formed either directly by, or in contrast to, this constellation of popular culture events. This is my own view of Generation X. I feel that a precise definition of boundary years is not possible. As a rough-and-ready sketch, however, I think of Xers as those born from the early 1960s to the late 1970s.

This is not to say that examining social data within particular years lacks value. Charting social and economic factors enriches any generation's story, including that of GenX. Although this book focuses on specific forms of popular culture and does not use socioeconomic categories as its primary interpretive lenses, it is important to note that participating in the forms of popular culture that I discuss requires at least middle-class status (because it often requires access to disposable income). In addition, racial integration seems to be more common for Xers than for previous generations, but I have barely touched on the variety of rich cultural forms among the many ethnic groups that may be included in the generation. In other words, my book begs for conversation with studies that explore other groups and cultures within the generation.

I envision Generation X as including the cross-section of Americans with whom I shared live music, bohemian living, and mud romping at Woodstock '94. In my informal observations at the three-day concert, I found most revelers to be in their early twenties through early thirties. They had varying sexual identities and were largely middle-class. To my unscientific eye, the concert attracted a racial spectrum similar to the diversity of those born in the 1960s and 1970s. For the birth years 1965 to 1974, for example, approximately 70 percent are white, 13 percent are

African American, 12 percent are Latino or Latina, 4 percent are Asian, and 1 percent are Native American or another ethnicity (Holtz, 1995, pp. 191, 271). The percentage of minorities within this cohort is slightly higher than that within the general United States population and will increase in the coming years.

Assuming that we can identify a generation born in the 1960s and 1970s that has a common bond to popular culture, recent social and economic history tells us that such a generation has many challenges to confront. GenX political activists Rob Nelson and Jon Cowan have written *Revolution X*, a manifesto that lists "100 harshest facts" about the generation that should continually be borne in mind. For instance, they note the following trends: a decline of real wages and an increase in the length of the average workweek over the past twenty-five years; an increase in young adult poverty and a concomitant decline of real income; the devastation of AIDS, the top killer of Xers in many cities; the continued socioeconomic crises of many minority communities, particularly of young African American men; continuing crises of divorce and suicide; overqualification of college graduates for available jobs; unacceptable levels of violence in schools and neighborhoods; a steady drumbeat of drug abuse; and a high percentage of young adults without health insurance (1994, pp. 209–221). These authors provide the context in which we theologically interpret GenX popular culture. As Mahedy and Bernardi have noted, these conditions collectively amount to a "critical mass" of social pathologies that help mark the uniqueness of this generation, aside from whatever else sets Xers apart in history (1994, p. 75).

Uses of Theology

Theology has everything to do with culture. To understand a Generation X theology, we must understand Generation X culture, and vice versa.

When I first studied theology, I thought I was going to be living with my head in the clouds, floating in an airy, spiritual nothingness. I imagined myself returning to earth at the end of each day to find myself back in my own culture. I was completely wrong.

Theology has to do with culture because theology has to do with living religiously, which always takes place within a culture. *Theology*, by its very name, makes the great assertion that we can express a *logos* (word or reason) about a *theos* (God). Theology means "talk about" God, because it is first possible to "talk with" God, or to encounter revelation about God. Despite the airy claims of some theologians, then, there is no theology apart from life in the world, from life in culture.

Theology and culture are deeply intertwined. Whenever we use theological language, such as the phrase *kingdom of God,* our cultural concepts make it possible for us to understand what *kingdom* and *God* mean. For us to understand even the word *theology,* a theology must take the form of terms and ideas that we can grasp, which means that it must be articulated in the language of our culture. Even though theology always adopts the style of a particular culture, however, it can still bear witness to a reality *beyond* the limitations of language and culture. For instance, although my conceptions of God derive from my culture (even my popular culture!), God may still exist beyond my limited language.

But traffic between theology and culture travels both directions. Just as culture influences theology, theology influences culture. A simple (if overused) example is the way in which America's Puritan ancestors still hold sway over morality hundreds of years after their heyday. The great influence of their lived theology on the way our culture functions makes it difficult to easily separate theology from what we call "culture."

Theology is always found and created within a particular cultural perspective. In order to understand our culture, therefore, we must think theologically. And in order to comprehend our theology, we must know our culture.

God in Everyday Things

If theology is about our religious experiences in our own GenX cultural settings, it is important to establish what *religiousness* means. (Throughout this book I generally use the phrases *the religious* or *religiousness* instead of *religion,* because of the common association of *religion* with a particular institution. In this sense, Xers have their own "religiousness" but not their very own "religion.")

A key component of the *religious* is a profound experience of a limitation. From guilt or awareness of death to ecstatic love or joy, David Tracy reminds us that the experience of religiousness is evoked when we find an "ultimate limit" to our human existence (1978, p. 105). That is, religiousness is present whenever we find ourselves at the boundary of our existence and need to go beyond ourselves to make sense of life. The religious reveals fundamental meaning about our existence. Lutheran theologian Paul Tillich calls this sense of the religious "the aspect of depth in the totality of the human spirit" that points to what is "ultimate, infinite, unconditional" (1959, p. 7). Tillich was convinced that this aspect of religious "depth" underlies all culture. Thus, all forms of culture—and human experiences within culture—have a religious character that may be plumbed—even, in my view, pop culture and the human experiences it describes.

Catholic theologian Karl Rahner writes that "the very commonness of everyday things harbors the eternal marvel and silent mystery of God" (1967, p. 14). Although Rahner is not referring directly to popular culture, his theological insight about "everyday things" is applicable to GenX popular culture, especially for a generation whose popular culture is an "everyday thing."

But can pop culture, from rock songs to Barbie dolls, reveal the "mystery of God"? Certainly, many people think that popular culture—especially if it is thought of as culture for the masses—is driven by the irreligious values of the marketplace. Pop culture, its critics say, is different from "high culture," such as museums and ballet. They note that pop culture's heavily commercial, lowest-common-denominator character cannot be considered religious at all.

Popular culture, however, is not simply mass-produced detritus. Pop music scholar Simon Frith (1996b, pp. 415–416) notes three ways of defining pop culture: first, as produced by a culture *for* the people (people consume what is fed to them); second, as the culture *of* the people (people consume what resonates with their own values); third, as the culture *by* the people (popular ways people live daily life). I am approaching GenX pop culture mostly through Frith's second definition. I see GenX culture as the culture *of* the generation (as an expression of popular religiosity). Even though I have called our pop culture a form of "surrogate clergy," I do not mean to imply that it is merely preached to us or forced on us; it is "produced" by us as well. Fashion, cyberspace, and music video are forms of culture in which our own religious needs and interests help make items popular. Xers, in other words, are "creators" as much as "receivers" of pop culture.

Scripture and Popular Religiousness

The Scriptures provide some guidance in imagining how culture can bear religious truth. The Bible's description of ancient Jewish culture is a good place to start; God seemed to work constantly through the culture of ancient Israel. Theologian Langdon Gilkey summarizes this aspect of the Hebrew Bible well when he writes, "Israel's culture was, if there ever was one, one explicitly with a 'religious substance,' one founded directly by God and one preserved and ruled by the divine actions in history" (1981, p. 68). Because the culture of ancient Israel was grounded in

God, Gilkey concludes that we can "regard as 'biblical' the viewpoint that *each creative culture, insofar as it lives on a religious substance, is established in and through the presence of the divine*" (p. 68, italics mine). Here we have biblical evidence that culture itself (even, I suggest, popular culture) and people's lives and practices may indeed be religiously revelatory. This is not to suggest uncritically that all culture is always religiously meaningful.

To think of pop culture as having religious meaning strikes many (especially theologians!) as a complete reversal of what is expected. This proposal resonates, however, with the reversals of fortune described in the Christian Scriptures, particularly in Jesus' parables. Throughout the Christian Scriptures, the kingdom of God is constantly revealed and enacted through the least likely person or circumstances. If the first are to be last and the last first, then popular culture itself, as a quintessential instance of what counts as "last" in importance for many cultural high priests, may be granted its moment of significance.

In keeping with the Jewish tradition mentioned by Gilkey, both Paul and Jesus seemed to accept that popular culture practices could be religiously revelatory. Paul argued that even "pagans"—those commonly thought to be most distant from God—can know the divine. He wrote in his letter to the Romans that "ever since the creation of the world, [God's] eternal power and divine nature, invisible though they are, have been understood and seen through the things [God] has made." Pagans "knew God," although Paul felt they wandered astray with the knowledge (Romans 1:20–21). If God is ultimately the Lord of culture, it would seem that Paul affirmed the possibility of God's being revealed in that culture. Paul also alluded to Greek popular culture in explaining religious truths to his audience. For instance, he used examples from Greek athletics (as in 1 Corinthians 9:24–27) to illustrate the importance of discipline for a life of faith.

Jesus' parables refer to popular practices to reveal what God or God's reign is like. It was apparently Jesus' habit not to belabor the point by offering literal theological explanations of each popular practice that he cited; ordinary people could intuit the religious meaning for their lives. Jesus invoked common images: sowing a mustard seed, attending a wedding feast, baking bread, searching for a lost coin or lost sheep. Popular practices, the Bible attests, can yield theological meaning.

GenX pop culture should not be exempted, as if it were a uniquely irredeemable case. As theologian Bernard Cooke suggests in accord with the scriptural evidence I have just cited, "The *basic experience of life* that each of us has is the first and fundamental word that God speaks to us" (1983,

p. 32, italics mine). For Xers, this basic experience of life both shapes and is shaped by popular culture.

Signs and Senses

The Second Vatican Council of the Catholic Church (1962–1965) saw the necessity of bringing theology and culture into conversation by "scrutinizing the signs of the times and . . . interpreting them in the light of the gospel" (Abbott, 1966, pp. 201–202). The signs of the times would seem to include beliefs, practices, and questions alive in the culture. One of the clearest signs of the GenX times is the prevalence of popular culture and its trafficking in religious images. Thus, understanding the signs of the times is one of our contemporary religious responsibilities (especially if one is convinced that God works not only through religions but also through cultures).

One way to imagine pop culture's influence on institutions such as the Church is to consider the theological concept of the "sense of the faithful" (or *sensus fidelium*), also endorsed by Vatican II (Abbott, 1966, p. 29). The person in modern times most responsible for reviving this concept was the Anglican-turned-Catholic theologian (and later cardinal) John Henry Newman. A man ahead of his time, he wrote in the nineteenth century that the sense of the faithful includes "a sort of instinct . . . deep in the bosom of the mystical body of Christ" (1961, p. 73). This sense is not only a *response* to the theology proposed by Church leaders but a *source* of lived theology as well. That is, one way to arrive at a clearer theological understanding is to take stock of the lived witness of the faithful.

This theological view, that the communal experience of faithful people can be a source of religious truth, has not exclusively been the preserve of Catholicism. From a Protestant perspective, theologian Richard Mouw suggests that the concept of the sense of the faithful is consistent with two core Calvinist convictions: God's sovereignty and human depravity. If God is truly the Lord of all, then "popular religion is the experience of people who bear God's image" (1994, p. 28). Popular religious expression (even, I will add, pop culture religious expression!) is always undertaken by people who are made in the image of God. Calvinism also teaches that depravity—degradation and corruption—are central to the human condition. For Mouw, this means that "educated people are in no better position than the uneducated when it comes to knowing about God" (p. 28). Mouw's insight therefore deflates any claims about the inadequate religiousness of pop culture, which is often caricatured as simply the fruit of "uneducated" (read: pagan) impulses.

The lesson Mouw draws from these points is that Christians "all need other Christians" (p. 28). This is indeed true and is a pithy summary of the whole point of the sense of the faithful. This sentiment is not enough for Generation X, however. In this multireligious generation, people of various religious traditions (and none at all!) need each other in a dialogue about the religious.

To meet the needs of GenX's situation, I suggest expanding the concept of the sense of the faithful and calling it the *sensus infidelium* (the sense of the unfaithful). Basic to my proposal is that people (or forms of pop culture) who profess to know little or nothing about the religious may indeed form, inform, or transform religious meaning for people of faith. The term *infidelium* is not meant to cast aspersions on those who identify as nonreligious by resurrecting the disparaging term *infidel*; I use *infidelium* to state rhetorically the offensive and yet powerful possibility that truth could emerge from those least assumed to be in possession of it.

Certain forms of pop culture—and some Xers themselves—may be described as "unfaithful," and yet their religious "sense" may challenge and helpfully criticize the "sense" of those who call themselves "faithful"! This sense of the unfaithful is often evident in our daily lives. Whenever friends or colleagues from non-Christian religious traditions challenge or deepen my own faith, I am incorporating the sense of the (seemingly) unfaithful into my own life. (Of course, my non-Christian friends may be very faithful to their own traditions; I only mean that they are "unfaithful" in a very narrow sense in regard to Christian claims of truth.)

I think this sense of the unfaithful is emerging in Christian theology and is also evident in Scripture. Within contemporary Asian theology, Catholic theologian Aloysius Pieris suggests that non-Christian conceptions of Jesus can help Christian theologians understand Jesus. For Pieris, poor, non-Christian Asian "religious seekers" who have encountered Jesus within their own religious "pilgrimage" can make a real contribution to Christian theology (1988, p. 64). There is an analogy to GenX pop culture here—GenX music videos frequently feature images of Jesus. These images might likewise help Christians understand Jesus.

I see this sense of the unfaithful, surprisingly, in the Christian Scriptures. Even Jesus, who is for Christians the ultimate "revealer" of God, receives a revelation from outside his own religious tradition. His encounter with the Gentile Syro-Phoenician woman in Mark 7:24–30 illustrates my point remarkably well. A Gentile woman asks Jesus, a Jew, to exorcise a demon from her Gentile daughter. Jesus does not initially grant her request, saying that children (that is, Jews) should be fed before dogs (that is, Gentiles) have an opportunity to eat. In other words, Jesus' responsibility is to Jews before anyone else. The Gentile woman—using Jesus' metaphors—cleverly retorts, "Sir, even the dogs under the table eat the children's crumbs." In other words, the Gentiles are worthy of being fed the same "food" (Jesus' teaching). This changes Jesus' mind. In his reply, he acknowledges her retort: "On account of this word," he says, she may depart, and the demon will leave her daughter. In a radical reversal, a woman gets the punch line in a Gospel story, and Jesus gains a new insight about his mission, which thereafter in Mark's Gospel expands to include the Gentiles. In the large cast of characters that interact with Jesus in Mark's Gospel, she is the only one who wins an argument with Jesus. The man at the center of Christian faith receives a word of truth about his own religious understanding from someone outside his religious tradition.

Those who are thought "unfaithful" can greatly influence and even teach religious individuals, traditions, and institutions. As Mouw rightly observes, theologians are "more likely to show appreciation for a popular religious culture when it is located in a Third World context than when it is close to home" (1994, p. 19). It is necessary to import these insights from "Third World" theology and from the "Third World" of the Scriptures, to our own, more familiar theological context in order to gain a new sense of the unfaithful. Ultimately, I will claim that the supposedly "unfaithful" GenX pop culture has much to teach religious individuals, traditions, and institutions, even as these religious traditions have much to teach GenX and its pop culture.

Just as the sense of the faithful tradition has been based on an assumption of fidelity to the Church, so, too, a sense of the unfaithful, which is manifest in popular culture, must be subject to certain criteria. I think that the sense of the unfaithful should be consistent with core truths of the religious tradition it is addressing, subject to correction by that tradition, adequate to lived human experience, and life-giving.

A sense of the unfaithful is one key way of understanding the religiously revelatory power of culture, especially the popular culture of Generation X. To honor the possibility of finding the religious in culture is, to adapt the words of Dietrich Bonhoeffer (1971), to live in a world "come of age," a world in which adulthood is mandatory in regard to the religious life. It is a world in which Xers cannot pretend that the religious and the cultural are two entirely separate worlds. In this world, God might be working through pop culture or through other people from foreign religious traditions. In such a world, religious meaning can be expressed in and drawn from popular culture. This religious adulthood is a theological gift brought to you by the letter X.

о

This emerging GenX theology, a lived theology, cannot be understood apart from its context in a culture heavily prone to simulating reality. GenX uses the wider culture's fascination with "virtual" reality as we practice religiousness. It is appropriate, then, to turn to a discussion of the "virtually" religious, which I will undertake in the next chapter.

3

BEING VIRTUALLY RELIGIOUS

APPRECIATING GenX IRREVERENCE

WHAT DO YOU GET WHEN YOU CROSS performance with worship? A concert with a mass? For music scholar Katherine Bergeron, you get a "virtual liturgy."

Her essay "The Virtual Sacred" (1995) describes a virtual liturgy—a staged imitation of real worship—and its significance for contemporary culture. Although her topic is Gregorian chant, Bergeron provides an opening to my discussion of Generation X, the religious, and popular culture. Through an analysis of popular chant music, she finds that religious experiences are increasingly packaged and sold in contemporary culture, giving us a kind of "virtual religiousness." I think her description not only illustrates a religious direction in American culture at large but also helps to explain an important way in which GenXers are religious—in and through popular culture.

Bergeron examines reasons for the popularity of the *Chant* album (Benedictine Monks . . . , 1994), a collection of Gregorian chants by Spanish monks that found tremendous market success and popular influence in the United States in the 1990s. Contrary to the popular perception that chant is ancient music, Bergeron argues that chant is not a venerable musical form at all. Indeed, it arrived only recently in the long history of Western music; Gregorian chant is about 170 years old.

In the small French village of Solesmes, around 1830, Catholic Benedictine monks were rebuilding their order from the ruins of the French Revolution. Part of this renewal involved the reinstitution of singing at daily worship, which occasioned a rediscovery of chants from ninth-century Catholic rituals. A full millennium later, after decades of careful retrieval and musical recalibration, these monks of Solesmes developed what is now called "Gregorian chant." (The attribution to Gregory refers to the legend of a divine revelation of chant to Pope Gregory in the sixth century.) What many today take to be an ancient form of music, sturdily linked in an unbroken chain of tradition to the Church of the first few centuries, is actually a relatively direct heritage of the mid-nineteenth-century French Benedictines. According to Bergeron, they "restored (some might say reinvented) the tradition in modern performance" (p. 31). In this restoration, the monks were influenced by their own musical, liturgical, and cultural surroundings, so that so-called timeless Gregorian chant includes what Bergeron calls a strong "French aesthetic."

The popular music of the *Chant* phenomenon today, then, is merely a *simulation* of nineteenth-century chant, itself a simulation of ninth-century chant. Despite this, each generation usually claimed that every incarnation of chant was a timeless form of music rooted in ancient Christian tradition.

For Bergeron, the *Chant* album exemplifies a noteworthy religious trend, one that she senses in the broad popular interest in chant music. Fundamentally, chant allows its hearers (or its hearers allow themselves!) to create an illusion of an "other" time, of sacred time outside normal experience. The music's illusionary "otherness" enables it to seem removed from the consumerist cycle of buying and selling and so to stand as a pure religious object. Bergeron expresses the logic of the experience: "I relax simply by being presented with an image of time that I do not have" (p. 33). She suggests further that insofar as many consumers have purchased the album and have not listened to it, *Chant* works like a magical talisman, continually promising a sacred future time, always within the consumer's grasp.

One of Bergeron's key conclusions is that the "virtual religion" represented by *Chant* has one critical difference from "real" religion: it does not demand anything of the listener. She relates her own experience of watching a professional chant group perform at San Francisco's majestic, neo-Gothic Grace Cathedral. The company's dress and assemblage, the crowd's demeanor, and the musical order and selection too closely mimed a "real" liturgy for Bergeron. Like the ambient religious space created by *Chant,* the "concert presented a *virtual liturgy,* one in which we were *invited to participate,* but also one that *required nothing of us* whatsoever" (p. 34, italics mine).

Bergeron subtly connects her experiences of the virtual religion of both the chant "performance" and the *Chant* album. "It is the condition of being between two realities," she writes, "both of which are offered and both of which are denied, that creates the desired effect of this music" (p. 34). The music offered a new way to think about what authenticity really is for us today, "in the virtual space of a neither/nor," neither authentic nor inauthentic. "It is in this unreal space that we now find chant, and the idea of the sacred, and ourselves, at the end of the millennium" (p. 34). For Bergeron, religion (or what I am calling "the religious") is now characterized by its lack of reality, cast as something not quite authentic but not completely false, either.

I disagree with Bergeron because I think virtual religiousness can make claims on its participants. This happens when virtual religiousness is allowed to criticize real religiousness; virtual liturgy (as Bergeron describes it) can comment on and criticize real liturgy, and vice versa. By simulating a liturgy (or real religiousness), we can find out how "real" liturgy (or religiousness) works. As we consider how the simulation is faithful or unfaithful to its "real" counterpart, virtual liturgy may influence the way we think about "real" liturgy. We may come to realize, for instance, that "real" liturgy itself does not always make claims on the participants! (This is difficult to see until you set up a simulation of a liturgy, such as the one Bergeron attended. Then it becomes absolutely clear. In observing the imitation, you wonder, "Why doesn't this challenge me spiritually?" Then you think, "Why does the real liturgy make claims on me in the first place? Well, I guess it doesn't necessarily do so, either!") This is one way of using the virtual to comment on or criticize the "real."

At the same time, virtual liturgy exposes the amount of "simulation" in a real liturgy, and real liturgies illuminate the amount of "reality" in a virtual liturgy. They influence each other in a way that can clarify the spiritual demands each makes on the participant. In sum, simulating the religious—making it virtual—may lead to a more thorough religious practice, not the opposite!

Another example of the relationship between virtual and real religiousness is the footprint of Jesus in Jerusalem. When I last visited Israel in 1994, I climbed up a long stone walkway from the Garden of Gethsemane and, on arriving at the summit of the Mount of Olives, stumbled on a site marking the ascension of Jesus to heaven. A guide charged me a shekel to enter and told me that the tiny building in which the footprint was housed was a former mosque that had preserved the footprint's integrity for centuries. When I stepped inside, I saw a rectangular slab of plaster, which was dirty and cracked. In the middle was a large depression, made not by a foot but instead by some kind of boot or perhaps a sandal. Unless Jesus just had a taste for oversized sandals, I thought, he must have had about size eleven feet.

There was something parodic about the entire event. I imagined the disciples' hustling to procure a bucket of plaster right before Jesus ascended to heaven (Mark 16:19, Luke 24:51) and Peter's attempting to make a plaster cast as Jesus left the ground or inscribing his initials in the wet plaster after Jesus disappeared. Of course, given what we now know of physics and our universe, I cannot believe that Jesus would actually have pushed off from the Mount of Olives to go "up" to heaven. (As it was, Jesus must have been partly off the ground, because they were only able to cast one of his feet in plaster.)

Nonetheless, Jesus' footprint is a terrific common example of the virtually religious; it imitates "real" religiousness, can lead to a deeper understanding of "real" religion, and can criticize real religion. The footprint imitates "reality" by simulating what Jesus' foot might actually have looked like and by placing it at a likely spot on the Mount of Olives, which is traditionally viewed as the ascension site (the "historical" Jesus probably traversed this area several times).

This virtual religiousness can lead to greater "real" religiousness by reminding Christians of the very materiality of Jesus' bodily existence. They may realize that Jesus actually *did* leave footprints around Jerusalem during his lifetime, and likely not very far from the contemporary plaster site. The weight of his labored steps, like those of modern pilgrims to the holy land, gently stirred up the dust of the Mount. Such a banal connection can at the same time be a profoundly human insight about Jesus for someone to whom Jesus seems only a spirit on earth, quite apart from the dirt of daily existence.

Jesus' footprint can criticize real religiousness by raising questions about the ways in which our regular religious practices and beliefs rely on dubious "facts" such as this footprint. Jesus' footprint is virtually religious (and recognized as such, can be enjoyed with a wisened innocence) but has obvious implications for real religiousness such as those listed above.

Throughout this book, I will attempt to highlight ways in which GenX popular culture (and GenXers themselves who "make" this popular culture) are "virtually" religious. In showing this, I intend to clarify "real" religious practice. GenX pop culture's simulated religiousness is both "real" and "unreal."

The security of what people previously considered simple "reality" has—for many Xers—molted like a snake's skin. In this space of fresh and frightening indeterminacy, religious pop culture images roam freely and Xers abandon themselves to grace. This grace comes at a cost—the abandonment of the comfort of past generations, of a once-and-for-all final reality. Having grown up too quickly anyway, Xers will not go back to the childhood of presimulational religiousness. Abandoning themselves to video culture, cyberculture, and fashion, Xers' lives can become lived prayers for the embrace of the religious in the pop culture milieu, which is the virtual location of GenX salvation.

GenX's culture of virtuality, of both reality and its imitation, uses irony to communicate religious ideas. Irony is often misunderstood, especially when Xers use it, as a purely negative attitude toward the world. Irony mocks, to be sure, but it does not just poke fun. Irony undoes the supposedly self-evident meaning of a statement, idea, or image, and empties that image of what it was previously thought to contain. Irony on the part of Xers is a way of marking distance from what is received as religious in order to collapse that religiousness playfully, to iron(ize) it flat. Then, through pop culture, Xers suggest something else in its place, however vague that replacement may be. To operate ironically, as GenX pop culture does, is not merely to take a negative, dismissive tone. It is to engage for the sake of reclamation—but only after the devastation of an engagement that destroys. Irony sucks the air out of its object, only to reinflate it later.

GenX practices its pop-cultured, ironic religiosity in the context of the both-and. The generation celebrates the real and the artificial, reality and unreality. It is in this arena that I have distilled key theological themes.

Religious Themes in Popular Culture

In Generation X's popular culture, I have found four main themes that represent strands of a lived theology. This "practical" theology is both *actual and potential,* both self-consciously lived and awaiting further exploration.

These themes are not confined to the religious universe of the generation; they are the generation's gift and challenge to others, including religious institutions. Neither are these four themes wholly new in the history of religions or theology. GenX popular culture both reclaims forgotten themes and cloaks familiar ones in new images, defamiliarizing them, making them more acutely "religious" again.

The first theme that emerges from GenX popular culture is deep suspicion of religious institutions. Three types of popular culture suspicion illustrate this distrust. First, Xers challenge religious institutions in general. Second, GenXers specifically assault the Catholic Church. Third, they frequently pit Jesus against the Church.

The second religious theme is an emphasis on the sacred nature of experience. Lived experience becomes a key indicator of what counts as religious. More specifically, pop culture often features experiences that fuse either the human and divine or the sensual and spiritual. A more communal view of sacred experience, as mediated by communities of faith and as lived in the political and everyday world, rounds out popular culture's theological experimentation with experience as sacred.

The religious dimension of suffering characterizes the third theme. Suffering is seen in religious context in three primary ways. First, several popular culture events plumb the varieties of suffering that the generation has endured. Second, flowing from this is pop culture's interest in the religious significance of suffering servanthood. Finally, a focus on the prophetic and apocalyptic carries the theme to a dizzying and destructive height.

The final religious theme brings the three previous themes not to a gentle completion but to a wobbly teetering, an exploration of faith and ambiguity. This theme encompasses unique ways of being religious, ways in which faithfulness happens with (or as) a question mark. A series of instabilities fills up this theme, raising the following questions: Can Xers be faithful in the space between orthodoxy and heresy? What happens to faith when space and time are indeterminate? To have faith, must one know one's own identity with certainty?

As I suggested earlier, one overarching "metatheme" that runs through each of the individual themes is that of "virtual" religiousness. This imitational way of being religious permeates GenX pop culture. Thus, my interpretations of pop culture's themes will attend to both "real" *and* "virtual" religiousness.

In an examination of the GenX relationship between the "really" and "virtually" religious, the word *religiosity* is key. I find the term very useful, because it is paradoxical. On the one hand, *religiosity* refers to how formally "religious" (usually understood as "pious") a person is. On the other hand, *religiosity* also refers to an affected or fake sort of piety, even a mockery of what is commonly considered "religious." *Religiosity* is the perfect word for the sort of authentic and fake, real and unreal religious practice that much of Generation X popular culture indicates. Its ambiguity will ironically serve to clarify interpretations of this culture and its relation to the religious.

Forms of GenX Popular Culture

"The first spiritual want of a barbarous [person] is decoration," wrote Thomas Carlyle in 1838 (Rubinstein, 1985, p. 243). Whereas most people would not consider fashion a spiritual need, to GenXers it has been as dear as any of our grandparents' religious devotions.

Much of the generation's disposable income has ended up in the hands of untypical clothing retailers. Xer fashion not only hails from the flashy, climate-controlled atmosphere of the mall. It also originates in second-hand or "thrift" stores, in parents' (or grandparents') outmoded outfits, or in creative reconfigurations of "mainstream" clothing. Thus, disposable income was not an absolute necessity to participate in Xer clothing trends, much less to fall within their influence. One need not have participated in every or even most aspects of popular Xer "fashion" in order to acknowledge various trends as meaningful.

In this book, I interpret *fashion* broadly, as costume and bodily adornment. Fashion is a way for the body, or even the self, to communicate itself to society. Xers produced and displayed their own "fashion," but those styles are also evident in movies, music videos, television, and other popular culture forms. Thus, I will sample a variety of fashionable adornment, fashion both "on the ground" and "in the media."

To begin any fashion-oriented interpretation of pop culture, one must choose which fashion "events"—that is, which particular costumes and bodily adornments—to take into consideration. To select fashion events for analysis in this book, I went by my own memory of fads in the 1980s and 1990s, trends that fellow Xers noted as popular in interviews and discussions, and styles included in various studies of fashion culture. I have culled several popular fashion "events," including heavy-metal clothing styles; crucifixes as accessories; body piercings and tattoos; ripped clothes; the gothic look, grunge, and camouflage; undergarments as outerwear; oversized styles; and blue jeans. Obviously, not all Xers participated in the fashion events I describe. My own experiences and those of others I interviewed, however, lead me to believe that one can be sympathetic to a clothing (or other pop culture) event even if one did not directly participate in it. In other words, pop culture events speak for more than just the direct participants.

Cyberspace is the second form of GenX popular culture I interpret. For the purposes of this book, *cyberspace* mainly refers to the Internet and World Wide Web. Although the Internet (as a popular communications medium) and the World Wide Web gained prominence in the 1980s and early 1990s, involvement with these media can be seen as continuations of two older technological developments: the computer and the video game. Generation X grew up on intimate terms with these machines, and our smooth entry into the nether reaches of cyberspace is directly linked to this technologized upbringing.

Although the number of Americans on-line has been frequently exaggerated, GenXers have generally constituted around one-third of the total number of those in cyberspace. In addition, of the many users of cybertechnologies, particularly the World Wide Web, the average age has consistently dovetailed with the age of the generation's oldest members. The actual number of Xers (and others) on-line represents a great mass of people, but nevertheless accounts for only a small proportion of the U.S. population. This "wired" minority, however, exercises a far greater influence on popular culture consciousness than these small percentages would initially suggest. The significance of cyberspace lies beyond its seemingly endless metastasization into diverse cultures, media, and realms of knowledge; its importance has more to do with its effects on ways of communicating, on the pop culture imagination of a generation, and on our entire society.

The components of cyberspace that I will consider include virtual communities, virtual conceptions of space and location, religious sites in cyberspace, access to "religion" in cyberspace, types of discussion and interest groups, individual virtual communication, the cyberspatial "self," the significance of hypertext, and the bodily experience of being on-line.

Music television's centrality in Xers' lives makes it a worthy candidate for my third form of popular culture. The most common venue for viewing music videos was the twenty-four-hour cable music video channel MTV, which first appeared in 1981. (There have been other avenues for viewing videos, though, including other video channels, network television video specials, "bootleg" taping and trade of music videos, and purchase of music videos packaged individually or as collections.) For at least the first decade of its existence, MTV's viewers were primarily GenXers.

In surveys conducted from 1990 to 1992, when most of the generation was in late adolescence or young adulthood, statistician George Barna found that almost half of Xers (for him, those born from 1965 to 1983) "believe[d] that the values and lifestyles shown in movies, television programs, and music videos are an accurate, representative depiction of the way Americans live and think these days" (1994, p. 71). Barna also found that four out of ten Xers watched MTV every week, a habit certainly related to the fact that nine out of ten Xers had televisions and that two out of three had cable (pp. 80, 85). One study in 1986, when the heart of the generation was in mid-adolescence, found that eighty percent of the Xers surveyed watched MTV, averaging two hours of viewing daily (Sun and Lull, 1986, p. 117).

Why this compulsion to watch? There is a popular assumption that videos offer a "definitive" interpretation of a song (Roe and Löfgren, 1988, p. 311; Sun and Lull, 1986, p. 121). This idea frequently colors Internet discussions of music groups; when people cannot agree on a song's meaning, they shift the discussion to what is perceived as the ultimate authority—the music video.

Music videos employ a plethora of formats, from edited concert footage to science fiction narratives to realistic urban cityscapes to cartoon adventures, each dramatizing a particular song. Those who have never seen a music video need only imagine the numerous creative ways in which a "story" about a particular song could be told. Then, the multivalent, evocative possibilities of video making become apparent.

From the thousands of music videos that exist (hundreds of which I have seen), I have chosen six to discuss. I selected those with which I was familiar and to which I attributed religious significance. These videos were also popular, increasing the chances that they are meaningful to others. Most, but not all, were shown in heavy rotation on MTV and appeared on popular video countdowns. During the two-and-a-half years in which I spoke with GenXers, gathering information for this book, these videos were among the most common that Xers cited. In treating only a small portion of the videos available, my theological interpretation is in no way exhaustive.

The videos I will consider include Pearl Jam's "Jeremy" (1991), Soundgarden's "Black Hole Sun" (1994), Tori Amos's "Crucify" (1991), R.E.M.'s "Losing My Religion" (1991), Nirvana's "Heart-Shaped Box" (1993), and Madonna's "Like a Prayer" (1989). I will occasionally refer to other videos, as well.

The Religious in Fragments

Nourished on the milk of popular culture, Generation X has developed a keen way of finding meaning in fragmentary and disparate pop culture "moments," from magazine advertisements to television commercials to styles of footwear, in a series of endless reassociations with popular culture ephemera.

One way of recognizing this "meaning in the moment" is to consider our popular music. Simon Frith argues that as we (all of us, not just Xers) listen to modern music, we experience time as "fragmented and multilinear" (1996a, p. 243). Frith calls contemporary music, and by implication our sense of time, "experience grasped in moments" (p. 243). The larger "musical" picture, a coherent sense of "time," seems lost to us today. Our fragmented, sampled music can therefore be understood as a momentary "quotation," an example of the way in which we experience time and find meaning in the rest of our lives.

This insight applies to the popular culture of Generation X and indeed guides my interpretation of popular culture. Because GenX lives in a "culture of moments," I call my book an interpretation of pop culture events.

These "quotations" from the popular culture need to be assembled and reassembled so that we can find or make meaning. In our fragmented culture, ambiguity becomes the norm rather than the exception; experiencing the moment and determining its meaning overshadow any longer view.

In this "culture of moments," music video's exceedingly quick cuts and dizzying mania of montage suddenly make sense. Not only are the cuts quick—the viewing is, as well. The popularity of frequent, short visits to MTV inspired Douglas Coupland's neologism *nanotune,* which is "a brief zap over to MTV during a televised political debate" (Rushkoff, 1994b, p. 14). MTV pilfers moments from other programs. The medium itself derives its momentary nature from its ability to combine an instant of music with a frame of film, to "nail sounds . . . onto visible space and spatial segments" (Jameson, 1995, p. 300).

When viewed as part of a "culture of moments," cyberspace appears as a powerful technological bridge between the ephemeral and the eternal.

In regard to fashion, scarification of the body seems not solely masochistic but also a way to get beyond this "now," this moment—a way to ensure a continuity of the body. We are a fashionable generation, constantly reimagining each moment, assuming the future to be a chain of unending renegotiations of moments, and sensing the possibility of the instant. Our popular culture is predicated on a continual demise and rebirth, on a continual recycling, on moving in and out of style. Slippage of context and historical amnesia are the fruits of a "culture of moments"; together, they shape our struggle to make meaning from popular culture.

This culture of moments derives from—and fuels—what Douglas Rushkoff calls the "datasphere," popular culture's massive media system of recycling stories and images (1994b, pp. 4–15). The datasphere's prevalence becomes apparent in snippets of Generation X conversations, which are frequently "a regeneration of imagery already in the media" (1994b, p. 8). I would include in the datasphere an intimate pop culture linkage that goes beyond electronic media; fashion, cyberspace, and music videos are constantly shifting constellations of popular culture that are continually reconfigured in new meanings. The recombinatory nature of the datasphere means that time, meaning, and experience are bound to be "momented." Even when individual Xers boldly step out and define their sense of meaning *against* the datasphere, against the menagerie of MTV, fashion, or cyberimages, they still explain themselves *in relation to* the datasphere. Resisting the datasphere is one way of recognizing its omnipresence, its authority.

This datasphere is largely a culture of autonomous images. My three forms of popular culture frequently appropriate or suggest religious images. If we gently touch such images with our interpretive handkerchiefs, we may see that they are still damp with religious residue.

The image is the ground, the unit of experience, the frame for each of the pop culture forms I interpret. Music video is a collection of televisual "musical" images. Cyberspace is a series of virtual images. Fashion conveys the image of the self and the self as image.

What unites all these images? Each image in pop culture is a sign (whether a pierced navel, a crucifix, or a fish on a cutting board) that refers to something else. A reference to sensual religious art in a music video reminds us of worship, sex, devotion, passion. What, we wonder, does *passion* mean, where is it found, and to what does it refer? A pierced navel recalls pain, the body, the belly. The belly is full of religious history and meaning, opening more religious paths of interpretation. A virtual monastery in cyberspace signifies a place of peace, of scholarship, of community, further representing other theological signs.

Thus, any GenX pop culture interpretation is a chain of signs, with one image leading to another. The more these signs evoke the ground, horizon, or "limits" of our human experiences, the more "religious" our interpretation of the image may be. My task as a GenX theologian is to plumb, inquire, interrogate, associate, unleash, be playful, and look for traces of theological residue on the surfaces of these images, if only to see God moving away from us, sensing the egress of the divine, as Moses did (Exodus 33).

Religious imagery bestows its blessings of religious simulation on the popular culture, and the culture bestows on the religious its own blessings of relevance. Just because the popular culture uses these signs does not mean that it has corralled or entirely commodified the religious impulses that emanate from fashion, cyberspace, and music video. Popular culture has a field day with the religious, reconstituting the sacred precisely in the midst of a multimillion-dollar culture industry. An interpretation of popular culture that attends to GenX's culture of moments may well yield a theological interpretation by, for, and about this X generation.

○

In later chapters, I will turn to the particulars of that interpretation, illustrating the GenX focus on experience, suffering, and ambiguity. Before looking at these positive qualities of GenX religiosity, however, I must first turn to a negative characteristic, examining the ways in which GenXers harbor deep suspicion about religious institutions.

PART TWO

HOW RELIGION STILL MATTERS

FOUR CENTRAL THEMES IN GenX RELIGIOSITY

4

INSTITUTIONS ARE SUSPECT

"IF YOU WANT TO TALK ABOUT CHURCH, I'm not very interested."

This was perhaps the single most common sentence that I heard from Xers over the past several years in discussions and interviews. Most frequently, this statement was followed by something like, "I still think people can be spiritual or religious without going to churches or synagogues." Some even added the rhetorical question, "Do you think it really makes a difference to God?"

Many people, especially our elders, cannot think about what it means to be religious without conjuring up an image of a particular institution. For Catholics, in particular, the institution of the Church holds pride of place as an instrument of God's grace and salvation on earth.

Those who practice their faith completely apart from institutions do not usually belong to a religious movement for very long; a religion's stability seems to depend on its becoming institutionalized, which means that it evolves rules, authorities, and worship rituals. For example, in the history of the early Christian Church, there was a long and uneven process of institutionalization. What began as a radical and inclusive movement of Jesus' followers soon threatened to become a Church that took its basic structures from the surrounding culture.

When religious institutions become too institutionalized, however, their atrophied ministries often encourage boredom, indifference, or outright rebellion on the part of the faithful. This has been particularly true throughout history in my own Christian tradition, once people sense the difference between Jesus' radical message and the institutions that minister in his name.

When religious institutions come under attack, what is at stake, therefore, is the very viability of the future of their message. If the institution withers, the abuses and inadequacies it represents may end . . . but so, too, may the tradition that inspired the institution's critics in the first place.

Generation X approaches religion with a lived theology that is very suspicious of institutions. Indeed, Xers have a heavily ingrained (one could say "institutional") suspicion or skepticism (even cynicism) in general. This skepticism surfaces most acutely in regard to those who purport to be looking out for the generation's good. As the self-appointed guardians of Xers'—and all—souls, religious institutions are therefore frequent objects of GenX criticism.

Through pop culture, GenXers attack religious institutions. These assaults are not just an anonymous bludgeoning of wide-bodied targets, though. Xers find their more specific marks by deriding the Catholic Church, in particular, and reclaiming Jesus against Christian Churches. Although this theme could be stated more positively as an "embrace of the noninstitutional," the "deconstruction" of religious institutions precedes the "reconstruction" of religious alternatives.

Criticizing Religious Institutions

Several music videos illustrate this GenX suspicion of institutions, employing provocative metaphors to make their attacks memorable.

The Cross in a Birdcage

Tori Amos's videos are both passionate and personal. She has risen to stardom not only because of her idiosyncratic, sensual singing and songwriting but also because of her unusual visual presence, including long red hair, expressive lips, and an animated Jaggeresque mouth.

As the daughter of a Methodist minister, Amos is in intimate touch with an institutional embodiment of the Church. She honestly shares her ambivalence about growing up in a religious home. In a short interview segment (from a collection of Amos videos) that precedes the "Crucify" video, she states her personal distaste for the Church as an institution.

In Amos's *Little Earthquakes* video collection, the interview fades into the "Crucify" video. As it does so, Amos speaks over two simultaneous images: a cross on a swinging chain in the foreground and the shadow of a birdcage in the background. In the birdcage stands what looks like a cross. The foreground cross swings lazily in slow motion.

This opening sequence dramatizes Amos's conviction that she has little fondness for the Church as an institution. The cross, swinging on a chain (or is it a leash?), mesmerizes the viewer, suggesting that this cross, the institution's precious (metal) religious truth, hypnotizes its adherents. Slowly pitching from left to right, the cross takes on a metallic shine as the background fades to black. The camera's close-up of the glinting cross represents the Church's gilded fetishization of religious truth. The cross oscillates and scintillates, shining briefly in the darkness, making a final pass through Amos as her torso comes into view. To my reading, the images suggest that she has internalized (during her childhood?) this fetishized object of the Church, a golden bird that the Church keeps in its gilded cage. Artful and subtle, this is an attack on the Church as an institution that selfishly cages its glinting, dubious truth and hypnotizes its adherents with a gilded message. It is all brilliantly articulated in about ten seconds.

Spilled Milk

The video for "Losing My Religion" begins with a shot that lasts several seconds in near silence before the song starts. Michael Stipe, the lead singer of R.E.M., sits near a pitcher of milk resting on a window ledge. A gentle rain falls outside. The camera tracks a couple of band members as they jog slowly in a semicircle in opposite directions, crossing paths and looking up in the air. The pitcher suddenly falls off the ledge, splattering milk across the floor.

This scene foreshadows two interrelated themes in the video. First, the band members look heavenward to find a (fallen) Jesus, who eventually falls to earth. Second, the spilled milk raises critical questions: Should we cry over spilled milk? Is the loss of religion, of an institution, something to be mourned? What exactly have we lost? The milk represents religion; the spill indicates the liquidation of its authority in the lives of Xers.

The next series of images continues the meditation on spilled milk. Michael Stipe looks desolate as a band mate lovingly rubs his shoulders and then appears in front of Stipe in cruciform—his arms are outstretched, in the form of Christ or a cross. Cut to Stipe, who sits brooding in front of a white cloth taped to the wall. A shaft of light plays across the blank cloth (but what does the cloth cover?), which points to the absence of a proper religious icon. In doing so, the cloth itself functions as an irreverent icon of impropriety, of lost religion. Whereas Madonna prefers to croon in front of crucifixes or other religious icons, R.E.M. emphasizes that the icon is definitely absent from the scene. In front of this anti-icon, Stipe sits, troubled.

That's me in the corner,
That's me in the spotlight
Losing my religion
Trying to keep up with you
And I don't know if I can do it
Oh, no, I've said too much
I haven't said enough
(1991)

In the space between saying too much and not saying enough, the singer hesitantly and ambiguously feels the loss of religion. As is true of many Xers, he stands outside the institution, outside formal "religion," feeling both hidden ("in the corner") and exposed ("in the spotlight") in his loss.

Sinister Ministers

Like R.E.M., Soundgarden takes up the theme of lost religion, of standing outside the institution, but in my view adds to that the criticism that institutional religion itself is lost. The setting for Soundgarden's "Black Hole Sun" video is a picture-perfect suburban neighborhood, where bright blue skies are interrupted only by lolling, marshmallow clouds. This was an ideal or real setting in the upbringing of many Xers—particularly those who watched MTV. To illustrate just how middle-class (and white) the neighborhood is, a montage of suburban images flickers by, including a middle-aged white man in a trendy jogging suit mowing the lawn in front of a big white house, which has carefully groomed flowers and lawn furniture. In the kitchen, a suburban mom with carefully coiffed hair prepares a meal. Innocently, their daughter jumps rope in the plush grass of the big yard. Yet there is something unsettling and synthetic about the entire scene. The colors are a bit too sharp, and everyone is a little too happy and manicured—or sedated. Only later in the video does the charade of the suburban lifestyle emerge clearly with the "dawning" of the black hole sun (as I discuss in Chapter Six).

Soundgarden's mockery of suburbia is directly linked to a strong critique of Christian religious institutions. Early in the video, four men gather under a sign declaring The End Is Near. The men are caricatures of Christian ministers. One, clad in black, is likely a priest. Another wears a lavender suit and a prominent crucifix. A third is bearded with dark glasses, a top hat, and large crucifix. The last is a clean-cut man wearing a white tuxedo and pink shirt. A gold crucifix rests on his chest and two small golden crosses adorn his lapel. (The latter men, according to their clerical garb, might not be Catholic, but they wear crucifixes nonetheless.) Their prominent religious jewelry binds them together visually.

These representatives of religious institutions do not appear to be genuine men of faith; they remind us of what Eric Hoffer calls "true believers"; they are blind adherents to a cause who "breed fanaticism, enthusiasm, fervent hope, hatred, and intolerance . . . demand[ing] blind faith and single-hearted allegiance" (1951, p. 9). If the ministers seem shallow, it is because their faith is so deeply implicated in American middle-class culture that they are as uninteresting as the "average" family we viewed at the outset, but they are more sinister because of their authority.

These four stop in front of the man who is mowing his lawn, and they smile. The girl who is jumping rope looks up to see them. While the priest holds aloft his Bible, which is draped with crucifixes that dangle like sacred, dainty tendrils, the group beckons to her, holding a sign that reads Faith Saves. Here, the video invokes (and lampoons) a theological slogan, drawing on a distinction popularized during the sixteenth-century Protestant Reformation—the contrast between salvation for Christians by "faith" in Christ or by good "works." Classical Protestant theology makes more of a distinction (but not a separation) between the two than Catholic theology.

The Faith Saves sign indicts the institutionalization of Christian traditions that have made what should be merely a *distinction* into a clear *separation* of faith from works, where works of justice and mercy are no longer required of believers. This separation of faith from works is made playfully ironic by the amount of "work" these ministers—and by implication, "Christianity"—undertake to proclaim "faith alone." The video, then, sides with the Epistle of James (2:14) from the Christian Scriptures, "What good is it, my brothers and sisters, if you say you have faith but do not have works? Can faith save you?" The video suggests that there is no resurrecting this way of being religious, separating faith from works. "Faith by itself, if it has not works, is dead" (James 2:17).

In the next scene, an elderly man rests on hands and knees like a domesticated animal, poised in front of his television, observing the face of the bearded minister. This is the image of the televangelist with whom Xers are familiar. The steady fall in the 1980s of preachers—"victims" of sexual scandal and monetary mismanagement—is a standard part of the Xer grudge against religious institutions. The video hardly needs to elaborate on this theme to ensure that Xers understand it, so it spends little time on the image.

What these opening scenes illustrate is the extent to which official "Christianity" has become intimately bound up with American middle-class culture. In this way, the gospel's radical message has been liquidated and made to support the American dream of middle-class (white) Americans.

Catholic theologian Johannes Baptist Metz explores this problem in his native bourgeois German culture. Metz wonders whether Christianity in the West Germany of the late 1970s became so bound up with bourgeois culture that it nearly sacrificed the radical, countercultural essence intrinsic to Christianity and accommodated itself to the contemporary economic, political, and cultural situation. Metz muses whether Christianity has become too subject to the influence of money to be able to oppose the prevailing culture at all (Metz and Moltmann, 1995).

In the prophetic mode of Metz, but with the *use* of popular culture, the Soundgarden video voices Xers' righteous rage at a Christian Church that has fused and confused itself with the American dream so deeply.

Electronically Leveled Institutions

Insofar as cyberspace influences Xers' worldview, they are increasingly participants in a subtle attack on religious hierarchy and rigid institutions. The environment of cyberspace provides resources that are ripe for upsetting hierarchies. Access to e-mail is fairly widespread, and one does not need to be part of the cultural elite to set up a Web page. The most socially unacceptable topics can become the subjects of discussion groups. Fugitives from orthodoxies of all sorts become the kings or queens of their own hills (or home pages) in cyberspace and expect that many will read what they have to say. It is a new, experimental, and imaginative space in American culture, as yet largely unregulated, and certainly beyond the control of religious institutions. Based on these modes of operation, media theorist Douglas Rushkoff suggests (with some hyperbole) that those who actively use cyberspace to their advantage can "topple systems of thought as established as organized religion" (1996, p. 15).

Philosophers Mark C. Taylor and Esa Saarinen summarize these qualities of cyberspace in their book *Imagologies*. They write poetically of the Internet: "The register of the imaginary is anarchic. Images proliferate, the net spreads, the volume rises. No one is in control" (1994, "Simcult," p. 9). It is the sense that "no one is in control" that makes cyberspace hostile to the hegemony of religious institutions.

Such a view, however, must be tempered (and I do think Taylor and Saarinen wrote the above line with a touch of melodrama). Hierarchy and "institutional power" (through corporations) still make their presence known on the Net. Access to cyberspace is costly, and only a technical elite can fully understand and use much of the available technology. There *are* still people in control. It seems reasonable, however, to envision cyberspace as a site of resistance to the hegemony of religious institutions.

Cyberspace also threatens the stability of religious institutions because it is a radically pluralistic space. Cyberspace unsteadies many religious dichotomies: private/public, holy/unholy, sacred/profane, Jewish/Gentile, Christian/pagan. The divisions that set one religious institution off from another are not immune to this leveling effect.

Xers thrive, for example, in a cyberspatial realm in which the distinction between public and private space is blurred or demolished. When I sit down at my computer and dial in to a local Internet access provider, I immediately connect via the World Wide Web to any of several million once-disparate "locations": from Cambridge City Hall to the French Ministry of Culture to museums in Israel. Where my "personal space" begins and ends becomes impossible to answer, particularly because I can electronically mark places that are geographically distant but virtually nearby; if I use an electronic bookmark, I can arrive more quickly the next time I log on.

As bits fire at the speed of light, the local and the global sizzle into one another. In cyberspace, one has as much opportunity to associate with the Mexican government as with the European Economic Community. Xers lead the way in reading, writing, researching, and surfing every day with a community of scholars of Norwegian culture, feminist theology, chicken recipes, environmental awareness, or television trivia.

This pluralist character leads to a "relativizing" of religions and their truth claims for those in cyberspace. That is, someone surfing the Net can easily assess any number of religions, which raises the question of their relative equality. Both "orthodox" and "heterodox" religious groups and traditions exist side by side in cyberspace, becoming equally accessible in a new way. In fact, the "heterodox" user may find fellow travelers more easily in cyberspace. In a study of discussion groups on Usenet (a collection of thousands of Internet discussion groups), futurist Jay Kinney found that discussions about "traditional" religions were heavily outnumbered by "a proliferation of alternative spiritualities," including astrology, Scientology, and paganism (1995, p. 769). Cyberspace as religious space is a fascinating place in which the "orthodox" must confront the "heterodox"; the heterodox heretic and orthodox hierarch meet each other in "space" that is theologically fluid. More profoundly, the Net exposes the fluidity of the orthodox and heterodox positions and gives ever wider scope to the catholicity (universality) of religious belief. The Net brings it to virtual light. If the Web is taken by Xers as an ontology (a way of being) or an epistemology (a way of knowing), will this continue to affect Xer conceptions of religion?

Part of the radical leveling of religion in cyberspace seems a result of the fact that religious spaces—like all Web spaces—are assigned a Net address (such as "www.my_religion.net") that is as transient and manipulable as any cyberephemera. The more such religious space comes to be associated with a cyberaddress, the more the uniqueness of that religious space is diminished. Simply by changing a few letters in the address, one arrives at a completely different location in cyberspace. This is a wholly different experience from physically moving a certain distance to visit various religious sites in the "real" world, some of which may not even be open for "browsing." When religious devotees note the ephemerality and heightened access of religion in cyberspace, they may begin to doubt the absolute claims of sacredness and permanence that a religious site can make in the "real world."

In this way, a cyberaddress and its religious referent (such as an institutional Church) exist in constant conflict. The cyberaddress (an ephemeral set of letters and numbers) and its religious site (representing eternal truth) strive to subvert each other—but given the very medium, they must both strive and be denied in their striving: the Web site will never become a stable location, and religious claims to absolute truth will not subside.

Transience and Disposability

This criticism of religious institutions has several implications about lived spirituality, both for Xers and institutions. The GenX theology "happening" in the pop culture, the general insufficiency of religious institutions, and the plurality of religious options in cyberspace all invite Xers to open themselves to many different religious traditions. Whether on the Web or in the real world, Xers are not as bound by institutions as their grandparents were. In this regard, Xers challenge religious institutions to clarify the uniqueness of their spiritual message and tradition. Religious institutions can creatively rise to this challenge. In my own preaching, for example, I often try to touch on explicitly Catholic themes, as much for the visitors (many Xers) "shopping" our church as for the "regulars."

Xer religiosity calls out the ways in which religious institutions become ill, institutionalized (as the caged cross in "Crucify" represents), and irrelevant. Xers continue to explore how religious institutions, at least in their outward structures, are all socially *made,* not divinely *given,* and can thus be unmade. This can be a liberating spiritual discovery, particularly for Xers who grew up with religious institutions that valued the institution's success over preaching and practicing a religious message.

In highlighting institutions' imperfect and finite character, Xers can examine their own relationships to religious institutions, to find out whether they are "in the corner," brooding, or "in the spotlight" of shame in relation to their own religious tradition. Xers must take stock of their place in religious institutions as they reconstruct their spirituality; they can challenge institutions while holding onto their own irreverence.

Xer religiosity challenges institutions to examine the space between their concrete expressions of religious traditions and the assumptions of the surrounding culture. For example, say that a particular religious institution preaches favorite themes on a regular basis. Do those themes also appear on the radio, in popular psychology books, or in newspaper editorials? Xers might as well choose those media, instead. GenX religiosity is hardest on institutions whose relationship with culture compromises the religious message preached. Likewise, Xers provoke institutions to level their own bureaucracies, to ask whether they are ephemeral, evolving, or fixed.

Institutions can learn from this GenX criticism, taking to heart their own disposability. Institutions entrenched in and colluding with middle-class culture tend to assume that they have an inalienable right to an infinite existence. Accepting their own ephemerality means being willing—paradoxically—to make the institution's future secondary and to focus instead on the religious message to be lived.

If religious institutions speak authentically from a position of weakness and not from a rigid belief in a divine entitlement to preach, it can teach Xers that transience does not necessarily mean spiritual irrelevance. For Xers, who are so immersed in an ephemeral culture, this would be a blessed message to hear.

Indeed, to minister to Xers, institutions are challenged to engage this transience by entering cyberspace in all its plurality and ambiguity. They must be willing to bring a uniquely religious message to the raucous cyberspace public square. Of course, Xers may find the public face presented in cyberspace even more unwelcoming than their local religious institution seems to be. It is a terrific and sad irony, for instance, when Catholic dioceses set up Web sites that adorn themselves in Catholic garb from past centuries. These dioceses use the latest technology to show off a Church of the past, not the future.

For their part, institutions offer spiritual challenges to Xers in regard to the same theme. Institutions may well ask Xers how their own spirituality can be immune to the deep influences of culture, such as bourgeois suburbia or multicultural urban centers. Institutions may wonder whether Xers interrogate their own spirituality as intensely as they criticize institutions.

In regard to cyberspace, institutions can challenge Xers to examine criti-
cally whether a cyberinfluenced spirituality is too much of an accommo-
dation to Western capitalist culture, where choice, convenient shopping,
and individual purchasing power reign supreme.

In these ways, GenX pop culture's criticism of religious institutions puts
hard questions of religious practice to both Xers and institutions.

Attacking the Catholic Church

Catholicism is not immune to GenX popular culture's criticism of religious
institutions. Among all Churches, in fact, the Catholic Church suffers the
most regular attacks. (The biggest kid on the block is the easiest target.)

Crucifix/ations

Crucifixes would seem to be the least likely fashion statement in the heavily Protestant United States. Crucifixes, which differ from mere crosses by
bearing an image of a crucified Jesus, are among the most identifiable
pieces of Catholic jewelry. Xers' interest in crucifixes as fashion accessories
dates back to the influence of pop artist Madonna. In her 1984 video hit
"Like a Virgin," she wears a long rosary with large beads as a necklace.
The rosary, replete with a crucifix, whips around her neck and waist as
she dances in a gondola down a scenic canal. With this video, she became
one of the first entertainers to turn a crucifix into a fashion statement.

Xers wear crucifixes in many ways, from small and unobtrusive golden
ones to more explicit, large, silver crosses with writhing Jesus figures pinned
to them. I often see Xers wear overly dramatic crucifixes, with crossed nails
forming the beams and an oversized Jesus figure on the cross. Moderate-
sized crucifixes are more common as fashion accessories, however.

As a quintessentially Catholic artifact, its use as popular adornment is
a playfully ironic appropriation of something at the heart of Catholic
identity. Whereas previous generations took the crucifix (often along with
a rosary) as a very serious and pious expression of religiousness, Xers have
turned the crucifix (and rosaries, as well, when worn as necklaces) into a
free-floating religious talisman in our ready-made "religiosity." This is an
indirect, subtle, and almost undetectable poke at the Catholic Church.

It is an ambiguous appropriation, however. Why have Xers borrowed
this particular religious symbol, so heavily identified with Catholicism, as
a fashion statement? It symbolizes something with which some Xers identify, no matter whether they come from various religious traditions or
none at all. It is less likely that Xers would wear simple, small crosses in

ironic religiosity, because those crosses have a strong identification with Protestant, usually conservative traditions. Very few evangelical Protestant artifacts are appropriated in this way. Evangelical tracts, Jesus shirts, or other conservative Protestant paraphernalia rarely enter GenX popular culture. Catholic kitsch is more successful with GenX. Because this is a religious symbol dear to an earlier generation of Catholics, its fashionability and appropriation as an accessory function as a subtle mockery of the institution.

Wearing the crucifix as fashion also makes an ironic statement about those in our culture who continue to wear it out of (pre-Xer) piety. By turning it into an accessory, Xers highlight the extent to which those who pretend to wear it as a symbol of piety are also wearing it as a fashion statement—they are presenting their religious self-image to others. Xers first show that there is nothing so sacred about a religious symbol that it cannot be turned into a fashion accessory. They then have the ironic audacity to claim that we are not the ones responsible for turning the crucifix into fashion. Xers merely make explicit what previous generations have already been doing!

Xers will rarely bother to protest against the institution directly; they simply turn its most hallowed symbols into fashion statements in a way that both honors the religious image and yet takes an ironic stance toward it. At the same time, Xers irreverently skewer the excesses of earlier generations, showing that we were not the first to confuse piety with fashion.

Jesus in Oz

If the use of crucifixes represents a subtle attack on the Catholic institution, I interpret one Nirvana video as making a harsh and direct assault on institutional Catholicism, partly by mocking a "living crucifix." Nirvana's last and perhaps most popular video was "Heart-Shaped Box," from the song on their album *In Utero*. As a preface to those who *claim* Jesus against religious institutions, this video *ridicules* Jesus as a way of taking a lance to the side of the Church.

In the opening scene of "Heart-Shaped Box," a bearded old man with long hair lies motionless in a hospital bed to one side of a sparsely arranged room. The shadowy setting and stillness of the scene suggest that his berth is a deathbed. From an aerial shot, we see that a black cross dramatically marks the floor in the center of the room. The three band members sit opposite the bed. They look bored, affecting stereotypical Xer ennui. The slightly parted curtains admit a thin stream of bright sunlight that slices across the floor.

As Kurt Cobain forces out the first lyrics, the scene cuts to the old man. Wearing nothing but a loincloth and a Santa Claus hat, his bony, frail body cuts a sorry figure as he examines poppies in a field. The identity of this tragic figure is revealed as he begins to ascend a nearby cross with a ladder leaning against it.

Immediately, the video reveals its playful attitude as several associations coagulate. The scene evokes *The Wizard of Oz*, with fields of bright flowers and narrow forested paths between ominous trees. This figure of Jesus hangs from his own cross like a scarecrow in the Land of Oz. His surroundings confirm his tragicomic appearance, making his crucifixion like something from a fairy tale.

This Santa Claus–Jesus has been not only denuded but also unmasked as a fraud, a childhood hoax, a useless claus(e) deserving his own (death) sentence. Through several close-ups, we see how aged and frail this pseudo-messiah really is. Resigned to hang on the cross, he is stripped not only of physical strength but also of purpose and will. The crucifixion has become an act, a charade performed by a red-capped weakling atop a cross in Oz.

This is, in my view, the Jesus that has been presented institutionally to many Xers in their childhood and young adult years. This Jesus, which Xers and their popular culture justly mock and ironize, has been domesticated and drained of any spiritual energy. Not only does he wearily climb the cross of his own accord as an empty ritual, but when he does so, no one else is looking. No one cares, not even an apostle who can later note the event for posterity or for a gospel. As Jesus hangs amid the poppies (Jesus the hallucination? Jesus the hallucinogen?), crows alight atop the cross and pick at him. It is as if he is so domesticated that he no longer instills any emotion, including fear. Any positive feelings about Jesus are mocked as sentimentality. Thus, the video illustrates both the image of Jesus as preached by many churches *and* the critique and mockery of that image.

The video next follows a young girl who wears white clerical dress. She resembles a pope or bishop, as well as a witch. This image subtly captures the Church's historical ambivalence toward women, who have been both glorified and denigrated in Church history.

We first see her jumping, grasping for objects hanging from branches. Upon closer inspection, we see that she is trying to grab fetuses in the trees. As she does so, an obese woman "angel" waits for the girl with open arms. The angel wears a costume that makes her innards appear exposed; the muscles in her torso and stomach are visible and bulge grotesquely. This disturbing series of images is again a montage of mockery directed at the institutional Church. With these bizarre images, the video rolls out an attack on what is considered to be a Catholic control of women and the female body.

As the video unfolds, it employs more and more Catholic images and themes, which help to establish the context of the song's outcry. By showing a girl dressed in clerical robes, the video seems to reproach a religious institution that bars women from its highest positions of clerical authority (later in the video, this girl will, ironically, be the only one who comes to Jesus' side in his suffering). The little girl could not dream—even in Oz—of becoming a bishop in the Catholic Church, the ironic suggestion of her attire. The fetishization of fetuses by the girl and by the camera itself mocks what the video takes to be the Catholic Church's preoccupation with preserving the unborn. This is a rare video attack on the Church in regard to abortion. The provocative image of the fetuses actually helps us understand the obese female angel. With her body seemingly transparent to all, we become voyeurs of her innermost organs. This clever, if distasteful, reduction to absurdity of the Church's intrusion into women's bodily rights adds further to the video's criticism of organized religion.

This constellation of criticism comes to a head as the girl wanders up to Jesus, who is on the cross and is suddenly seen wearing a papal miter (the traditional triangular head covering of Catholic bishops). The denuded and unmasked Jesus is also a defrocked pope. While the bejeweled miter twinkles in the twilight, the girl jumps up to grasp the Jesus-pope. Both, of course, are unreachable. The scene has become intriguingly tragicomic and confrontational; far from Jesus' suffering servanthood, contemporary papal splendor and power are parodied at the same time as the overglamorization of Jesus' crucifixion is intensely criticized.

In the final series of images, the girl's white cap blows off into a murky puddle, becoming a witch's black hat. Employing another reduction to absurdity, Nirvana completes the transformation of the girl into a witchy "other"; the association with witchiness symbolizes how she is insufficient in the Church by dint of her sex. In black robes, she attends Jesus' bedside, the symbols of her outcast status now doubling as garments of mourning. The video's critique of the institutional Church's stand on abortion continues in this scene as the ailing messiah's intravenous tubes are connected to a fetus that floats in red liquid. These images—which are as religiously shocking and offensive as any I have ever seen on MTV—seem to illustrate the extent to which even a bedridden Jesus is barely sustained by the lifeblood of the unborn, which the video takes to be one fet(us)ish of Catholicism.

These scenes give us some insight into a lyric that I interpret as being uttered by the Jesus figure. If so, he is talking about the little girl who grabs at him; she is the one who looks at him, as the lyrics suggest, as if she is looking at a frail fish.

Jesus was symbolized in early Christian tradition as a fish; the letters of the Greek word *icthus* (literally "fish") stood for Jesus Christ. This is not a story, however about the obstinate "one that got away." The Jesus mocked by "Heart-Shaped Box" is viewed as a fish, the lyrics suggest, only when he is frail. The Jesus whom the video presents is shorn of will and identity and is packed (in ice?) snugly into a full-blown system of institutional religious trappings from which he cries for liberation in his deafening resignation. This Jesus is all too well known to Christian (and formerly Christian) Xers, because this is the Jesus to whom their Church has exposed them.

A lyric suggesting a seductive slip into something like quicksand refers to the difficulty of separating oneself from the religious images of one's upbringing and even from the importance of faith to contemporary life. This quicksand snares in two ways. First, it continually draws in the spiritually curious, who are fed a fairy-tale meal of a watered-down Jesus who is Church property. Second, it snares those who, ironically, ought to have a better place within the Church, given its core message. Thus, the girl who is most kind to the suffering old Jesus is still imaged as a witch or anticleric because she was sucked into the quicksand. The lyrics also mock the institutional Church's promises and threats of heaven and hell, which at this stage in the video have been rendered all but irrelevant.

The video's final moments return to the opening scene, with the old man flat on the bed. But is Jesus any closer to death or to life now? We cannot tell. He remains inert. A band member stands up and throws open the curtains. He is bathed in blinding white light, arms extended in cruciform. This brief moment of transfiguration, wherein "his clothes became dazzling white" (Matthew 17:2), is not a conclusion at all. Rather, we are taken up into hope, into possibility. After the video's devastating—some would say heretical—attack on Jesus and the Church, Nirvana concludes with a hopeful moment.

A Return to Jesus

In accord with this pop culture theme of Catholic institutional suspicion, Catholic Xers can continue to claim their own faith and not just passively accept what their Church teaches them. We witness again and again that although the Church may ideally be sacramental—a living sign of God's presence—faith in God and faith in the Church are not the same thing.

Catholic Xers can make sure that their criticisms are as direct as possible by immersing themselves in the history and tradition of the Church.

This becomes a necessity for Catholic Xers, because so much of what people claim to be "Catholic" today is in tension or outright contradiction with the depth and breadth of Catholic tradition and history. By using knowledge of this history and tradition as a resource to criticize current Church arrangements creatively, Catholic Xers make their criticism even more pointed.

If the Church as an institution can hear this harsh criticism, it can learn from GenX. At a fundamental level, it needs to bring its practices and preaching back to its origins and its center—Jesus—in order to appeal to Christian Xers. As Gustavo Gutierrez, a Catholic Peruvian theologian, writes, "The church cannot be a prophet in our day if she herself is not turned to Christ. She does not have the right to talk against others when she herself is a cause of scandal in her interpersonal relations and her internal structures" (1988, p. 70). GenX pop culture would strongly endorse that prophetic insight.

The Church, surprisingly, may find itself in a position to teach Xers something of utmost importance: countercultural witness in the name of faith. For example, at its best, it can teach concern for the poor and excluded, care for immigrants, and economic justice for all. Our generation, which so frequently takes ironic stances as it reappropriates the materialism it has been given, might even reject such materialism in favor of a countercultural witness if the Church toward which it is so skeptical inspired it to do so.

Gaining Jesus, Losing Religion?

Pop culture's suspicion and criticism of social and religious institutions have a pungency that would seem to reflect the depth of Xer skepticism sufficiently. GenX popular culture, however, does not just catapult attacks on the institution from outside the walls. It takes its suspicion of institutions right to the center of Christianity, to the person of Jesus. In the ultimate act of criticism, GenX pop culture uses Jesus *against* the very institution that claims to witness to his memory.

A Fallen Angel

In "Losing My Religion," the first intimation of Jesus is an old man resting against an angel, both seated on the limb of a tree. Is the man weary or just asleep? Grey-haired and bearded, he is fitted with a pair of angelic wings and clothed in orange robes. His age is striking; he looks to be in his sixties or seventies. According to the Christian Scriptures, Jesus was probably in his early thirties at the time of his crucifixion and resurrection. The videos of "Losing My Religion" and "Heart-Shaped Box" are two of the very few representations of Jesus as an old man in contemporary art. This older Jesus is the central figure of the "religion" that is being lost in the video.

The spotlight turns to Jesus (marking him briefly as a star). He tumbles out of the tree, becoming a fallen star, and lands in a heap on the ground ("like a hurt, lost and blinded fool," lead singer Stipe opines, but is this the narrator, Michael Stipe, or Jesus?). As a rotund, bearded man helps him stand up, we realize that the man we took for Jesus also appears to be a "fallen angel" with his own wings.

The scene segues into a series of biblical pictures as Stipe sings:

> Consider this, consider this
> Hint of the century
> Consider this slip
> That brought me to my knees
> (1991)

If one does not check the "official" lyrics, it sounds as if Stipe is singing, "consider this *hit* of the century." What is this "hit" of the century? Is it literally a "smack"—the thud that Jesus makes as he strikes the ground as a fallen angel?

As Stipe sings the phrase "consider this," the plump, bearded man motions in a disgusted and outraged manner toward the antihero, the fallen angel. This phrase and hand motion in the direction of the Jesus character suggest Pilate's exclamation (John 19:5) to the chief priests and Roman soldiers: "Behold the man!" Behold this man, who was purported to have been a messiah, fallen from heaven, hardly strong enough to stand on his own two feet! "Behold the man!"

The man is indeed beheld, even probed. One of those standing next to Jesus sticks his fingers into the wound in Jesus' side. According to the scriptural accounts, the wound was created when a soldier thrust his lance into Jesus' side as he hung on the cross. It is disgusting to watch the man violate Jesus' body. As the would-be doubting Thomas explores the wound, Jesus grimaces. The incident is nothing like the anesthetized account in John's Gospel (John 20:26–29), which omits any details of how Thomas places his hand in Jesus' side, even though Jesus invites the inquiry. The video's version is humiliating for Jesus and perversely fascinating for the Thomas character. The Gospel story ends with Thomas's expression of faith: "My Lord and my God!" The parallel scene in "Losing My Religion" ends with an implied "My God, you're my Lord?"

There is nothing and no one in the video's mininarrative to believe. We are not witnessing a risen Jesus, confidently striding through a locked door and emanating authority to the disciples (John 20:19–23). The Jesus of "Losing My Religion" looks exhausted, worn out, and sorry—not any sort of messiah inviting friendship or faith at all. Like those who mocked Jesus while he hung helplessly on the cross, we want to chant at the screen the words from Mark 15:31: "He saved others, why can't he save himself?" But we have no history of this Jesus in the video and therefore no reason to feel sympathy for him. This Jesus is just a haggard old man, acting as if he were not quite sure why he is on earth in the first place.

In the next series of shots, several people attend the ailing Jesus. One of them holds a crutch, which represents a clever twist on the biblical miracle stories. A traditional retelling of a Gospel story would have the man with the crutch toss it away as Jesus heals him. In this story, though, the crutch is meant for Jesus! Clothed only in a tunic, Jesus leans on those attending him. As he does so, the portly comrade reaches his hand to Jesus' head and pulls off a grey wig. Remarkably, Jesus is even older, more frail, confused, and farcical than everyone (including the viewer) thought. No wonder the narrator loses his religion, uncertain that he can follow this man any longer. Stipe sings:

> Losing my religion . . .
> Trying to keep up with you
> And I don't know if I can do it . . .
> Consider this, consider this
> Hint of the century
> Consider this slip
> That brought me to my knees
> Failed
> What if all these fantasies come flailing around?
> Now I've said too much
> (1991)

As if realizing that his faith has crossed too deeply into doubt, the narrator tries to pull back ("now I've said too much"), but it is already too late. Jesus' attendants laugh heartily at him. They lash him to crossed beams and throw stones at him. In this richly parodic scene, those who criticize Jesus are the first to throw stones, and Jesus himself is the victim of the stone throwing (compare the famous story of the woman caught in adultery in John 8:3–11). As is true earlier, he cannot save himself. Indeed, this stone throwing may contribute to his death.

The ambiguity of the final Jesus scene is disturbing; in a brief shot, his associates work with rope that is wrapped around Jesus' body. Are they releasing him, or are they binding him to the beam, hoping to get him up on the cross so that he might really be the messiah they are hoping for in the end?

The spilled milk signals the end of the story, a very unlikely passion narrative (a Gospel story of Jesus' suffering and death). As this dispassionate narrative of a dispassionate Jesus concludes, Jesus is slumped on the ground (dead?) and the same group huddles over him with concerned expressions. One distraught woman has her arms outstretched.

In the video's closing shot, Stipe remains in his chair. Behind him lie a pair of wings and an open book. (This represents the closure of an extended religious frame that began with the cruciform image at the video's beginning). Even in the parting seconds, R.E.M. cannot resist taking more subtle jabs at institutional religion; the open book, which looks very much like a Bible, sits between the two stylized wings. The Bible, it is implied, has been given heavenly wings and been made divine in Jesus' absence. Meanwhile, Jesus' wings (which do not work, symbolizing how earthbound he is) become the prototype for a stylized, formalized pair of "official" wings on which blacksmiths toil throughout the video in furtive shots. Because Jesus' own wings never carried him beyond the sphere of the mundane and the weak, these stylized wings, the video implies, are based on a fabrication, on wishful thinking. It is suggested that the Bible, then, is divinized folly built on a divine fantasy.

Sympathy for the Fallen

What is happening here theologically and spiritually? The first several times I saw this video, I thought "Losing My Religion" was simply chronicling Jesus' irrelevance by depicting him as a useless old man who might not even want to be the messiah in the first place. Several viewings later, however, I began to think that my first interpretation was too simple. After all, the video's quest wouldn't be worth pursuing unless it were something more than "Look, Jesus never really amounted to much, did he?" The band and the video are more subtle. "Losing My Religion" did not create an elderly, haggard Jesus, ridicule him, and then put him up on the cross just for sport.

Instead, the video is taking seriously the (elderly, haggard, largely irrelevant, but still somehow affecting) Jesus that is preached by so many

Christian Churches. In response to this Jesus, "Losing My Religion" asks, What we are supposed to do with this sorry figure? The milk of the sacred cow, Christianity, has been spilled, and it is not certain that this is worth crying over! Ironically, the sort of "religion" that the video is ridiculing was hardly Xers' to be lost in the first place. "Losing My Religion" puts this Jesus—the one so many Xers have been given—back where the band supposes he belongs. He returns to a suffering situation; sad and pitiful, he tries to return to the cross.

This is not a hostile attack on Jesus to get at the institution, as in "Heart-Shaped Box." There is a more subtle separation of Jesus from the institution here, and that separation is a way of criticizing the Church. In "Heart-Shaped Box," Jesus is pathetic. "Losing My Religion" is sympathetic; there is a human sadness about this fallen Jesus, a disappointment that we can't make him be what he is supposed to be. Yet in that failure to live up to what the Church has made him, we understand him. He is with us, down on the ground, fallen from the sky, where he was out of our reach. Like the uncanny scene in the video, we are caught somewhere between the binding and releasing of Jesus, which has everything to do with Xers' own uncertainty about our freedom and captivity in contemporary culture, about the agonizing moments between hope and nihilism in our private and public lives. I am even tempted to say that Jesus has let the institution down and that the Church has capitalized on a Jesus they do not really seem to know.

I hesitate to draw further theological conclusions about what Xers see in Jesus. The fascination with Jesus in music video is as much an ironic stance toward Jesus as a reclamation of him, showing the emptiness of what many Churches offer. What is an important backdrop to Xers' suspicion of institutions is the implied charge that in fetishizing the cross and suffering, the Church has forgotten why the Romans killed Jesus in the first place. The Church has distanced itself from the dangerous memory of Jesus' revolutionary practice.

Lambs Bleating to Death

In a more veiled but even more provocative way than "Losing My Religion," Soundgarden's "Black Hole Sun" video subtly pits Jesus against the institution.

In one revealing scene, a minister in a white tuxedo bends down delicately, displaying the leash that he holds in his hand. A young lamb waits with gentle expectation, tethered to the other end. In slow motion, the preacher reaches out a hand that holds a baby bottle, squirting a milky, creamy substance. After he places the bottle in the lamb's mouth, the tiny animal sucks the mystery liquid. This craftily constructed sequence can be interpreted as a swift but subtle jab at Christian ministers. This parodied preacher acts as a condescending "shepherd," in implied contrast to the following biblical passage: "The good shepherd lays down his life for the sheep. . . . I lay down my life for the sheep" (John 10:11,15).

The major clue in interpreting this scene occurs during the singing of a lyric which, apart from the video, would be indecipherable. The odd lyric describes the narrator's being personally addressed through a frothy, milky substance.

Meaning froths over, threatening to cream viewers. So often treated as helpless lambs in churches, some Christian Xers can still discern the call of Jesus through the fluff of institutional religion. That is, I interpret the lyrics as suggesting that Jesus' message makes a claim on the lives of Christian Xers, despite the attempts of institutional leaders to make the gospel less sharp, less direct, less countercultural, less political, less cur-dling—in effect, to make it smoother and creamier.

At the same time, the video suggests that it is Jesus himself, the "lamb of God" (John 1:29), who is being suckled and *tamed* by the conde-scending minister's creamy offering. The protectors of institutional Chris-tianity, like the author of the Letter to the Hebrews in the Christian Scriptures, have the "gall" to tell Jesus: "You need milk, not solid food. . . . Solid food is for the mature, for those whose faculties have been trained by practice to distinguish good from evil" (Hebrews 5:12,14). (Perhaps, in this uncanny scene, Soundgarden has mopped up and bottled the evidence of broken institutional religion, the spilled milk from "Losing My Religion," which is why the minister is so eager to feed it to the lamb.)

In a masterfully ironic stroke, Jesus, the lamb of God, is stuck with a bottle in his mouth and bleats to death, screaming in agony. The lyrics turn to describe the recognition of a shriek, and a biblical passage (Matthew 27:46) immediately seems apposite: "My God, my God, why have you forsaken me?"

Christian Xers join in this scream of holy abandonment, which is one source of their serious challenge to the institutional Church. Perhaps more than any recent generation, Xers see behind the curtain; they scoff at the minister's pretense that this lamb of God is on a leash. As if Jesus and his message can be reduced to such simpleminded domesticity. As if the gospel does not elude every attempt to articulate its final meaning. As if it makes sense for those who identify most closely with American middle-class cul-ture to call themselves "ministers" in the name of Jesus. Concurring with Latin American theologian Jon Sobrino, who is "indignant that the reality

of Christ has been manipulated, distorted, commandeered, 'kidnapped'"
(1988, p. 12), Xers see right through this distorting religious institutionalism. The result is a video like "Black Hole Sun."

Suspecting Institutions Through Real and Virtual Religiousness

GenX pop culture and GenX religiosity are profoundly marked by irreverence. Such irreverence can be found in Amos's depiction of a cage containing a cross and a shiny cross hanging from a leash, the iconoclasm of
"Losing My Religion," and the illustration of institutional representatives
in "Black Hole Sun." The appropriation of crucifixes and the music video
images of Jesus are all so irreverent that it almost undercuts their impu-
dence to name the irreverence explicitly.

This irreverence drives the suspicion of institutions found in GenX popular culture in fashion, cyberspace, and music video. Although each
medium has its own mode of addressing institutions, all of them display
evidence of critical attitudes. This is a religious stance we inherited from
the baby boomers, who taught us how to keep a distance from all social
institutions, including religious ones (Roof, 1993). Our skepticism of religious institutions has taken on a uniquely video-centered approach, as is
common in our image-heavy generation.

What does this suggest about GenX religiosity? On the one hand, real
religious institutions lose any privilege they might once have been given,
for example by our grandparents. On the other hand, the "virtual," imi-
tative aspect of GenX religiosity emerges in this suspicion of institutions.
In cyberspace, for example, a new institution of religion is mimicked. Yet
cyberspace is not a real religious institution at all, however much institutions try to inhabit it and proclaim their truth. In fashion, using the crucifix as a fashion accessory both mocks religious symbols and appropriates
them in a new way to disclose personal identity. In music video, the imitation of Jesus unravels and exposes the claims of the institution, as Christian Xers hammer away at the effigy while reclaiming their own lives as
virtually Jesuslike.

The use of irony is a signal element of the virtually religious in Xers'
skeptical depictions of institutions. Irony is evident throughout GenX culture. It is part of the "virtual" element of GenX religiosity and is key to
understanding GenX popular culture. Irony works by negating whatever
is supposedly the most immediate, most obvious meaning, emptying it
out. This emptying-out process may indirectly imply a deeper truth, which
is far more effective than a didactic, forthright statement. Crucifixes as

GenX fashion, for example, are ironic, draining the "expected" meaning from the symbol (an expression of solemn piety) and reappropriating it as an accessory. In a similar way, images of an elderly, weak Jesus are ironic when they show how "empty" the received Jesus really is. In so doing, they suggest a new way of understanding Jesus in GenX religiosity. With both the crucifix and Jesus, as we have seen, a key part of this Xer religiosity is a strong critique of religious institutions.

—————— o ——————

This criticism of religious institutions is only the first step in a Generation X theology. Along with a strong skepticism about institutions, Xers turn inward to focus on their own personal experience. Indeed, it is only in light of this personal experience that the generation has rendered its verdict on religious institutions. Chapter Five will examine this personal emphasis.

5

EXPERIENCE IS KEY

GROWING UP IN A FAIRLY RESERVED suburban Catholic parish, I never understood the religious importance of personal experience until I attended a charismatic Mass in the late 1970s, when I was about ten years old. All around me people were dancing, raising their arms in the air, or gently swaying. A woman sitting next to me folded her hands, raised them close to her lips, and chanted, "Homily, hominy, homily, as they kill our till. Homily, hominy, homily, as they kill our till." I'm not kidding; I still remember the words. For the next several years, I thought she had been chanting a Catholic prayer I had never heard, and I was intrigued by what these vague and mysterious words might have meant (a spiritual meditation on grits, a sermon, and the collection?). Only later, after I watched a television special about the "charismatic movement," did I realize that the woman next to me was speaking in tongues. I was awed by such an intimate religious experience that could so carelessly flout social convention. Thereafter, personal religious experience had a ring of authenticity that remains for me to this day.

Personal Experience as Religious

In this century, personal experience has not always counted so heavily in what it means to be religious. Different eras and cultures have placed more importance on an intellectualized faith or assent to creeds or doctrines. In our own times, submission to an outside authority (an institution or a member of the clergy) has sometimes counted as more religious than personal experiences. For the last few decades in mainstream institutional religions, however, there has been an attempt to recover the religious significance of experience. Xers are heirs to this renewed emphasis.

An expert on baby boomer religiousness, Wade Clark Roof, credits boomers with reintroducing personal experience as a legitimate font of religious truth. As Roof observes, they "are inclined to regard their own experiences as superior to the accounts of others, and the truths found through self-discovery as having greater relevance to them than those handed down by way of creed or custom" (1993, p. 67). Feminist theologians, too, have sought to recover the centrality of experience. Catholic theologian Elisabeth Schüssler Fiorenza writes that "the experience of women struggling for liberation and wholeness" is important for feminist theology (1984, p. xvi). This recovery of experience is especially important for those whose own personal and religious experience has historically been marginalized, particularly women and ethnic and racial minorities in the United States. In valuing experience highly, then, we Xers find ourselves among a great cloud of witnesses to its importance in contemporary spiritual life.

Xers generally find the religious in personal experience, particularly in an emerging form of sensual spirituality. In this turn to experience, there is a constant yearning, both implicit and explicit, for the almost mystical encounter of the human and divine. This turn to experience also manifests in a new interest in communities of faith, as well as in faith lived in the everyday experience of the world. Key to this discussion is the theological concept of *sacramentality*. This pop culture sacramentality suggests that the body and personal experience represent signs of God's grace in the world.

Sacramentals (miniature, personal signs of God and God's grace in the world) emphasize the personal dimension of faith and underscore the sacramentality (visible signs of God's invisible presence) of lived experience. Grounded in accessible, quotidian practices, sacramentals help Xers see their own experience as religious. The divine may be present in the artifacts that attend Xer quests for the religious life. Sacramentality and personal experience both imply that Xers feel a sense of freedom and personal responsibility in regard to their spiritual lives; Xers will not simply receive religious truth paternalistically from a religious authority. What counts as religious must meet the ultimate test: Xers' own personal experience.

Madonna and Saint Martin

The idea that personal experience grounds religiousness surfaces frequently in Madonna's popular video "Like a Prayer" in the form of sacramentals. In the video, the stigmata, a kiss, a crucifix, a small church, and even the main characters all suggest a sense of sacramentality.

In a key opening scene of "Like a Prayer," Madonna gazes admiringly at a statue of a black man behind an altar grate. The votive candles, crucifixes, and other iconography confirm that we are with Madonna in a familiar place for her—a Catholic church. But who is this black man, the object of her devotion? Whereas many viewers see him as Jesus or a priest, I agree with historian of religion Colleen McDannell, who thinks the statue is likely Martin de Porres, an Afro-Peruvian saint (1995, pp. 63–64). The attraction of Madonna, a white woman, to the statue of de Porres, a black man, raises one of the most troublesome race relations issues in the United States—that of interracial relationships, particularly between white women and black men. One of the keys to this video is the significance of Martin de Porres in the Catholic tradition.

Saint Martin (1579–1639) was a lay brother of the Dominican order. He carried out his ministry, centered in Peru, on behalf of the sick, the poor, and African slaves. Pope John XXIII, who called the Second Vatican Council, canonized de Porres in 1962, making him an official Catholic saint. Saint Martin, the child of a Spanish father and a free black woman from Lima, has become known as the patron saint of interracial justice.

Madonna's relationship with this important saint represents a strong critique of American race relations. She means to overcome racial division through a shared religious experience with de Porres. (That may also explain why her hair is brown in this video, not blond; getting back to her hair's probable roots symbolizes a return to her Catholic roots (Rettenmund, 1996, p. 41). This might be further confirmation that the black man is indeed Saint Martin, who is also known as the patron saint of hairdressers!)

Her gaze upon the statue is interrupted by rapid-fire cuts of a crucifix, a prayer card, and statues of Jesus, Mary, and Joseph, which are all very Catholic symbols. These sacramentals are typical aspects of Madonna's work. With the prevalence of prayer cards, statues, crucifixes, holy water, rosaries, the cross she wears, and other Catholic paraphernalia, Madonna's videos use artifacts with theological significance. Suffused throughout Madonna videos, these sacramentals and the experience of sacramentality are irreplaceable pieces of GenX's lived theology. I also think they partly account for her popularity with Xers for the last decade.

Subversive Sacramentals

Sacramentals rank in importance somewhere between "official" sacraments and the ordinary material world. According to the *Catechism of the Catholic Church*, sacramentals act as "sacred signs *which bear a resemblance to* the sacraments" (1994, p. 415, italics mine). Thus, sacramentals are virtual sacraments, simulations of true sacraments. Sacraments—which include baptism, confirmation, the Eucharist, confession, anointing of the sick, marriage, and holy orders—are the ultimate grace-conferring experiences in the Catholic Church. Immersion in simulation is one characteristic of contemporary culture and one way in which GenX pop culture engages the religious. Sacramentals, then, are eminently appropriate for GenX religiosity! They offer a way of thinking theologically about how our lived experiences can be manifestations of God's grace.

Grasping sacramentals' theological role in GenX religiosity (and hence in GenX popular culture and practice) requires a brief detour into an interpretation of Catholic theology. It is worthwhile to note a key tension about sacramentals as we think about them theologically. There is a tension between sacramentals as locally approved by "ordinary" laypeople, on the one hand, and as officially approved by the Church hierarchy, on the other hand. (The *Catechism* calls this tension the "wisdom" and "discernment" of the *faithful* versus "the care and judgment of the *bishops* and . . . general norms of the church" [1994, p. 417, italics mine].)

In addition to being somewhat free of Church hierarchy, sacramentals are more personal and fallible conduits of grace than full-fledged sacraments. The grace conferred by sacramentals is not "automatic"—it depends on the believer's spirituality, whereas sacraments can confer grace regardless of the priest's spirituality.

As symbols that mediate the divine in a very earthly context, sacramentals are ideal "media" for the experience of GenX spirituality. For Catholics, although the hierarchy has officially licensed sacramentals, they operate somewhat independently of institutional religion. Because of this independent existence, they continually threaten to undermine the official institution's monopoly over the dissemination of religious experience and access to grace—as well as pronounce judgment on the institution itself.

That the theme of experience in GenX religiosity threatens institutions is clear even in the *Catechism,* as it quotes a document written by Latin American bishops. The wisdom of the people, according to the bishops, manifest in sacramentals in the forms of popular piety and devotion (and, I would add, pop culture!), "is also a principle of discernment and an evangelical instinct through which [people] spontaneously sense when the Gospel is served in the Church and when it is emptied of its content and stifled by other interests" (p. 417).

Sacramentals fit the GenX religious imagination. They frequently show up in pop culture, as well as in everyday experience. Rooted in the *experiences* of individuals and groups, sacramentals become integral to GenX's irreverent spirituality. Appropriately enough for Christian Xers, and unlike official sacraments, sacramentals are easily personalized, responding to "the needs, culture, and special history of the Christian people of a particular region or time" (p. 415). Like Xer spirituality, sacramentals refuse to be confined to religious institutions.

By frequently employing graced everyday artifacts from common experience, Madonna participates in the symbolic and sacramental life of her Catholic Church while unhinging sacramentals from their exclusive relationship to Catholicism. She both reinforces *and* undercuts Catholic authority, displaying the extent to which official Church teaching carries the seeds of its own subversion. It is this paradoxical reinforcing and undercutting, I believe, that causes Catholics to feel ambivalent about Madonna's style of Catholicism.

Mark of a Generation

In 1986, when I was a high school junior, I had my left ear pierced at a shopping mall. I wore an earring for a few years, then tired of it. The mark on my ear remains, however, and will stay with me for the rest of my life. Like its related trend, tattooing, this permanent cut is more than just teen folly. My interpretation will suggest that the experience of the body is a source of religious meaning for one's life.

By the late 1980s and early 1990s, body piercing and tattooing were increasingly common Xer fashion statements. My high school students, friends, and Xers at large appeared with a plethora of body adornments throughout the 1990s, including multiple ear piercings; rings in the navel, nose, tongue, eyebrows, and sundry other body locations; and a great increase in tattooing. Tattoos also appeared on all parts of the body in a variety of images ranging from Mickey Mouse to religious or rock band symbols. On the first day of the new school year in August 1993, half a dozen students of mine stopped by my classroom to show me new rings in their navels, ears, and noses. It had become a rite of passage that they knew a fellow Xer would understand.

Piercing signifies immediate, bodily, and constant attention to the intimacy of experience. To pierce one's body is to leave a permanent mark of intense physical experience, whether pleasurable or painful. Though it has been more than a decade since my own piercing, the mark of indelible experience is ever with me, as proof that something *marked me, something happened.* This permanence or deep experience indicates why piercings have religious significance across cultures, and why rites of cutting or piercing the body are common in many religions.

For Xers, marking the body has various layers of meaning. This vague sense of being indelibly marked signifies the childhoods that have permanently but ambiguously marked (or even scarred) many Xers. And despite—or perhaps because of—the religious significance of piercing, Xers pierce themselves outside the religious context. Whether in the cathedral-like anonymity of an antiseptic mall or the cloister of a friend's basement, they administer to themselves gold or silver rings—which in some cases function as their own sacramentals. This is partly because religious institutions today are unable to provide for deeply marking, profoundly experiential encounters. At the least, then, this turn to piercing and tattooing reflects the centrality of personal and intimate experience in Xers' lives.

There may also be some truth for Xers in English professor Andrew Ross's suggestion that piercing and tattooing signify identification with "semicriminalized codes of the outcast," as such outcasts are identifiable by various sorts of body markings (1994, p. 296). This would be consistent with Xers' history as a generation unafraid to explore the margins, the psychologically marginalized recipients of a critical mass of social dysfunctions. This history surely has encouraged many Xers, particularly those with "punk" styles, to choose scarification out of sympathy toward the possibly romanticized outcast.

That mind-set would also explain why so many punk Xers ironically use safety pins in piercings. Because they frequently lacked safety in their childhoods (or even in their adult society), a pin named *safety*—an artifact meant to avoid harming babies—becomes a social statement about harm, danger, and social effrontery.

We are a generation willing to have experience, to be profoundly marked, even cut, when religious institutions have not given us those opportunities. It could even be said that our indulgence in tattoos mocks the hypercommercial world in which we live; tattooing is the only way we have control over "branding" ourselves, instead of being name-branded to death.

One common trend among Xers throughout the 1990s was particularly revealing—the exposure of pierced navels. Aided by half-shirts and a healthy dose of self-assuredness, many Xers (particularly women) bared their midriffs (including many of my students, which created a dress code crisis at our high school). The popular GenX guide *alt.culture* features a stark picture of a pierced navel as the sole image on its cover (Daly and Wice, 1995), emblematic of a generation's fashion. To interpret this phenomenon is to draw attention to the belly's religious significance. When the abdomen, or the navel, is seen as the center of the self, this seemingly innocent fashion trend can be interpreted as GenX theological playfulness about the exposure of the person's center.

Historian of religion Mircea Eliade notes that the navel represents the center of human fecundity in Jewish and other religious traditions (1987, p. 44; 1996, pp. 377–378). This was true in the Hebrew Scriptures, which reported that the monster Behemoth's "power [was] in the muscles of its belly" (Job 40:16). Similarly, one Proverb reports that turning from evil brings "health to thy navel" (Proverbs 3:8). There is a double exposure at work; when women bare their navels, it means that the more socially concealed sex is exposing that which is most revealing about themselves— the part considered to be at their center. They let it beam out as a beacon of irony, casting darkness instead of light, confounding our final attempts to understand it.

The term *navel-gazing* is key here, suggesting a preoccupation with the self. The fashion trend of exposing a pierced navel invites all who see it to navel-gaze (the ring draws attention to the navel), to dwell on one's own experience, by gazing at another's navel. This can be a gift of religious experience and reflection from the fashionable Xer: "Out of the believer's belly shall flow rivers of living water" (John 7:38). With a fleet of exposed bellies unleashing flowing water, Xers seem to have formed their own navel academy. If the belly is the seat of deep humanness and even fecundity, navel piercing is also an example of Xer religiosity; it implies finding the spiritual in the sensual (which I will discuss in the next section).

There is something gendered and ascetic about pierced navels. Rarely are they found on men. That women most often wear navel rings is not surprising, because piercings are usually only displayed on firm bellies. Thus, the pierced navel is a fuzz of contradictory suggestions: the authority of bodily experience, the sensual life of the spiritual body or belly, the reinforcing of popular social expectations about women's bodies in regard to thinness and firm bellies, and the suggestion of an ascetic refusal to indulge in the overconsumption of modern culture (signified by a slim abdomen). Call it an ascetic aesthetic.

(Although the fashionable navel has refused to overconsume, it invites consumption by all who will see it, deploying a navel convoy of suggestions that sail to the rich port of personal experience.)

Body and Soul Together

"The body is a temple," wrote Paul in the Christian Scriptures (1 Corinthians 6:19). The way Xers adorn their temples helps us see that a lived theology emphasizing experience is well under way. Through this trend, Xers indicate their spiritual need for truly *marking*, transformative spiritual experiences. This sort of spiritual change may happen on retreats with religious groups, or (often better) during days or weeks spent alone as guests at monasteries or convents, or perhaps on road trips across the United States, as for several friends of mine. It likely only happens when we put our selves, our futures, and our stubbornest needs at risk—when we enter God's future for us. Each of us must find these transformative initiations, as institutions so rarely provide them now as part of spiritual maturation. (Of course, these change-inducing experiences may not always happen at the mountaintop; they might require years of spiritual drudgery. But that yearning for the mountaintop is alive and well among Xers.)

Institutions that ignore the way Xers need to be marked, religiously branded, and body oriented cannot fully minister to them. With their accumulated wisdom of tradition, institutions can give Xers tools for a discriminating sense of the sacramentality of personal experience; this is necessary because not all experiences reveal God, particularly in a culture that frequently offers a great deal less than graced experience. If institutions dignify the sacramentality of experience for GenX, they can express their concern that what Xers interpret as grace may instead be sin. Among the various sins in which pop culture and personal experience can indulge, the denigration of the human, for instance, cannot disclose God's grace. Anything that demeans people—even if cloaked as sacramental—must therefore be considered sinful or distorted, not graceful. Catholic mystic Thomas Merton's warning bears remembering: "By no one is more harm done in the world than by men who were at the point of becoming mystics, but whose mysticism [or, we may add, whose sense of sacramentality] degenerated into an irrational surrender to every passion that knew how to dress up as an angel of light" (1981, p. 200). Although it is critical for the Christian interpreter of popular culture to be vigilant in regard to sin in pop culture, the overemphasis on sin by religious interpreters has masked the sacramental potential of GenX culture and experience.

It is into this unpredictable world of the passions that GenX's lived theology marches, declaring sensuality a potential arena of grace.

Sensual Spirituality

Pop culture highlights the sacred potential of human experience by frequently fusing or juxtaposing sexuality and spirituality.

This focus on the close relationship between sensuality and spirituality is first of all about understanding Xers' experience at the edge of our own limits—that is, of interpreting our experience religiously. Even though sexuality at its base is mysterious (a gift in faith and love of oneself to another), that does not mean that Xers, or popular culture, cannot say anything of consequence about sexuality (indeed, as we shall see, we are saying a great deal about it!). What makes our experience mysterious (particularly our experience of sensuality) is our continued ability to find depth and meaning—deep relationality—in it. The mystery of human experience is a rich symbol—an inexhaustible theological resource.

"Like a Prayer" illustrates this connection of spirituality and sexuality. Catholic sociologist Andrew Greeley rightly suggests that Madonna "dares to link her sexuality with God and religious images" (1989, p. 449). Madonna initiates this fusion of spirituality and sensuality when she kisses the feet of Saint Martin. Calling again upon Catholic tradition, her action alludes to the ancient practice of venerating the cross. On Good Friday, two days before Easter, Catholics venerate crosses at services. A frequent form of this obeisance is kissing the feet of Jesus on the crucifix. In my view, by honoring Saint Martin with this intimate, sensual act, Madonna humbly acknowledges the mystery of experiencing intimacy with him, even suggesting that he has a sacred character akin to that of Jesus.

She opens the doors of the altar grate, and her sensual touch brings Saint Martin to life. (The spiritual awakens and enlivens the sensual, and vice versa.) His first response is also sensual; he kisses Madonna on the forehead, reciprocating the action that is at once sensual and spiritual. The juxtaposition of the sensual and spiritual ends the video. In a church, Saint Martin and Madonna share a kiss before he returns to the life of a statue behind the altar grate.

This video is not alone in suggesting an interplay of the spiritual and sensual. At seemingly random intervals throughout "Losing My Religion," a young boy appears who could readily pass for a young girl. In several scenes, this transgendered youth is either tied to a tree or stands erect in a field with arrows taped to his mostly naked body. The scene bears a strong resemblance to Botticelli's classic fifteenth-century painting *Saint Sebastian,* a creative rendering of a third-century Roman martyr. In this painting, Sebastian (clothed only in a tunic, just like the boy in the video) is a smooth-skinned male. He is sexually ambiguous, with shoulder-length, curly hair. His head is cocked seductively to one side, and one foot is slightly in front of another so that his hips pivot slightly. His hands rest behind him, and he stands against a svelte tree. Small arrows pierce his body. Culture critic Camille Paglia calls him a "Christian Adonis" (1991, p. 148). In reproducing this famous painting as an "animated" image in video, and by splicing it frequently and unexpectedly throughout a video meditating on the loss of religion, the question of the relation between the sensual and the spiritual is subtly raised, suggesting that attentiveness to the religious is often tethered to sensuality.

In fact, according to one exhaustive study, sexual and religious images are frequently combined in music video. Researchers Carol Pardun and Kathy McKee discovered that "religious imagery is twice as likely to be found in videos that also use sexual imagery than those without" (1995, p. 444). After randomly selecting 160 videos to analyze, they found that religious and sexual images were combined in more than one-quarter of the videos. The religious images were not satanic, as some would expect; rather, they were "highly recognizable Judeo-Christian symbols" (p. 445).

Although Pardun and McKee title their study "Strange Bedfellows," religiousness and sexuality have been paired before—to the surprise of many today—in Christian tradition. Many mystics, for example, in Christian history have explored the deep congruities between sexuality and spirituality and the ways in which the two share language and experience.

Bernard of Clairvaux (1090–1153) employed erotic imagery in his advice to young monks on leading a spiritual life. He was aware that in order to reach them effectively, he had to use the language of the world from which they came and their own personal sexual memories. Bernard depicted progress in the life of Christian prayer as an increasingly intimate kissing of Christ. He took this striking metaphor (and stressed that it was *only* a metaphor) from the Hebrew Scriptures' Song of Songs. The acts of kissing Christ's feet, his hands, and then his lips parallel the salvific work of repentance, grace, and union, according to Bernard. Pleasing though the Lord's goodness (or kisses) may be, the highest level of union with the divine, a brief ecstasy, is best achieved by way of a spiritual and immortal body when all fleshly "entanglements" have been left behind. Then our spiritual bodies will be united with the God who has "no particularities" and yet is as close to us as we are to ourselves. God can be *known* fully in the next life, *loved* wholly in this one. Bernard's introduction to the sermon on this topic is wonderfully relevant for GenX's lived theology. His focus is not on the holiness of the Bible or the Church but of life itself. "Today," Bernard wrote simply, "we read the book of experience" (1987, pp. 221–226).

Women mystics, too, have explored this theme, perhaps even more daringly than men. According to historian of mysticism Grace Jantzen, medieval women mystics frequently exhibited "a direct, highly charged, passionate encounter between Christ and the writer" (1995, p. 133). Hadewijch of Antwerp, a mystical writer from the thirteenth century, recounts her experience of Christ on a Pentecost Sunday:

With that he came in the form and clothing of a Man, as he was on the day when he gave us his body for the first time; looking like a human being and a man, wonderful, and beautiful, and with glorious face, he came to me as humbly as anyone who wholly belongs to another. Then he gave himself to me in the shape of the sacrament. . . . After that he came himself to me, took me entirely in his arms, and pressed me to him; and all my members felt his full felicity, in accordance with the desire of my heart and my humanity. So I was outwardly satisfied and fully transported . . . but soon, after a short time, I lost that manly beauty outwardly in the sight of his form [1995, p. 135].

This intimate encounter with Christ, sensate and erotic, also appears in other works by mystical authors. Teresa of Avila referred to herself and others who seek God as his "lovers," and said that God sometimes torments these lovers to test them (1957, p. 80). Unlike Madonna, who can sing through the ecstasy, Teresa's intimate contact with Christ overwhelmed but did not completely drown out her senses: "By the command of the Bridegroom [Christ] when He intends ravishing the soul, the doors of the mansions and even those of the keep and of the whole castle are closed; for He takes away the power of speech, and although occasionally the other faculties are retained rather longer, no word can be uttered" (Teresa of Avila in Underhill, 1990, p. 377). Madonna would feel right at home in these works, inasmuch as her video stands so firmly on this branch of her Catholic tradition.

The lesson Jantzen draws from several women mystics is timely for the spirituality of Generation Xers: "It is precisely through actual eroticism that lessons of God are to be learned" (1995, p. 134). There is for Xers, then, an expression in pop culture of an emerging understanding of the relation between sensual passion and faithful passion—indulging in finite sensual passion is analogous to indulging in the infinite passion of faith in union with God.

This fusion of the sensual and spiritual has unfortunately been a minor theme in Christian history and theology. Early on in the Church's history and frequently thereafter, for complex reasons, the disjunction between sexuality and spirituality was more commonly seen as appropriately Christian. GenX pop culture recovers a subversive strand of Christian tradition, offering a reversal of the significance of the body and sexuality in religious institutions' preaching and practices.

An interesting liturgical tool (if used in church) or evangelical tool (if used on music television) would be to play Madonna videos while scrolling texts from Teresa of Avila or Bernard of Clairvaux along the bottom of the screen.

Some would deride this sacrilegious juxtaposition, but it might accomplish much for both a "secular" and a "churchy" audience; they could each appreciate that mystical writings and GenX lived theology seem to be pointing in the same direction—the unabashed reintegration of sexuality and spirituality.

Xers are way out in front of religious institutions on this issue, as institutions are largely hesitant to suggest that sexual intimacy can be correlated with spiritual intimacy. They prefer all-or-nothing (usually nothing) approaches to sexuality. This GenX theology of sexuality can inspire institutions to change their position; rather than trying to control sexuality, they can start encouraging Xers to see it in a spiritual perspective. Indeed, Xers and institutions can have a common interest in attending to the degradation of sexuality still at work in popular culture. To do this, however, institutions must abandon simplistic interpretations of popular culture's sexual content.

Intersection of the Human and Divine

As evidenced in sensuality, bodily experience, and sacramentality, Xer religiosity explores the experience of incarnation, that is, finding the divine in human form. I interpret this quest for incarnational experience as a desire for the encounter of the human and divine. To experience the divine is to go beyond the confines of human limitation, but the deep enfolding of Xers in culture suggests to us that the divine can only be present through the mediation of the human. To engage experience at this intersection of the human and divine is a key characteristic of the turn to experience in a lived GenX theology. While this theme may cut across religious traditions, for Christian Xers and for some forms of popular culture, this nexus of human and divine is a result of a turn to rediscovering and reexperiencing Jesus, who is Christians' decisive disclosure of the divine and human.

"Like a Prayer" is about the power of experiencing the intersection of divinity and humanity. In the video, Madonna herself functions as a Christ figure and liberates a Christlike person, Martin de Porres. This encounter of the human and divine, the video suggests, takes place both in the church *and* in the world. "Black Hole Sun" is even more interesting.

Jesus the Cleaver

The presence of Jesus is startlingly insinuated in several scenes in "Black Hole Sun." In one scene, a quaint suburban mother smiles hungrily at the fish she is about to chop. Wielding a huge cleaver in her right hand, she pauses before bringing it down on the fish. Suddenly, the fish escapes the cutting board by flopping away, much to the cook's chagrin.

Among early Christian communities, the fish symbolized Christ and Christian solidarity. Early Christians played with the Greek word for *fish*, or *ichthus*. They discovered that the Greek letters for *ichthus* could also signify Jesus Christ, Son of God, Savior *(Iesous Christos Theou Huios Soter)*.

Quite independently of Soundgarden, biblical scholar Stephen Moore has played theologically and linguistically with the idea of Jesus as a fish by scaling the Gospel of Mark in Christian Scripture:

> Dragged from the muddy river in [Mark] 1:10 ("and when he came up out of the water"), Jesus slithers across the surface of the text. Who can ever grasp him? Mark itself comes closest. Mark's plotlines are fishing lines, as are the lines of its page. And its genre is that of the fishing manual: "I will make you fishers of men [*sic*]" (1:17). Caught and taught by these fishermen, Jesus' followers will be a school of fish. But first, Jesus himself must be caught ("they . . . seized him"—14:46), and so Mark's book becomes a hook, a clawed fishhook or X. From the four sharp corners of its page Jesus-*Ichthus* dangles, gasping for air [1992, p. 56].

Similarly, in "Black Hole Sun," the fish "slithers across the surface" of the cutting board. Limp but still breathing, it escapes the cleaver (and escapes the Cleavers?). Ironically, though, *ichthus* is himself a cleaver—one who cleaves families:

> Do you think that I have come to bring peace to the earth? No, I tell you, but rather division! From now on five in one household will be *divided,* three against two and two against three; they will be *divided*: father against son and son against father, mother against daughter and daughter against mother, mother-in-law against daughter-in-law and daughter-in-law against mother-in-law [Luke 12:51–53].

The experience of cleaving to Jesus cleaves families apart along generational lines, tearing fathers from sons, mothers from daughters. This radical cleaving of Jesus—typifying the countercultural demands of the gospel—interrupts a previously comfortable life, "drops like a bomb on our complacent present" (Metz and Moltmann, 1995, p. 18), and threatens to cleave the suburban household, upending those who have sold their lives for a materialistic American dream and their spiritual advisers (read: the country club ministers depicted earlier).

My theological reading of GenX culture, as expressed in this video, offers hope that Christian Xers can reclaim the dangerous memory and experience of Jesus against the domestication of the Gospel message. As theologian Johannes Baptist Metz (Metz and Moltmann, 1995, p. 28) has pointed out, "Was Jesus not crucified as a traitor to all the apparently worthwhile values? Must not Christians, therefore, expect, if they want to be faithful . . . to Christ, be regarded as traitors to bourgeois religion?" Equally and appropriately radical is the plea of Latin American theologian Jon Sobrino: "Christ must not be forced to leave reality in peace" (1988, p. 59).

For Christian Xers, such creative reconceptualizations of Jesus, and return to experience of him in memory and reality, can break new ground for a spirituality both irreverent and gospel oriented. Christian Xers are well situated to understand Jesus' cleaving call. In the Gospel of Mark, he identified as his true family those who do the work of God. Jesus thereby offered the ultimate blended family, perfect for the generation that grew up with more than half of marriages ending in divorce and with frequent remarriages. By following Jesus, a new family formed, one to which Christian Xers could have cleaved: "Then his mother and his brothers came; and standing outside, they sent to him and called him. A crowd was sitting around him; and they said to him, 'Your mother and your brothers and sisters are waiting outside, asking for you.' And he replied, 'Who are my mother and my brothers?' And looking at those who sat around him, he said, 'Here are my mother and my brothers! Whoever does the will of God is my brother and sister and mother'" (Mark 3:31–35). As biblical scholar John Dominic Crossan has argued, Jesus' teaching is "an almost savage attack on family values" (1994, p. 58). By placing the work of God over blood relationships as constituting a true family, Jesus catches us off guard with our assumptions about "families." My interpretation of "Black Hole Sun" shows that Xers can be particularly poised to claim this familial theology as their own, by seeking an experience of Jesus in the present day.

Jesus is decisive for a Christian understanding of the embodiment of the human and divine. Cyberspace, however, can be interpreted as a metaphor for the experience of the human and divine. Although cyberspace and Jesus should not be confused, these emerging GenX-heavy technologies are worthy of theological attention. Engagement in this medium implies a widespread search for a site of the encounter—however analogous—of the divine and human.

Cyberspace and the Quest for the Divine

The chief characteristic of cyberspace is speed. Many of the qualities that interest people in virtual reality and enable them to experience life in cyberspace revolve around the cult of the current: ever-faster computers, breakneck modem connection rates, advanced multitasking, supercharged networks, increased hours and modes of access, and increasingly "real" forms of communication. If computers began to operate at the speed people seek, it would culminate in a fullness of presence on-line. A "perfect" speed, whether in virtual reality games or in Internet communication, would guarantee the most "real" simulation possible and would therefore enable full presence in a realm that lies beyond the limits of reality.

In this search for perfect speed and full presence, cyberspace is a metaphor for two quests. The first is full interpersonal interaction, or what Jewish philosopher Martin Buber called *I-Thou* relationships. The second is an attempt to transcend human experience, which is why Xers often experiment with imagining the Web as a metaphor—however imperfect—for God. Perhaps the GenX plunge into cyberspace evidences a yearning for full presence in both divine and human relations.

Cyberspace highlights our own finitude, reminding us that we can never be fully cognizant of all that is happening. We are just solitary souls among the millions in cyberspace, exploring less than one hundredth of one percent of all that is out there. In this way, cyberspace illuminates our human limits. Yet it also mirrors our desire for the infinite, the divine. Given the direction in which technology is moving, cyberspace seems increasingly omniscient and omnipresent, which may be what the obsession with speed is all about theologically. To search for this fullness of presence, one that spans and unites the human and divine, is to operate in the field of a divine-human experience in which spirituality and technology intersect.

What I am suggesting, then, is that cyberspace is not just a playful diversion for Xers. There is something deeply theologically compelling about this medium with which Xers are so comfortable. Xers implicitly or explicitly may experience cyberspace as an analogue or a metaphor for experiencing the human and divine.

Filippo Marinetti, a futurist who foresaw the coming of this technology as early as 1909, wrote, "We already live within the absolute since we have already created an omnipresent speed" (Marinetti in Taylor, 1993, p. 186). Theologian Mark Taylor has elaborated on Marinetti's revolutionary observation: "The increase in speed creates the hope of breaking the barriers of space and time and entering a fourth dimension where it is possible to experience an eternal now" (p. 186). This eternal now in cyberspace is always deferred, because it is still being sought. The "hope" that Taylor infers indicates the religious thirst of a generation. For Xers, cyberspace "incarnates" and carries forward this theological desire.

Cybercommunities of Faith

If cyberspace offers a metaphor for divine-human experiences, those experiences happen concretely through cybercommunities of faith. Cyberspace—particularly the Internet—is an appropriate medium to serve as a communal center for Generation X. The Internet originated as a national defense communication system designed to remain functional throughout a nuclear war. Given this hypothetical apocalyptic setting and lack of central authority (to avoid collapsing the whole system), how could such a medium *not* appeal to Generation X?

Opportunity for Community

Despite some popular perceptions, those who surf the Net are not exclusively rugged individualists. There are many opportunities for communitarian action on the Net, including organizing relief for victims of natural disasters, circulating protest petitions, and gathering like-minded people from around the globe (particularly those denied access to "mainstream" media). The communities that form can be as bonded as some physical communities and are therefore no less "real." Indeed, cyberspace seems to have great potential for Xers as a site of religious community-gathering. The medium is uniquely able to accommodate both like- and different-minded users who want to form cybercommunities of faith.

In this regard, the interrelationship between Net identity and community is important. It has been suggested that in order to sustain a "persona" on the Net, one must participate frequently in cybercommunities. Routine involvement in discussions establishes a user's (or persona's) reputation and "presence" on the Net. Thus, to "exist" in cyberspace itself demands involvement and discourages one from being an electronic wallflower (MacKinnon, 1995, pp. 125–131). Because the medium demands that users join individual identity with communal involvement, cyberspace is an opportune religious space.

Many resources needed for this sort of community exist on-line: Bibles, reference guides, and commentaries. A plethora of religious scholars inhabit the Net. In addition, one can reveal oneself more easily, given the "distance" between users on the Net. In other words, technology enables intimate discussion about spirituality, which benefits both Xers and Net-based ministries. This is perfect for Xers, who have grown up with such a tense relationship to formal communities of faith and who are so well suited to nonfamilial, ad hoc communities.

The Saving Remnant

Such a virtual community of faith formed during the two years I spent studying for a master's degree in theology at Harvard Divinity School. Half a dozen friends who identified themselves as Catholic began to meet regularly and discuss topics and readings of interest. Because we indulged in lengthy discussions about contentious issues in the Church and Catholic theology, we came to see ourselves as a tiny salvific community. With tongue firmly in cheek, we adopted the name "the Saving Remnant," a term from the Hebrew Bible designating a small group of faithful people who will renew the larger community. Our group of seven met consistently for over a year.

During our second semester of existence, we shifted several of our conversations to cyberspace. Moving our discussions on-line had many advantages, none of which we explicitly discussed (the on-line discussion simply happened because we all had Internet access). Suddenly, we no longer had such a difficult time coordinating appointment calendars so that we could all make discussions or other events. Individuals could log in whenever they liked and contribute whatever they wanted, or simply "lurk" during discussions. We often told each other about Web sites of interest, enabled by the easy interactivity between Web browsers and e-mail software. The medium provided a spatial and psychological distance that created a "safer" setting for discussions, which were frequently more frank and self-revelatory than when we met in person. Cyberspace also provided opportunities for the group to work out problems in a nonconfrontational way.

Midway through our year together, a problem arose about inviting other people into our cybergroup. The argument, extending over several days, was almost entirely carried out on-line. It included long sidebars on the meaning of such emotional words in the academy and Church as *inclusivity, exclusivity,* and even *Catholicism.* Participating in this difficult conversation would have been almost unbearable in person for some of the "saving remnant." On-line, however, group members felt more comfortable and took time to word their responses carefully, particularly because they were guaranteed a reading by the whole group. There is much anecdotal evidence that such cybercommunities of faith as our "saving remnant" can and do thrive in cyberspace.

Solitary Spirituality

Those seeking a religious context not for community but for relative solace may also find rest in cyberspace. The Net is increasingly becoming a virtual monastery for the spiritually dispossessed. As in "real" monasteries, a user may seek community at specific times or in particular sites, and there are myriad opportunities for self-reflection, prayer, meditation, and Scripture studies. There are even on-line monasteries, in which users can listen to chanting monks, gaze on brilliant iconography, and read holy manuscripts without interruption.

New Communities and Connections

Cyberspace gives Xers a voice in religious matters by way of a technology with which they are comfortable. It might even be said that cyberspace is where many Xers are most "themselves." Insofar as that is the case, cyber-communities of faith will continue to coagulate.

For a generation so hesitant to talk about its faith (for fear of sounding too "religious"), cyberspace affords opportunities for intimate faith discussion without necessitating face-to-face communication. The Net gives Xers opportunities to deepen their spiritual life by connecting with other spiritually curious Xers and people from around the world. Dedication to a religious cybercommunity can be as gratifying and important as allegiance to any "real" religious institution.

In this way, Xers challenge religious institutions to rethink the definition of *community*. As something that augments (but does not replace!) real community, religious institutions have an opportunity to use this virtual space to build community when ministering to Xers. Ministers may find it an even more effective way to relate to and counsel members of the flock. Institutions might challenge Xers not to limit themselves to religious cybercommunities. Although virtual communities give Xers one more sphere for religious interaction, we should not avoid the difficult religious tasks of loving and seeking justice in the real world. For Christian Xers in particular, there is an implied demand of real embodiment—based on Jesus as the incarnation of God—as an important part of community.

Experience of Living Faith in the World

As I mentioned earlier, Madonna brings the spiritual de Porres to sensual life through her sensual and spiritual touch in "Like a Prayer." As she does so, she becomes a saint of liberation, much like de Porres himself. This highlights another GenX religious experience—the practice of liberation and freedom, living faith in the world.

Works of Faith

With his new freedom, Saint Martin leaves the church to go out into the world. In the following moment, Madonna cuts herself. A messianic figure who has lived and spoken (or sung) incisive words that have cut open

the altar grate and sliced the division between heaven and earth, she ironically becomes the victim of cutting. Madonna picks up a knife and
receives on her palms the stigmata. They are a *simulation* of Jesus' wounds,
and yet true wounds they are, thus verifying her messianic calling. With
these stigmata, Madonna thereby joins the ranks of many of her stigma-
tized Catholic forebears, including Saints Francis of Assisi and Catherine
of Siena.

Thus marked with such a stigma and stigmata, Madonna herself moves
into the world. When she does, she sees a gang of thugs stab a woman in
a deserted alley. A black man bearing great likeness to de Porres comes to
the injured woman's rescue (employing his sixteenth-century barber-
surgeon skills to stop the bleeding?) and is falsely accused of the crime
and arrested by police.

Before Madonna liberates this unjustly accused man, she provides for
the viewer a bridge that is not so much musical as it is visual, a bridge from
this point in the drama to its stirring conclusion. The bridge is one of passionate fire; Madonna dances in front of a field of burning crosses in a
loose-fitting dress with the straps falling off her shoulders as flames light
up the night sky. As in the original scene of attraction to the black saint,
the video confronts the viewer by explicitly dredging up the racial anxieties at the core of the American soul. By showcasing many crosses on fire
with Madonna dancing in front of them, the video paradoxically and ironically reduces to absurdity these infamous symbols of racial hatred. Not
only can the flaming crosses be seen as emblems of Madonna's spiritual-
sensual passion, but they are also transformed into symbols of Christian
passion (a fire of love for God?) as they are drained of their racist referent.
Seeking racial reconciliation (an important issue for Xers) is a spiritual
task, and "Like a Prayer" reminds us again that spirituality and sensuality need each other. After de Porres steps back behind the altar grate,
Madonna wakes up from what seems to have been a dream. She proceeds
to release the accused black man from prison, completing her role as savior and racial conciliator.

As "Like a Prayer" illustrates, the world of the street can be a site of
religious activity and experience. Madonna liberates the saint, whose
blessings of racial reconciliation are desperately needed in American society right now. Through her own action, she claims resources from her religious tradition to address the real-life situations she faces, including
racism. The experience costs her personally, as the stigmata signify (I will
discuss this further in Chapter Six). The test of Madonna's faith is not
how it is contained within the Church but whether it can guide her experience in the world (where she acts to right injustice), just as faith guided

the historical Martin de Porres. Likewise, the first thing the liberated saint does is go out into the world to let faith shape not only his own actions but also his experience of being in the world, even in a dangerous situation. "Like a Prayer" cautions that the Church cannot be aloof from the world. Salvation happens in the world and in the Church, not in simply one or the other.

At this point, it is also worthwhile to recall "Black Hole Sun"'s mockery of "faith alone" when it strays too far from works of mercy and justice. As pop culture testifies, Xers have experienced counterfeit claims of faith and widespread disconnection between faith and works in the lives of those who claim to be Christian. Xers therefore know that faith does not "work" unless it lives in good works. In this sense, the popular exhortation "Work it, girl!" becomes a GenX theological commandment!

The Right Kind of Joining

In *Generation at the Crossroads,* social commentator Paul Rogat Loeb surveys in detail GenXers' political work and attitudes at campuses around the country. At the College of the Holy Cross, Loeb interviews a peace activist whose involvement in college with Catholic peace groups helps her see the interrelationship between her faith and politics in a new light. "I went from a workshop on campus activism to one on the elections and then to Mass," she recalls. "It felt empowering, *the right kind of joining"* (1994, p. 163, italics mine).

This kind of joining runs like a thread through the popular culture, with the political and the religious refusing to be relegated to separate spheres. For instance, Nirvana and R.E.M. both pointedly criticize a messiah who has nothing to say to the "real" world. Soundgarden's video turns comfortable, middle-class families' appropriation of Christian faith into comedy mixed with horror, revealing a massive absence of meaning. Tori Amos's video points out the ways in which crucifixion happens in and to a body in a very this-worldly fashion, and Pearl Jam's "Jeremy" prophesies a generation's revenge on a culture—both religious and secular—that has ignored Xers.

In cyberspace, religious and political sites bump elbows, vying for Xers' attention. Several religious Web sites, whether liberal, conservative, or somewhere in between, include links to particular organizations across the political spectrum. Whereas the sites of Christian conservatives may provide links to the Christian Coalition and the e-mail addresses of sympathetic senators, pages of the Christian Left may include links to Greenpeace or Amnesty International. Reared in a culture that has struggled over issues of justice and in a hyperpoliticized atmosphere, Xers have a special sensitivity to political action. No religious involvement can take this away from them, and as popular culture suggests, their political involvement is often linked to religious beliefs.

Xers can frequently cite exactly where religious institutions have fallen short in speaking to the world. According to Xer Rodolpho Carrasco, many "Generation X Latinos perceive that our faith sects (both Catholic and Protestant) have little to say about the issues that affect us most: technology-induced future shock, a national debt as frightening as a velociraptor, AIDS, and (perhaps most important) race and identity" (1994, p. 16). Carrasco retains more hope than many Xers, however. He writes: "I personally believe that the age-old wisdom of the Bible can affirm my generation in all its complexity, while pointing to a greater, eternal harmony. But will the church be able to *communicate* this to us?" (p. 16, italics mine).

Loeb observes that GenX students "were most willing to act when doing so did not require immediately confronting powerful institutions" (1994, p. 248). This is true of Xers not only politically but also religiously. Faced with Churches that do not ordain women, for instance, or that preach suspicion and fear of other religions, many Xers prefer to work from a practical faith that lifts them up by lifting the world up through them—and so lifting up the content of their faith in the world.

Separated unnaturally, institutional religion and politics are mere husks of what they could be. When they have joined together in our lifetimes, it is often for the sake of wielding power over others. Many Xers want "the right kind of joining," even if they have no clearly articulated theology to explain what they mean. Xers often sense this union intuitively. They know that if religion doesn't go into the streets, the streets will overtake religion. I have personally known dozens of Xers who have been spiritually kickstarted by working in soup kitchens and food pantries for the poor. One friend even said to me, "The reason I went from working for Congress to studying religion is that I can't understand what to do in one without the other." Religious institutions that heed this challenge from Generation X may find their comfortable positions destabilized, which means they will only be more authentic in many Xers' eyes.

Perhaps the most noticeable charade in this regard is the disavowal of politics many mainline churches make in favor of spiritual concerns. As we have seen, however, most Xers know that the two are not so easily separated. A GenX lived theology understands Catholic theologian Gustavo Gutierrez's plain talk: "The social influence of the church is a fact. Not to exercise this influence in favor of the oppressed . . . is really to exercise it against them" (1988, p. 76).

Religious Experience as Virtual and Real

As a key to religious living, GenX reveres personal and communal experience by way of ripely irreverent expressions in the popular culture. "Like a Prayer" is at once a narrative of irreverence, a reappropriation of Madonna's Catholic tradition, and a religious and social critique. The impiety of GenX's reclamation of sensual spirituality and spiritual sensuality manifests in videos and popular body adornments. Xers make what works in the world, as well as what works in cyberspatial communities, a criterion of religiosity that may strike some as irreverent churchiness. Embracing these ways of being religious, Xers trumpet them in the popular culture.

As I have already suggested, the irreverence of GenX spirituality is heavily dependent on pop culture's use of irony. Kierkegaard writes that irony does not want to be directly grasped, even though it eventually makes itself known. Irony has a peculiar way of "not wanting to be understood immediately, even though it wants to be understood, with the result that [irony] looks down, as it were, on plain and simple talk that everyone can promptly understand" (1989, p. 248). Irony is quite apposite as a GenX posture in popular culture, because it conveys not only what Xers try to say but also the attitude of many Xers themselves!

For example, the employment of sexuality in pop culture frequently has an ironic character. Many cultural critics look at GenX pop culture's deep immersion in sexuality and say, "How far GenX has run from God!" In contrast, I look at all the sexuality and think, "How deeply GenX desires God!" The reveling in sexuality that seems so characteristic of pop culture, from music video to cyberspace to revealing fashions, is not what it appears to be on its face. It empties out the viewer's presuppositions and points to something much deeper, a suggestion that the mystical tradition also affirms (if more piously). The deeper suggestion is that sexual desire is an analogue for desire for God, and that each type of desire may illuminate the other. As irreverent as this recombination of the spiritual and sensual may seem, it is a foundation stone in a lived GenX theology.

As grounded as it is in the individual and the community, the GenX emphasis on experience has a heavily "virtual" feel to it. Xers live a theology revolving around *incarnation*—the experience of the human in the context of the divine, and the divine mediated by the human. Thus, Xers express religiosity with *sacramentals,* which can evoke the religious depth of the most common objects or experiences. Because sacramentals are "imitations" of real sacraments, GenX religiosity once again seizes on the salvific experience of simulation. Cyberspace, the prototypical virtual experience for Generation X, can even function as what cyberculture essayist David Porush calls "sacramental architecture" (1996, p. 125). On the Web, Xers can simulate a community that may be as "religious" as any in real life.

This turn to experience has particular implications for Christian Xers in regard to experiencing Jesus. A new sort of GenX liberation theology is emerging, but it is not primarily about the poor, who are normally the focus of liberation theology. Instead, it begins with the liberation of Jesus from the clutches of the Church. Jesus himself needs to be liberated so that Xers can experience the power of his words and deeds, the blessing of his bodily and spiritual presence.

———— o ————

Such an extended meditation on experience as this must address a central category of experience in the life of the generation—that of suffering. It is to this drama of pain that I turn in the next chapter.

6

SUFFERING HAS A
RELIGIOUS DIMENSION

"WHERE'S THE SUFFERING? YOUR GENERATION has gotten everything you wanted," scoffed a man in the second row. "Your generation hasn't suffered," another added. "You are on top of the world because of the sacrifices we made." In a sense, of course, they were right. But few baby boomers at this ministry conference could understand why Xers were complaining about various forms of suffering. There was a surprising disconnection between these older ministers and me when I suggested that suffering is a key religious issue for Generation X.

Xer Pain as Sparking Spirituality

After three years of discussions with Xers about our generation and our popular culture, I am convinced that self-consciousness about suffering is an important trait that separates Xers from baby boomers. Perhaps this is because, as Wade Clark Roof writes, "Self-reliance is a tenet of faith among boomers" (1993, p. 46). If this is true, it might explain why many boomers dismiss or minimize Xers' awareness of suffering, which seriously challenges a glorified, make-it-on-your-own individualism.

But the questions linger: Where *is* the suffering? What right do we have to complain? Didn't we have access to some of the finest health care, universities, and technology in the Western world? Don't we thrive on luxuries such as three-dollar lattés, mountain bikes, and computers? There *has* been, it must be admitted, a certain amount of whining among Xers, exacerbated by press reports about a generation afraid to stake its place in the world. It is this whining, I think, that most immediately turns off intentionally self-reliant baby boomers.

Suffering Versus Whining

Expressing a sense of suffering is different from whining, however. It is one thing to whine about not being able to pay for a new skateboard, bike, or car. It is entirely another to point out that Xers earn 20 percent less in real income than people our age a generation ago (Lipsky and Abrams, 1994, p. 15). It is one thing to whine about political correctness on college campuses, and quite another to protest the average Xer's college debt, which reaches into tens of thousands of dollars, mortgaging our young adult years (even though many of us work part-time during college). It is one thing to complain that our elders do not understand the difficulties Xers face today; it is another to point out the extent to which our generation has been forced to parent our own parents. Finally, it is one thing to whine about what to wear tomorrow, and quite another to find that we do have a tomorrow after all—despite nuclear threats, despite AIDS, despite our unjustly allotted portion of the national debt.

In my own work with Xers, and in the popular culture, I have witnessed a sadness and anger about the generation's suffering and dysfunction, a suffering that—whatever its economic reasons may be—expresses itself in psychological and spiritual crises of meaning. Clothing styles and music videos suggest feelings of rage, with the videos expressing this in apocalyptic images. Despair is common and occasionally leaps overboard into nihilism.

Xers' relation to suffering lays the groundwork for religiousness. This knowledge of suffering sparks our spirituality, because suffering is a sort of "boundary experience" that forces us to confront questions about our own human limits. After all, when you suffer, you want to know why, for how long, and who or what is responsible. If you ask that question broadly enough, you wonder about God and religious experience, whether in emotional, resentful, dismissive, ironic, debased, or intellectual ways. Suffering is a catalyst for GenX religiosity.

Dulling the Scandal

Videos suggest that the sufferings of both GenX and Jesus have been institutionalized and trivialized. To interpret pop culture's depiction of suffering in Christian "language," as I will soon describe, it helps to return to a theme of previous chapters. This helpful theme is Christianity's domestication of Jesus.

The apostle Paul used language familiar to Christian Xers when he wrote that the cross, the horrific sign of Jesus' suffering, is a scandal and a stumbling block (1 Corinthians 1:23). The cross confounds any worldly attempt to "make sense" of it at last. Many in Generation X, more than any generation today, know what it means to be a scandal and a stumbling block to an entire social structure, to a hierarchy, and to institutions. After all, we have frequently disappointed our elders. American society has often passed harsh judgment on Xers.

Christian Xers wear their s(c)andals with the s(c)andaled Jesus as they liberate him from the cage in which the Churches have imprisoned him. In other words, after having our elders ignore, trivialize, and domesticate our suffering, our generation reacts by finding solidarity with Jesus in suffering. Christian Xers, however, are graced to know—as Christians—that their own suffering is taken into Jesus' suffering, and that just as Jesus' suffering and death resist all domestication, so—in an analogous way— does Xer suffering.

Salvadoran liberation theologian Jon Sobrino has argued that the domestication of Jesus' suffering on the cross was well under way in the earliest Christian communities. He shows that the early Christian attempts to come to terms with the meaning of Christ's suffering and death are manifested in the evolving interpretation of this tragedy in the Scriptures. Those early Christians viewed Jesus' suffering as befitting a prophet. This perspective was later supplemented by early Christian reflection that the Hebrew Scriptures predicted his suffering. Jesus' suffering and death were interpreted at a still later stage (in Acts 2:23 and 4:28) as happening "according to the *definite* plan and foreknowledge of God" (Sobrino, 1993, pp. 220–232, italics mine).

Sobrino's description of the progressive scriptural attempts to come to terms with Jesus' suffering and death is instructive here. It informs my interpretation of the GenX pop culture protest against suffering, as well as my view of the domestication of Xers' and Jesus' suffering. Sobrino suggests that because Scripture ultimately attributes Jesus' death to God's own will, humans themselves cannot "figure out" the cross's true meaning.

In the last resort, the attempt to find a meaning for the cross "at least in God, shows on the one hand the despair of human beings of finding this meaning for themselves, which is a sign of honesty in the face of what in itself is only tragedy and scandal. And it shows, on the other hand, the obstinacy of these same human beings in maintaining that there must be some meaning, in other words, that history is not absurd, that hope continues to be a possibility. They locate this meaning in God" (Sobrino, 1993, p. 221).

Sobrino points out that such a justification of God's actions may help people of faith, but it can also have dangerous effects. I will examine some videos that point directly and indirectly to these effects. Sobrino warns: "The danger is that in having our own answer to the 'Why?'—God's plan—*we dull the edge of the scandal of the cross* . . . because in the end it could not be explained. And it would be even more dangerous . . . to claim to know that and how, in God, Jesus' cross becomes something logical and even necessary" (1993, p. 221, italics mine).

For Sobrino, Jesus' resurrection from horrible suffering and a gruesome death signified God's affirmation of Jesus' entire life. This affirmation cannot be reduced to a simple salvific formula. By affirming through the resurrection that Jesus lived his life entirely in love, as Sobrino notes, God gave Jesus' life meaning.

To extend Sobrino's insight, Jesus' resurrection gives meaning to the life and suffering of Christian Xers. I posit that this is true, even though such meaning can only come by way of faith, not logical appropriation and domestication of Jesus.

I am not arguing that Xers have an intuitive sense about exactly what Jesus' death and resurrection mean in terms of sophisticated theological speculation. The fact is, however, that even when GenX music videos criticize institutional religion in the harshest terms, they still retain a striking fascination with Jesus. I interpret this fascination as GenX's sympathy with one who suffers unjustly and who is then caged, his suffering subjected to an *institutionalized interpretation* by the hierarchs of the Church and society. This tragedy is not just about Jesus; for Christian Xers, *it is also about us.*

As with Jesus's suffering, GenX suffering cannot be made logical and should not be domesticated or explained away. It can, however, be redemptive, once hope in God surrounds it. Christian Xers need not view suffering as an isolated, still object that one can fetishize but rather as existing within the merciful trajectory of liberation, freedom, and deliverance that God makes possible for each of us. As Dietrich Bonhoeffer wrote from prison in 1944, "Suffering is a way to freedom. In suffering, the deliverance consists in our being allowed to put the matter out of our own hands into God's hands" (1971, p. 375). Suffering sparks GenX religiosity.

Pop Culture's Expression of Suffering

With Xer-like wisdom, Marcel Proust wrote that "we are healed of a suffering only by experiencing it to the full." Those Xers who are pushed to the limits of experience and the experience of limits naturally turn to religious interpretations of suffering.

Most of pop culture's meditation on suffering—individual, social, generational—reflects a coming to terms with soul-deep anxiety or alienation. This suffering primarily derives from a deficit of real religious meaning in the autobiography of Xers. GenX pop culture expresses a psychological and philosophical—and to a lesser extent material—suffering in the heart of the generation.

The prevalence of images of suffering in GenX culture suggests that we are making a tremendous inventory of our suffering before imagining anything redemptive, anything beyond the crush of the moment.

Unadorned Adornment

One of the most surprising sources of information about GenX suffering is Xer clothing. What Xers have chosen to wear can be interpreted as an expression of their irreverent spirituality.

FASHION UNPLUGGED. When I started teaching high school in fall 1992, several of my students sported flannel shirts, ripped jeans, greasy hair, and combat boots. One of my colleagues said that they looked like furloughed prisoners. I knew better, though; being only a few years older than they, I was part of their culture. "Grunge," I realized, had arrived in the midwestern suburbs.

Under the influence of Seattle-based rock bands, grunge fashion dominated Xer styles in the 1990s. Like grunge rock music, grunge fashion was unvarnished and unwashed. Flannel shirts were its distinguishing mark. They were preferably aged and partly buttoned or left open with a plain shirt underneath. Xers augmented the flannel shirt with faded, often ripped jeans, and combat boots. Likewise, grunge hairstyles were unadorned. Men grew their hair long again (after a hiatus during much of the 1980s), and men and women could be completely "natural" about their hairstyles. Leaving it unwashed for days on end heightened the unprimped, antiglamorous look. Unlike punk styles, which favored wearing buttons to advertise musical and political allegiances, grunge let unadornment speak for itself. Unlike the 1980s with its big gelled and moussed hair, neon colors, and turned-up collars, grunge was stripped down. It was fashion "unplugged."

Grunge was very accessible. A visit to the thrift store and twenty dollars were the only prerequisites for an entire grunge wardrobe. Its lack of adornment and impoverished look were fundamental to the various ways that grunge could be interpreted: Not only could Xers who dressed in grunge styles seem unable to afford to care about expensive self-decoration, but they also could suggest that they themselves were uncared for. As if accepting this, the clothes themselves seemed to shrug, hanging loosely off the body, visually reinforcing the GenX "slacker" stereotype. Unlike the exposed belly trend, however, grunge did not leave the body open to inspection. The body was concealed, but not so tightly that it showed off fleshly curves or muscles, as did 1980s designer jeans and muscle T-shirts. The message is that there is no showing off here. (Of course, grunge shows off that it is not showing off.) Grunge underscores neediness; it highlights want.

Where did this preoccupation with poverty originate? How could my grunge-loving, upper-middle-class suburban high school students possibly consider themselves poor, especially when they had lived through the 1980s in all of its ostentation?

I interpret grunge as an outward expression of an inner poverty that Xers discovered as teenagers and young adults. We feared that there was something poor at the heart of who we were, and we expressed that deficit in what we wore. Many lived a suburban and young adult existence marked by a lack of meaning. (This is why we piece together our own meaning—our own religiosity—through popular culture. We cobble together a lived theology in a realm over which we have creative influence.) Chronology matters; grunge happened *after* the excessive 1980s. Poverty, a feeling of hollowness, followed the splashy fashions of the previous decade.

As secondhand clothing, grunge is appropriate for a secondhand generation—one that must pay for the excessive desires of its elders, from the sexual revolution to the national debt to easy divorce. This hand-me-down generation knows that there is a poverty in our hearts, born of our roles as both society's orphans and its cleanup crew. Grunge announces, "We are on our own." It does not rejoice at this, yet it does not despair. Grunge simply offers our own take on our reality—when left alone, as we have been, we will wear the disarray in which we live (psychologically, culturally, and fashionably). Tailoring and cleanliness be damned, small gestures though they are. It is no accident that grunge emerged from Seattle, where the rain is incessant. Those who wear grunge do not let others forget about the storm clouds of suffering that follow Generation X.

The epitome of grunge was the Seattle band Nirvana, fronted by Kurt Cobain. When twenty-seven-year-old Cobain committed suicide in 1994, it put a tragic face on the suffering bottled up inside many Xers. Fans viewed his death as a sort of martyrdom, with Cobain as the quintessential Xer killed by a life lived too quickly under the stress of too many expectations. His doses of prophetic criticism, enraged and heretical, proved too strong for most Americans. Revering Cobain as a misunderstood genius, his followers still mourn the anniversary of his suicide and erect elaborate shrines in cyberspace. Cobain was the first fallen (anti?)hero of the X generation. (Cyberspace makes it possible for suffering to unify Xers. Visiting the many Web sites honoring Cobain, one senses the sadness and religiosity-in-suffering that draws thousands of Xers daily to these virtual memorial grottoes.)

SOLDIER OF MISFORTUNE. In 1983, at the dawn of my high school days, I visited a military surplus shop in Independence, Missouri. The stocky, tense proprietor kept an eye on the handful of teenagers wandering around his store. My purchase of camouflage trousers big enough for a platoon was my initiation into GenX fashion trends. For the first time, I had enough spending money to participate. I jumped on the camouflage bandwagon, a fashion trend inspired by popular survivalist magazines, Vietnam movies, and paramilitary television shows.

Other friends with more disposable income bought full military fatigues and combat boots (later recyclable for the grunge craze). Whereas grunge adornment did not sexually discriminate, the camouflage craze was almost exclusively male. Aside from appealing to the macho, hard-edged persona into which many males are socialized, what else might this fashion trend, which lasted well into the 1980s, have represented?

The army outfit implied a fight for survival—but where was the war? Generation X never fought in a major, prolonged armed conflict. Instead, we survived the protracted Cold War. Wearing military clothes helped us imagine that we were part of the big "event" that never happened for our generation. I interpret the trend not as much about our losing ourselves in romantic notions about the military as about our acting out a slow-burning fight for social and economic survival, as well as the more important battle for meaning in our lives. The style perhaps also promised us our own moment of large proportion where we could transcend our allegiance to the local mall or other pop culture ephemera.

As with grunge, military fashions allowed us to say, "We are on our own." With camouflage, we did not pose as poor slackers but as individual soldiers of (mis)fortune. Even the military boots, which are made for lengthy, heavy-duty marches, implied a prolonged trek toward wholeness and out of suffering.

Military fashion may also have hinted at an emerging bunker mentality among Xers, who began in adolescence to cluster into fashion-bounded groups. Although all generations do this, ours did it to survive; in the absence of our parents (who were often "gone" even when they lived in the same house), we frequently felt more loyal to friends than to family. Popular culture, a fashion culture, bound us together. Despite its ephemerality, it was no more provisional for many of us than our own families.

SEPARATION AND SADNESS. Growing up in the aging suburb of Independence, Missouri, I did not have an exalted sense of our cultural status. Many large trends passed us by or arrived too late to be called fashionable. Grunge and camouflage trends did make it to town, but then again thrift and military surplus stores were common in our lower-middle-class neighborhoods.

We also embraced a trend that unusually unnerved our parents and teachers—the "gothic" look. I had barely broken in my oversized fatigues when, on the first day of my sophomore year of high school, five or six students congregated near my locker. They looked like punkers—but from the local cemetery. It is hard to say what intrigued me the most: their completely dark outfits (even their accessories were black, except for silver crucifixes), their jet-black hair gelled in gravity-defying arrangements, or their starkly pale faces (the result of expertly applied white makeup with black highlights around their eyes). They called themselves many things and were called even more, but the most common self-designation was *goths* or *gothics*.

Soon, I frequently noticed goths around Kansas City, all of them Xers. I continued to mingle with them in the city until I moved to Boston in 1994, where I again encountered small pockets of goths. In high school, my lack of an overbearing personality and uncertainty about my own niche gave me the freedom to hang out with almost any clique. This condition continued into young adulthood, and I found myself able to talk with punkers, grunge kids, goths, and a host of other genres of GenXers. I dated a gothic woman during high school, which was enough to give my parents chills, fatigued as they still were from my military-clothing ventures. It gave me access to a fascinating Xer world and helped me feel comfortable around goths thereafter, when others around me were intimidated by their unsettling appearance.

Whereas the camouflage trend was a males-only affair, goths seemed to have an equal-access policy; it was often difficult to tell male from female. Men and women wore similar clothing styles and colors, as well as striking makeup. There is a fastidiousness about gothic dressing that provides a strong contrast with the grunge look. Hairstyles are often moussed into elaborate sculptures. Goths in public are such a contrast with their surroundings that they often appear to be plucked from an extraordinarily somber fashion shoot.

Gothic fashions are the most stark expression of GenX suffering. The style indulges in mourning and death, an imitation or even parody of what one would normally wear to a funeral. The paleness suggests a mask of death, sickness, and a nocturnal life, lived away from daylight. But what is being grieved? By chance, as I took a cab home one summer evening, a gothic driver who worked by day as a hairdresser (Martin de Porres reincarnated?) helped me get to the roots of the style. "Gothic," he told me, "is all about separation. Separation from society and from God." He thought quietly for a moment and then summarized, "Most of all, it's about separation and sadness."

Whatever else the gothic look signifies, it indicates Xers' ironic take on President Reagan's "morning in America"; goths are highlighting their own mourning in America. As a psychologist friend told me a few years ago, "There are plenty of reasons for your generation to feel deeply sad." A series of negative experiences characterize GenX history. (I call this series the "litany of the *sans,*" borrowed from the Catholic "litany of the saints.") When a generation bears the weight of so many failures—including AIDS, divorce, abuse, poor schools, recessions, youth poverty, teen suicide, outrageous educational and living expenses, failure of governmental and religious institutions, national debt, high taxes, environmental devastation, drugs, parents that need to be parented, violence, unstable economic security, premature loss of childhood—how can suffering not be an important part of one's identity?

This litany of the *sans* is real, but does not tumble out at a moment's notice from every Xer's lips. Most know the reasons that they and their generation have suffered, but many tire of thinking about these painful realities in their lives, this series of deficits.

That is why, as in so much GenX culture, gothic fashion also takes a less-than-serious, ironic stance toward suffering. The gothic style is excessively funereal. Survival, it seems, is only possible by hyperbolizing death, by making an entire wardrobe out of bleakness. Paradoxically, this mimicking also explains the clownish element in gothic; the whiteface represents a mask of death but also of humor "in the face" of death.

All these fashion statements—the gothic look, grunge, piercings, and camouflage—emphasize the extent to which we each don a persona. Xer fashions illustrate how all living is an interchange of masks. By continuing to live despite the suffering, even by embodying the suffering foisted on Xers, goths ironically show that suffering can be commodified, commercialized, and fashioned. It can be mastered by Xers. It need not be a series of debts we owe but can ironically be a set of clothes we own. There may be something sad about this sort of comedy, but gallows humor is usually the most poignant.

Screened Suffering

If clothes can be religiously revealing, music video has even more vivid ways of meditating on GenX suffering.

CRUCIFYING A BOY(HOOD). The central suggestion of Xer fashion, that suffering is an integral part of the GenX experience, is taken to a violent extreme in Pearl Jam's "Jeremy." Amid lyrics of family strife and violent, apocalyptic utterances, a collage of images alternates between front man Eddie Vedder, who sits anxiously and strains forward angrily, and Jeremy, who paints pictures, argues with his parents, and struggles to stay awake and avoid abuse in school.

From the very beginning, "Jeremy" embodies GenX's list of grievances against its elders. The inattention of Jeremy's parents symbolizes the dysfunction in many Xer families. The lyrics suggest the American culture of violence. Even at this early point in the song, however, there are hints that Jeremy has been called to a destiny far higher than the depths to which his childhood has fallen; the lyrics suggest that Jeremy might be hanging on a cross.

During these opening stanzas, the phrase *Genesis 3:6* uncannily flashes and then disappears. Genesis 3:6 describes how, at the serpent's behest, Eve took fruit from the forbidden tree and gave it to Adam. Appropriately enough, a scriptural verse about the beginning of life on earth and the supposed entrance of sin into the world appears at the beginning of the video. The verse refers to lost innocence, a dirge for Xers who grew up too quickly (recall the litany of the *sans*), who lost their innocence at an extraordinarily early age. Jeremy appears to be about thirteen years old.

To depict this youthful GenX disillusion, the video shows a rebellious Jeremy in a shouting match with his parents at the dinner table. The familial fireworks touch off a series of images related to social ostracism, including a journey to a dark forest interspersed with scenes in which Jeremy's peers mock him, pointing condescending fingers and bobbing their heads in laughter.

Interpreting "Jeremy" as representing the prophetic Jeremiah—who some scholars think was about thirteen years old when called to be a prophet and eighteen when he began preaching—provides us with more clues that Jeremy bears a special gift and task from God. This calling exacts a price: "O Lord, you have enticed me, and I was enticed; you have overpowered me, and you have prevailed. I have become a laughingstock all day long; everyone mocks me" (Jeremiah 20:7). Jeremy is not only a prophet like Jeremiah but also a messianic figure, a type of Christ. Some believed that Jesus himself was a reincarnation of Jeremiah or one of the other prophets (Matthew 16:14). Not coincidentally, Jesus received a prophet's welcome (and leave) and was cruelly mocked before and during his crucifixion.

> Then the soldiers of the governor took Jesus into the governor's headquarters, and they gathered the whole cohort around him. They stripped him and put a scarlet robe on him, and after twisting some thorns into a crown, they put it on his head. They put a reed in his right hand and knelt before him and mocked him, saying, "Hail, King of the Jews!" They spat on him, and took the reed and struck him on the head. After mocking him, they stripped him of the robe and put his own clothes on him. Then they led him away to crucify him [Matthew 27:27–31].

> The people stood by, watching; but the leaders scoffed at him, saying "He saved others; let him save himself if he is the Messiah of God, God's chosen one!" The soldiers also mocked him, coming up and offering him sour wine, and saying, "If you are the King of the Jews, save yourself!" [Luke 23:35–38].

With head bowed, Jeremy raises his arms and faces an ominous wall of fire. The scene fades into a shot of Vedder, who walks by a shadow of Jeremy superimposed on a wall, an icon of a crucified boy(hood). Implicitly invoking the litany of the *sans,* the video lifts up Xers' crucified childhood.

YEARNING FOR A MESSIAH. That it may be easier for our generation than for previous ones to report abuse does not lessen the devastation of each instance of abuse. Xers still suffered from sexism and other forms of injustice, inside and outside the family and religious institutions. Tori Amos's "Crucify" uses Christian images to explore gender-related suffering.

In the video, Amos acts out the many ways in which women "crucify" themselves—or are crucified—for others. The clearest illustration of this sort of crucifixion unfolds as she changes from one fashionable outfit to another during the chorus. A high-heeled shoe dangles before the camera. Amos then dances in an expensive dress and shows off her expressive lipstick (for her equally expressive lips). She also dons a choker that resembles a dog collar.

The visual effect of these scenes is as important as what Amos is wearing. Throughout the exploration of women's appearance, Amos can only be seen in the middle third of the screen; the left and right sides are black. Significantly, this forces the viewer to be a voyeur. Are we looking through a door that is slightly cracked open? Are we peering through a peephole? Or are we spying on Amos through a two-way mirror? Because the very act of watching the video makes the audience into Peeping Toms, the video's "success" depends on viewers' acknowledgment of that voyeuristic role.

According to some cultural critics, one symptom that our culture is postmodern is the extent to which our technology has become interactive. Amos creates a disturbing postmodern video by inviting the viewer to stare illicitly at the evidence for her crucifixion. We leer at Amos, further crucifying her with our lancing looks, funneled through the narrow viewing slit.

We learn even more about this suffering if we consider the ironic way in which this scene is framed. Kierkegaard observes that irony (again, a key feature of GenX pop culture) lures its readers (or viewers, in this case) into revealing something about themselves. Irony, he writes, seeks "not so much to remain in hiding itself as to get others to disclose themselves" (1989, p. 251). Thus, this scene in "Crucify" is ironic because it forces us to assume the objectifying "male gaze"—the same one she seeks to undermine in this scene. Her "hiding" behind the keyhole makes viewers consider their complicity in Amos' crucifixion, as well as their contribution to sexism in general.

The lyrics intimate that Amos (or the song's narrator) seeks salvation in seamy places, undergoing yet another form of crucifixion. She does not want to be yet another casualty for God, the lyrics seem to say. Outside the institutional Church, the narrator explores fashion, street life, and sex as salvific alternatives and finds each of them wanting. In this suffering, like many Christian saints and even some contemporary Christians, the lyrics suggest that she experiences the stigmata, the wounds of Christ. Personal suffering is allied with that of Jesus.

Biblical scholar Joseph Fitzmyer, in a commentary on Paul's letter to the Romans, inadvertently helps us understand the video's theological implication: "Sufferings now endured must always be seen as a participation in the suffering of Jesus himself, in what he has already suffered. Christian suffering is never an individual, lonely experience; Jesus has suffered before, and Christian suffering is only the overflow of his" (1993, p. 502).

Suffering is not the last word, however; foretastes of redemption flash throughout the video's tale of crucifixion. (As Fitzmyer notes, "Through such 'suffering with Christ' the participation in [Christ's] glorification is already assumed" [p. 502].) From the beginning, water images leak through the video in the form of brief, subliminal shots of underwater scenes, including submerged chains and a handbag. These images foreshadow her later immersion. Amos enters the video clothed in a white robe (and white heels), clothing strongly reminiscent of Christian baptismal garb (minus the heels).

Her journey of lamentation through the rest of the video is destined to culminate in baptism. During the bridge of the song, Amos walks in slow motion into a bathtub vigorously flooded with a cloudburst of water from on high. The water travels torrentially under the song's bridge, beckoning to Amos. As she sings, she approaches the bathtub clad in formal dress. Without breaking stride, she steps right into the bathtub and sinks down, delighting in the water.

The video seems to be restating a Christian theology of baptism first offered by the apostle Paul. In Paul's letter to the church at Rome (Romans 6:3), he asked, "Do you not know that all of us who have been baptized into Christ Jesus were baptized into his death?" Christians believe that they die with Christ in baptism so that they might have new life, both here and in the hereafter, as Christ did. To be baptized into Christ's death is gruesome; it involves the call and challenge to endure in life contemporary analogues of all the horror and humiliation of crucifixion, that most inhumane of punishments. This suffering is proof of solidarity with Christ, even kinship with him. "We are children of God," wrote Paul, "and if children, then heirs, heirs of God and joint heirs with Christ—if, in fact, we suffer with Christ so that we may also be glorified with Christ" (Romans 8:17). George Eliot wrote somewhere: "Deep, unspeakable suffering may well be called a baptism, a regeneration, the initiation into a new state."

Amos's full immersion in the water—perhaps the most ancient form of Christian baptism—marks the culmination of the video's drama. Interestingly, however, there is something beyond this apex; Amos emerges from the bath still wearing the dress. While she is in the bathtub, the camera pans seductively across her body. When she comes out of the bath, in waterlogged dress, Amos dances for the camera. The voyeuristic view is gone now, replaced by an unusual head-and-shoulders shot that downplays her body. This implicit reference to what the apostle Paul meant by a "spiritual body" (1 Corinthians 15:44) is a sign—as it was for Paul—of resurrection.

Salve for Wounds

For the spirituality of GenXers and the mutual teaching-and-learning dynamic that could exist between Xers and religious institutions, our pop culture's inventory of Xers' suffering offers several implications. Pop culture can prompt Xers to reflect on the suffering in their own lives and attend to the ways in which they seek to heal those incompletions and wounds. The pop culture provides an opportunity to examine the crises of meaning in Xers' lives that call for religious responses.

GenX pop culture challenges religious institutions to "undomesticate" GenX suffering, to take it seriously and not explain it away. Indeed, for Churches it is a welcome opportunity to reopen Sobrino's question, which appeared at the beginning of this chapter, about the meaning and significance of Jesus' suffering. Our pop culture gives institutions the impetus to examine the extent to which their interpretation of Jesus' suffering (as lived in their preaching and practice) is bound up with their sense of their own suffering—or lack thereof. Institutions are challenged to interrogate the roots of that sense, to be self-critical about how they view suffering. In addition, institutions are challenged to examine how they perpetuate various forms of social suffering, such as those alluded to in "Crucify," particularly the degree to which they further the suffering of women.

GenX pop culture also reminds institutions of Xers' awareness that we are on our own, seeking the religious outside of their framework. Whereas boomer self-reliance partly results from the economic and social advantages they had in their upbringing, Xer self-reliance is a form of "making do." Xers challenge institutions to prove that they will not let us down.

Institutions can challenge Xers, as well, in regard to these themes. The first challenges institutions can offer are simply spiritual gifts to Xers; Churches can provide local, down-to-earth heroes or exemplars in religious communities, as well as experiences of family that are more than simply provisional.

In addition, institutions could challenge Xers to see themselves as part of a larger "movement" of a religious tradition, as some compensation for the absence of a theme and the theme of absence in the generation. Institutions can do this by forming small communities of solidarity for Xers; this will allow them to become responsible for their religious tradition (an issue I take up in Chapter Eight).

Finally, with their institutional memory, religious institutions can challenge Xers to see their suffering relative to that of past generations, such as those who endured the depression. This is not a matter of domesticating or explaining away the "scandal" of GenX suffering. It is using the resources at the disposal of institutions (in this case, a long memory about past generations in religious communities) to give Xers a larger story into which they can put their own suffering. There is much evidence that Xers thrive on stories, on narrative. Institutions should provide Xers with resources for imagining their lives—both the suffering and the success—as part of a larger religious story.

Suffering Servanthood

I came close to being accused of blasphemy as I presented some of the ideas in this book to various groups, in schools, churches, conferences, and on-line. Especially when it came to talking about suffering servant-hood, many felt that I had gone over the edge. After seeing a draft of this chapter, someone e-mailed me the following message: "When you wrote about the suffering servanthood of GenX in particular, I could see more clearly than ever that your generation's culture is trying to exploit the Bible for profits." He was close; Generation X is trying to exploit the Bible for prophets.

The image of the suffering servant appears in the Hebrew Scriptures in the book of the prophet Isaiah. The suffering servant is depicted as one who undergoes injustice for a good cause, who endures great torments in order to do God's will. According to Isaiah's testimony, "The Lord God opened my ear, and I was not rebellious, I did not turn backward. I gave my back to those who struck me, and my cheeks to those who pulled out the beard; I did not hide my face from insult and spitting" (Isaiah 50:5–6). Isaiah's testimony continues: "He was despised and rejected by others; a man of suffering and acquainted with infirmity. . . . Surely he has borne our infirmities and carried our diseases; yet we accounted him stricken, struck down by God, and afflicted. But he was wounded for our transgressions, crushed for our iniquities; upon him was the punishment that made us whole, and by his bruises we are healed" (Isaiah 53:3–5).

The suffering servant is also an image in Christian tradition, applied very early to Jesus. Peter's first letter in the Christian Scriptures alluded to the book of Isaiah, stating that Jesus "bore our sins in his body on the cross, so that, free from sins, we might live for righteousness; by his wounds you have been healed" (1 Peter 2:24).

Generation X's place in American history suggests some affinity with the suffering servant image, and the music videos I have interpreted allude to this affinity. In "Black Hole Sun," the lamb of God bleats with a bot-tle stuck in its mouth. There is a suggestive lyrical allusion to Jesus' cries

(Matthew 27:46) at the pinnacle of his suffering servanthood: "My God, my God, why have you forsaken me?"

"Losing My Religion" alludes to suffering servanthood by asking whether a servant who simply suffers can serve anything but the interests of an institution. Because Jesus is confused, old, and weak, other people end up serving him in this video. Finally, his image is served up as a pair of metal wings.

Whereas R.E.M.'s video wonders in evanescent glimpses whether a suffering servanthood is even possible, Madonna's video affirms that it is. In "Like a Prayer," Madonna receives Jesus' wounds, the stigmata, for freeing a fellow liberator (Saint Martin de Porres) and moving out into the world with her "religion." (As a suffering servant, according to Isaiah 58:6, Madonna is to "loose the bonds of injustice, to undo the thongs of the yoke, to let the oppressed go free." Madonna surely undoes every thong.) The stigmata symbolize her suffering for this servanthood by being a person for others and setting them free.

Society calls Xers to a suffering servanthood. Our society has unjustly demanded something of us, and we have responded by giving what others ask. For example, our generation pays a higher proportion of its income to fund our elders' retirement. We were also the objects of educational experimentation for trendy pedagogues of the 1970s and 1980s. Furthermore, we were the children who bore the brunt of no-fault divorce. Then, too, we suffered the ambiguities and hurts of sexual experimentation and the negative effects of the sexual revolution. In more ways than these, we are called as a generation to suffering servanthood, a religious way of framing secular demands and responsibilities. Whether Isaiah or Jesus is the ultimate referent, suffering servanthood illustrates one religious dimension of our pain.

As I suggested earlier, GenX can deepen its lived theology if Xers can see and experience their suffering as rooted in a salvific religious story that ties in with their respective religious traditions. Indeed, there is an invitation for us to be more conscious about who and what our particular suffering is "serving." Is it the poor? Corporate America? Ourselves? If Xers can take the spiritual challenge of Isaiah to heart, perhaps they can begin to ask whom they are making into the objects of their suffering. Whom are we forcing, as it were, to carry *our* individual and generational salvation?

GenX pop culture challenges institutions to dignify Xer suffering and to build preaching and theology around the surprising possibility that GenX suffering might be a form of servanthood. In return, institutions should challenge Xers to direct their suffering servanthood toward those in need and toward their own religious communities.

The End of the World as We Know It

"In this place I will make void the plans of Judah and Jerusalem, and will make them fall by the sword before their enemies" (Jeremiah 19:7). Thus does Jeremiah the prophet predict the violent end of his sinful people. Likewise, the video "Jeremy" rages from the Hebrew Scriptures, using prophecy and apocalypticism to express suffering in a religious context.

Apocalypticism and prophethood (or prophecy) share a theological kinship, so it is not surprising that they appear together in this video. *Apocalypticism* is a belief in a radical future revelation, usually envisioned by a prophet. As we approach the end of the millennium, for example, apocalyptic anxiety—fear or hope that the third millennium will bring about a radical change in the world—is on the rise. Jesus is sometimes characterized as an apocalyptic prophet who predicted that the end of the world and the beginning of God's reign were rapidly approaching. Apocalypticism is a characteristic religious stance for communities who suffer (making it ideal for Xers), because it inspires faith and hope and anticipates a radical revelation.

Suffering Prophethood

Jeremy, the adolescent star of the video, is symbolically associated with Jeremiah and Jesus as a suffering prophet. Meek and worn, Jeremy even poses with an American flag draped and sagging around him like Jesus in tatters before Pilate. The flag is too big for Jeremy (Xers were always forced to be more adult).

The video suggests that, like Jeremiah, Jeremy and Xers live lives of prophetic lamentation, which may explain Jeremy's deep disturbance. What biblical scholar Jack Lundbom says of Jeremiah could be true of Xers as well: "Jeremiah is a true divine mediator, which is to say his own personal grief upon receiving the divine word is every bit as intense as his preaching is of that word to others" (1992, p. 688).

How does the video depict the voice of Jeremy, the young prophet? Here is where "Jeremy" falls sadly short of its own challenge, yet is nonetheless instructive. The closing scene is one of the most shocking conclusions in any music video. In a classroom, students recite the Pledge of Allegiance and give the Nazi salute. Jeremy saunters into the room barechested. Blithely, he pitches an apple to the teacher and turns deliberately to face the class members, all clad in school uniforms. In one seamless motion, he pulls out a gun and sprays bullets. A snare drum's stark pulse substitutes for the firearm's sound. The camera pans across the classroom, and we see horrified adolescents frozen in time, their arms lifted to cover their heads. Bright red blood spatters their pressed white shirts.

Although this nihilistic and apocalyptic conclusion is an easy, almost predictable ending to a complex story, it is not completely at variance with our prophetic guide Jeremiah. The burden of prophethood received from God fosters violent wishes in both Jeremy and Jeremiah, and perhaps even violent fulfillment. The prophet Jeremiah laments:

> For whenever I speak, I must cry out, I must shout, "Violence and destruction!" For the word of the Lord has become for me a reproach and derision all day long. . . . But the Lord is with me like a dread warrior; therefore my persecutors shall stumble, and they will not prevail. They will be greatly shamed, for they will not succeed. Their eternal dishonor will never be forgotten. O Lord of hosts, you test the righteous, you see the heart and the mind; let me see your retribution upon them, for to you I have committed my cause [Jeremiah 20:8, 11–12].

(Neither this passage nor the video should be read out of context as condoning aimless violence. The passage should be interpreted in light of Jeremiah's criticism in 22:13–17 of King Jehoiakim's use of violence, as well as his mistreatment of the poor.)

The possibility of a deranged sort of messiahship for Jeremy remains, because there could be a different interpretation of the ending. The spattered blood on the students' uniforms may not be their own; it could be Jeremy's blood. Did Jeremy shoot himself in the final scene? (The frozen students would then be raising their arms in fear of him and of being splattered with blood.) Although this conclusion is unlikely, the final scene is ambiguous enough to make such an ending remotely possible. Regardless, "Jeremy" concludes with a will to destroy as blind as the unthinking patriotism it abhors, although it may be a result of the cumulative effects of violence of all sorts in Jeremy's culture. The nihilistic ending does not do "justice" to its rich content.

Jeremiah's own task—upending unjust institutions and lamenting the deafness of a people—involved a violence of a different sort. He was "to pluck up and to pull down, to destroy and to overthrow, to build and to plant" (1:10). This task paralleled the prophethood that Generation X is called upon to exercise in American religion and society today, as we shall see.

Jeremiah the biblical prophet could have provided Jeremy with more hope than the video does. Jeremiah's faith remained intact throughout imprisonment, through a lifetime of laments and painful prophecies:

"They shall come and sing aloud on the height of Zion, and they shall be radiant over the goodness of the Lord, over the grain, the wine, and the oil, and over the young of the flock and the herd; their life shall become like a watered garden, and they shall never languish again" (31:12).

Faith, which requires more courage and strength than the bloody recourse to nihilism invoked by the conclusion of "Jeremy" (and possibly the conclusion of Jeremy), is paradoxically within the grasp of GenXers. Because of the way America has treated them, Xers seem *least* likely to be people of faith. Paul's letter to the church at Corinth in the Christian Scriptures has particular significance for Christian Xers who identify with Jeremy/Jeremiah the prophet: "To shame the wise, God has chosen what the world counts folly, and to shame the strong, God has chosen what the world counts weakness" (1 Corinthians 1:27). Theologian Harvey Cox builds on Paul's assertion. Imagining Jesus as a mocked clown, Cox observes: "The clown is constantly defeated, tricked, humiliated, and tromped upon. He is infinitely vulnerable, but never finally defeated" (1969, p. 170). God may be working through our weaknesses, our folly, even our clownishness, giving Xers a prophetic place in American culture and religion.

Jeremiah's life corresponded roughly with the last half-century of ancient Israelite nationhood. Although we may not be living at the much-prophesied end of history, the life span of Xers seems to correspond with a radical decline in the quality of American life. The example of Jeremiah, however, gives Xers a model of survival. He withstood the destruction of the Temple and continued to preach. Xers survive the radical decline and deconstruction of the Church and American dream. Abandoned by their Churches, Xers can be inspired by fellow prophet Jeremiah to reconstruct the promises of America. As such, the GenX rebellion (evidenced in this video) can be interpreted as a postmodern jeremiad by some of the most authentic Jeremiahs around.

Xchatology

Xer suffering takes a bizarre turn through apocalypticism and prophecy in "Black Hole Sun." If Jeremiah cries that he will "make void the plans of Judah and Jerusalem," then "Black Hole Sun" declares simply and disturbingly, "I will make void!"

In the video, the suburban homemaker (who was featured in Chapter Five's discussion about cleaving the fish) looks out the window after the cutting episode. She beholds the absence of the sun that she had always expected to be there. Blood-red clouds overtake the sun, casting an eery twilight over the scene. The sky becomes the focus for the remainder of the video.

Where the sun used to be, a black hole develops, bathing the sky in deep red light. Around the black hole is a ring of fire. The gaping absence inhales and exhales chunks of red and black detritus. The black hole sun, a breathing uterus, eventually whips up a tornado, carrying away frightened suburbanites and threatening to engulf the entire neighborhood, if not the whole earth. The sun that no longer exists is now the "star" of the video.

As neighbors look to the sky, their faces—frozen in horror and delight—slowly melt in gruesome distortion. The melting faces are not merely a result of the savagely hot (or radioactive?) black hole sun. They are also intimately related to one of the video's deepest themes—the *plasticity* of suburban American culture, including the culture of institutional Church life, which is largely irrelevant to and insufficient for Xers. In one sequence of images, a Barbie doll turns on a spit over a flaming barbecue pit. As Barbie's body melts, a woman sunbathes near a swimming pool. Her bathing suit is similar to the one Barbie wears. Everything liquefies under the glare of a foundationless commercial culture, a nuclear meltdown, and especially a meltdown of *meaning*—the primary source of Xer suffering.

We now begin to grasp the nature of the "black hole sun." Once totally trustworthy, the old, comfortable sun no longer gives light from afar. It is distant from our daily lives and oblivious to our most basic needs. The ever-lasting, distant sun (in other words the transcendent, all-powerful, and distant God) has blinked out. It has been surpassed, supplanted, overtaken, sublimated, succeeded, and subverted by the black hole sun.

As the faces of the family in the video testify, this situation is both existentially terrifying and sublimely ecstatic. For Christian Xers, I interpret the black hole sun as none other than the black hole Son. (In other words, Jesus reappears after his earlier cameo as the little lamb.)

This arrival happened just in time, as Xers live in a black hole of meaning. With absolutes under attack, foundations crumbling, and cities degenerating into combat zones, there no longer seems to be any omnipotent, transcendent sun to guide our journey. Because so much of Xers' cultural experience can be characterized by a black hole, the only sort of Christian messiah that can emerge is a black hole Son/sun. This sun/Son speaks to the black hole of meaning in the lives of Christian Xers.

The parodied ministers of the video smugly warn, "The end is near." Having been around to give light and act as a fixed star for millennia, the sun is smothered by the black hole. The neighborhood is destroyed in an apocalyptic scene, the surreal melting faces of agony and delight recalling horrific predictions about nuclear holocausts. The end of the world seems to have arrived in "Black Hole Sun." This is a video about *eschatology,* which is theology about the end times.

An eschatological tone is evident in the lyrics as lead singer Chris Cornell heralds what I interpret as the final coming of the kingdom of heaven. The song's final (eschatological) lyrics have Cornell pleading in a firestorm of apocalypticism for the arrival of the black hole sun.

There is a striking similarity between Soundgarden's lyrical pleading for the eschaton (end time) and an eschatological saying of the early Christian Church. In Paul's first letter to the Corinthians (1 Corinthians 16:22), he invoked the brief but weighty exhortation, "Our Lord, come!" This is an Aramaic saying, Aramaic being a language closely related to Hebrew that Jesus may have spoken. This reference, from one of the oldest forms of Christian eschatology, serves as the implicit foundation for the video's searing critique of country club Christianity and vacuous suburban existence. The reference allows the introduction of Christian Xers' messiah, the black hole Son.

This Xchatology is illuminated by its proper cultural context. In the early 1980s, Xers who were mostly between grade school and high school age were subjected to a nationwide mini-hysteria prompted by the showing of *The Day After,* a television movie about a nuclear attack on America and the devastating nuclear winter that followed. Teachers organized classroom discussions, schools offered counseling for students frightened or disturbed by the possibility of a nuclear nightmare, and the press played up the drama.

This was the zenith of nuclear anxiety for Xers, who were too young to have lived through the Cuban Missile Crisis. Many schools in the late 1970s and early 1980s still carried out nuclear alarm drills and showed films in social studies or health classes about what to do in case of nuclear emergency. Indeed, few buildings had taken down their Fallout Shelter signs, with their ominous radioactive symbols implanting a slow-building anxiety in Xers from early childhood.

In October 1984, students at Brown University voted to keep the school's infirmary stocked with poison tablets in order to aid suicide in case of a nuclear war (Holtz, 1995, p. 64). A nationwide survey in 1982 of more than forty thousand teenage boys found that fear of nuclear war was their number one concern. Among the same number of teenage girls it ranked second, behind fear of a parent's death (Holtz, 1995, pp. 63–64).

The nuclear threat, however, was eliminated almost overnight. In the late 1980s, when a majority of Xers had entered their formative teenage years or young adulthood, the Soviet Union dissipated quietly instead of in the midst of nuclear mayhem. The Berlin Wall came tumbling down. More and more surveys showed that teens and young adults were apolitical, even grossly uninformed about the daily news and the basics of geography. Indeed, *alt.culture,* the early 1990s handbook of GenX popular culture, contains no entries in the index under *nuclear.* Such an absence is one indicator of how distant the nuclear threat seems to Xers.

In the wake of the decline of nuclear anxiety, an underlying crisis for Xers was exposed—a crisis of meaning. GenX pop culture addresses this anxiety of meaning, trying to fill the vacuum in Xers' lives. Given this cultural situation, the black hole Son beckons. In this context, Christian Xers plead along with Soundgarden for the arrival of the black hole Son/sun. Only a messiah who speaks from and to the black hole of meaning can be a Christ for Christian Xers.

Visions of the End

Inspired by our pop culture, GenX spirituality can radically orient itself toward the future. As we realize that the world is not ending, we can bear to imagine the end of our lives and the end of the world's life. The way we envision the end times, explicitly and implicitly, strongly affects the way we live (or do not live) spiritually in the present. Our pop culture also reminds us that many Xers must attend to a significant emptiness, a silence, and a darkness. We may overlook that void in our haste to live life at the edge. But living life at the edge should warn us that we are evading a spiritual vacuum, a black hole. That is the very place from which a renaissance of our spiritual lives can begin.

Xers challenge religious institutions to recognize the prophethood of all believers, not just those in control of religious institutions. Institutions can search out and heed these prophetic GenX voices. Despite protests to the contrary, religious institutions help spread nihilism within the generation; Xers can challenge institutions to close the wide gulf between their preaching and their practices and thereby to assuage Xers' despair. GenX pop culture also affords institutions an opportunity to reacquaint themselves with, and preach and practice, a God who is witnessed in Scripture and tradition as a God of nearness in emptiness and incompletion.

Institutions can push Xers to voice their prophecy inside institutional walls, not just in pop culture. Xers are challenged to see just how deep the generation's prophetic convictions run. That is, do we simply want to make a pop culture industry of suffering, apocalypticism, and prophecy, or are we willing to work within institutions to lend the strength of our divine word?

Irreverence and Suffering

One of the biggest spiritual challenges for Xers is to understand our poverty amid relative affluence. Some in our generation have been coopted by the seductions of big money, thinking their salvation lies down that road. Others have become so obsessed with their suffering that it seems there is no way out. Both are false roads.

While we try to make our way in a materialistic culture, it is our responsibility to attend not only to our physical or economic livelihood but also to our spiritual growth. The statement that we make with our clothing—that we are on our own—highlights the extent to which we need to find communities of religious inquirers. In struggling to make religious sense of our lives and the world, we must not slip into the vacuum of individualism that exists all around us. Claiming a spiritual quest that transcends our pop culture will paradoxically allow us to engage with our packaged, pop-cultured surroundings more meaningfully, which usually requires a healthy ironic distance. Because Xers indulge so heavily in pop culture, one of our prime temptations is to abandon the spiritual quest for the satisfactions of the moment. Resisting this temptation will ensure that we continue to master the pop culture instead of being mastered by it.

As I have repeatedly suggested, Xers master pop culture through the use of irony. Irony is one way out from under the weight of suffering. As I noted earlier, suffering communities tend to use apocalyptic visions as a means of hope for future meaning and relief from suffering. These visions are frequently communicated by prophets, like the prophets "Jeremy" and (Tori) "Amos." Suffering feeds apocalypticism, which is commonly given voice by prophets, and prophets often use irony. Kierkegaard, in fact, suggests that "the ironist is certainly prophetic, because he is continually pointing to something impending, but what it is he does not know" (1989, p. 261).

The great gaping nothingness of Soundgarden's black hole sun symbolizes this lack of certainty about what is actually impending. The image signifies GenX's typical stance toward culture, meaning, and our lives—that is, highlighting what is missing, mocking life, ironizing what is given, emptying it of meaning. Irony, says Kierkegaard, "enlivens by way of negativity" (1989, p. 14). Only by turning to the negative, drawing out what is missing, and puncturing what is supposed to be meaningful do Xers find their bearings. In the words of Kierkegaard, GenX pop culture often asks questions "without any interest in the answer except to suck out the apparent content by means of the question and thereby to leave an emptiness behind" (1989, p. 36). The black hole sun represents this great negativity.

If this all seems hopelessly allusive and incomplete, as if Xers are not articulating with extreme clarity their own theological vision of what lies *beyond* suffering, perhaps Kierkegaard has some insight into Xers' lack of answers. "It is essential for the ironist," he writes, "never to articulate the idea as such but only *casually to suggest it*, to give with one hand and take away with the other" (1989, p. 49, italics mine). Xers are skilled at being casually suggestive and at simultaneously creating and destroying.

In and of itself, suffering makes Xers at least pseudoreligious. They have a virtual religiosity. They are frequently willing to persevere in the midst of suffering, even to meditate deeply on it and produce explanations of their unhappiness. There is something virtually religious about a generation so acquainted with pain. There is also a "real" religiousness when a group understands that pain theologically, viewing it from the perspective of suffering servanthood, religious apocalypticism, or prophecy. In other words, "real" religiousness exists when people feel and explore suffering so that it becomes revelatory for their spiritual lives.

Suffering also prepares Christian Xers for further religious suffering. Who better to understand that there is a cost to discipleship—to a life of imitating Jesus in the present day—than Christian Xers? The cost of discipleship is what faith demands of us, what we must risk of ourselves to be faithful people. Lutheran theologian Dietrich Bonhoeffer argues that a central part of understanding discipleship is distinguishing "cheap grace" from "costly grace." Cheap grace does not "cost" us anything personally, does not force us to change what we hold dear. To attain cheap grace, we merely make our faith accommodate whatever we want; we suffer no discomfort in the process. In contrast, costly grace means making a sacrifice for faith. It is "costly because it costs someone their life, and it is grace because it gives a person the only true life" (Bonhoeffer, 1995, p. 45).

In this costly grace lies a hope that Xers can find peace. According to Catholic mystic Thomas Merton, "Peace, true peace, is only to be found through suffering" (1981, p. 25). In this suffering, Generation X has found a key piece (or peace) of its lived theology. Does it follow, then, that Jesus' reassuring "Peace be with you" (John 20:19) always means "Suffering be with you"? Real, costly faith digs out spaces within us, sometimes painfully, to lay a fresher foundation.

Suffering suffuses GenX religiosity with even more irreverence. There is irreverence in harshly mocking and ironizing the suffering Jesus and then adopting images that hint at the generation's similar, salvific suffering. We take on these pop culture images of pain because we feel we have suffered unjustly. In the appropriation of pop culture symbols of suffering, questions are also implicitly raised about who controls suffering, the domestication of suffering, and the freedom of the sufferer.

We do not want our suffering domesticated. So many Christian religious institutions have tamed Jesus' suffering, bundling it up into a logical explanation about his gruesome agony and death and selling it with a simple proposition: "Believe the bloodshed and you win eternal life." GenX pop culture challenges faith reduced to a logical assertion that can be bought and sold, diminished to a pin on a jacket or a clever T-shirt slogan.

The focus on suffering has something to teach our fragmented religious and social institutions in this postmodern moment when we are overwhelmed by diversities of all sorts. In our contemporary situation, it seems that everything we do and are is culturally "made" and not innately or divinely "given." In this moment of profound ambiguity, suffering is what unites Xers not only with each other but also with other generations.

As Catholic theologian Francis Schüssler Fiorenza has noted, suffering is at the "seam between interpretation and reality" (1991, p. 135). In other words, suffering cannot really be "interpreted." It occurs, regardless of how one interprets it, and it happens to everyone; it is one of the few experiences left that does not seem bound by culture or language. As Fiorenza observes, "Suffering brings us to the bedrock of human existence" (p. 135). With their pop culture meditation on suffering, Xers bring this theological insight to the attention of the wider culture. Suffering is a common starting point for all, and acknowledging GenX's suffering is a way to start recognizing its lived theology in the popular culture.

———————— o ————————

Even if suffering can be a unifying factor in a fragmented world, the fragmentation still needs to be accounted for, and GenX pop culture has entered mightily into this uncertainty. It is to this culture of ambiguity that I turn in the following chapter.

7

AMBIGUITY IS CENTRAL
TO FAITH

XERS MAKE GREAT HERETICS.

At times in my life I have seriously doubted or denied the existence of God, the divinity of Jesus, the Trinity, and original sin.

I have attended worship services in various traditions, including Southern and American Baptist, reformed and conservative Jewish, Presbyterian, Lutheran, Episcopalian, Greek and Russian Orthodox, Messianic Jewish, Roman Catholic, Evangelical nondenominational, Pentecostal, and Methodist. Although I do not agree fully with the teachings of any one of these, I found the presence of God in each place of worship. Which one of these faiths is "true"? To say "all" sounds like dangerous relativism. To take an exclusivist position by responding "only my own" is not only condescending to the others but also does not square with my experience.

In a different way—in cyberspace—I am also stuck between relativism and exclusivism. I have been an Internet junkie since 1988. In that time, I have created dozens of personae related to my "self" through virtual communications. Different selves that seem to belong to me emerge in on-line discussion groups, chat rooms, and private e-mail. Which one of these multiple virtual personae represents the real, singular "me"? To say "all of them" sounds like I am an unstable person with a plastic identity. To say "only who I am in real life" does not concur with my experiences of enacting these personalities in cyberspace.

I am not alone in these quandaries. Offending the canons of religion and psychology, posing as infidels, Xers practice a type of religiosity that experiments with heresies as new forms of faith. Trusting in betrayal as much as in a benevolent God, we erode stringent dichotomies between the orthodox and the heterodox. We search for faith in the midst of profound theological, social, personal, and sexual ambiguities.

Hesitation to Affirm Orthodoxies

The sacred and profane, spiritual and sensual, orthodox and blasphemous find expression in GenX pop culture. In typical Xer style, these categories are confused and re-fused in new ways.

Sin Against Light

When Madonna—and Xers—practice their religiosity with sacramentals, from prayer cards and holy water to ripped jeans, piercings, crucifixes, and dark makeup, they challenge the authority of the official sacraments and the institution that "dispenses" them. They threaten to displace the center with the margins. This is just the beginning of a larger blurring of what is considered orthodox with what was considered heterodox, or heretical.

Experimentation with heresy—even outright blasphemy—is a key part of GenX religiosity. Cyberspace, a refuge for many in the generation, provides holy home pages, as well as pornography and sacrilege. Music videos feature sacred images alongside profane ones. In GenX pop culture, the holy and unholy are removed from black-and-white categories and take on hues of grey.

In "Jeremy," for example, this play between the sacred and profane surfaces in the video's back-and-forth movement between the "demonic" (Vedder's crazed expressions, "profane" lyrics, and unsettling and bloody images) and the "religious" (Jeremy as a suffering prophet).

In "Black Hole Sun," heaven and hell are mixed up. What the suburbanites take to be their heaven of cheap grace has become a hellish vacuum of meaning. The video's salvific message implies that a heavenly salvation can only come at a cost—a full confrontation with the black hole Son who invites believers into the void of uncertainty. Salvation means giving up human certitude.

In "Losing My Religion," Jesus appears as a fallen angel, a mocked, irrelevant figure at whom people throw stones. The further irony is that even this "fallen angel" (usually a term for Satan) is as benign as the more orthodox version of Jesus! There is no "religion" to fear anymore. The video ponders what it means to "fear the Lord" or "fear the devil" for a generation losing its institutional religion.

In "Heart-Shaped Box," the octogenarian Jesus alternately wears a Santa Claus hat and papal miter. He is kept alive by a blood supply tank featuring a fetus and attended by a girl in the ambiguous garments of a cleric or witch. There is plenty of blasphemous fodder in these videos for those who take these images literally.

Heresy also seems apparent in pop culture's sexualization of the divine. This represents Xers' way of searching for a spirituality that reincorporates the sexual and the spiritual. As we have seen, music videos frequently set the sexual and sacred side by side. The consummate example is Madonna, whose work fuses and confuses the erotic and the spiritual. In her video "Take a Bow," her negligee slips off as a rosary falls to the floor. In "Justify My Love," cruciform images pad the video's erotic scenes. In "Like a Prayer," she kisses the dark-skinned Saint Martin de Porres and receives the stigmata while scantily clad. Madonna's live concerts have included the religious images of a kneeler and a stained glass window near a large bed; she confesses her sins before and after autoerotic playacting. Madonna seems to feel most at home in Catholic symbolic settings, and when she is in these surroundings, she sees no reason to check her sexuality at the (confessional) door. Neither do many Xers.

The myriad ways of fusing and confusing the sacred and profane distinguish GenX lived theology. In pop culture, Xers use images that are often considered blasphemous as a way of shocking and driving home their religious points. They understand, perhaps more than any other living generation, the extent to which the most religious people often flirt with heresy and that the line that divides orthodoxy from heresy is more ambiguous than commonly assumed.

Instead of proving that the generation is irreligious (as is often supposed), this familiarity with unorthodoxy may instead reveal a deep—if unorthodox—religiosity. Several theologians have recognized that offensive images or practices may indicate a familiarity with deep religious truths.

For instance, John Henry Newman, nineteenth-century Catholic theologian and cardinal, suggested that blasphemy could represent negative evidence of the presence of profound truth. Through its negativity, blasphemy can witness to something positive. A convert to Catholicism from the Anglican tradition, Newman defended himself against a critic who charged that he celebrated Catholic scandal and infidelity in his writings. Newman wrote apologetically, "There will be more blasphemy, more hatred of God, more of diabolical rebellion, more of awful sacrilege, more of vile hypocrisy in a Catholic country than any where else, because there is in it more of sin against light" (1989, pp. 393–394). In other words, the higher one's upward spiritual gaze, the more disastrous one's stumble may be. Newman thought Catholics could sin so deeply because they were in touch with profound religious truths.

Newman's ruminations on popular religiousness had a defensive and apologetic quality, such as when he wrote that "Catholics can sin with a depth and intensity with which Protestants cannot sin" (p. 393), which is a backhanded compliment if there ever was one. Nevertheless, I think his ideas have relevance for a theological interpretation of GenX pop culture. My interpretation of his basic intuition is that within popular religious practices, blasphemy and sanctity often appear together. Deep blasphemy can be evidence of an encounter with deep truth, because humans are always sinful and yet capable of finding God. He called this paradox our "intercommunion of divine faith and human corruption" (p. 394).

Like Newman, the great turn-of-the-century German philosopher of religion, Rudolf Otto, suggested that the abhorrent could be evidence of the religious. In his classic work *The Idea of the Holy,* Otto outlined the characteristics of experiencing "the holy" across religious traditions. He described this experience of the holy as a mysterious and overwhelming feeling of the "numinous," a sense of dependence on a great presence outside us. Something revolting could point to the "numinous." Any "horrible," "revolting," or "loathsome" images could be ways of expressing "numinous awe." These revolting images are effective because they are indirect paths to the holy. They could point to holiness despite their unholiness. For Otto, revolting or loathsome images are more "primitive" than other ways of expressing the holy—but they are avenues nonetheless. If what is revolting evokes the shudder of overpowering awe, he suggested, then we may reach the holy through the seemingly unholy (1969, p. 62).

Lutheran theologian Paul Tillich agreed that sometimes the loathsome may really be religious after all. In a discussion of art that depicts repulsive scenes, he suggested that a religious element "is present in those experiences of reality in which its negative, ugly, and self-destructive side is encountered" (1959, p. 73). Tillich's insight is consistent with those of Newman and Otto—the ugly or offensive might point us toward deeper religious truths.

Although some may criticize GenX pop culture for its heavy doubts about orthodoxy, Tillich pointed out that it is impossible even to express doubts about religious truth without first confronting its presence. Paradoxically, all doubt indicates an engagement with belief! Or, as Tillich phrased it, "The presupposition of doubt [is] the awareness of something unconditional" (p. 29). According to Catholic mystic Thomas Merton,

"Unbelief cannot arise until a [person] has found [a] way to God" (1981, p. 38). To be so "heretical," then, Xers must have strong spiritual intuitions.

The Never-Ending Scripture

When I first realized the degree to which GenX pop culture exhibited an experimental attitude toward orthodoxy, I became uneasy and looked for a firm theological foundation from which I could assess GenX culture. The foundation I found was Scripture . . . until cyberspace interfered, or rather clarified things for me.

In 1995, shortly after the World Wide Web became popular, I found a Web site with several chapters of various books of the Bible. But this was no ordinary Bible. The person who set up this site had put some Bible verses into *hypertext* format. In other words, *clicking* on many of the words with a mouse would produce Scripture verses, commentaries, or other information linked to the word in hypertext.

When I looked at Genesis 1:1, "In the beginning when God created the heavens and the earth . . . ," the phrases *In the beginning* and *God created* were colored (often referred to as *hot*) text, or hypertext. Clicking on the first phrase called up other Scripture verses—the Gospel of John 1:1 (another "In the beginning")—and offered further clickable links to scholarly commentaries comparing the two verses. I followed hypertext link after link, not exhausting this virtual meandering even after several layers of exploration.

My hypertext path went something like this: from the Genesis phrase *In the beginning,* to John 1:1, to commentary on John 1:1, to evangelical commentary on John 1:1, to collections of on-line evangelical commentaries, to other commentaries on John, and on and on. My hypertext path from the Genesis phrase *God created* brought me to general Genesis commentaries, similar creation stories in ancient literature, a site claiming Noah's ark never existed, a site dedicated to the search for Noah's ark, a list of archaeological digs, and on and on.

The possibilities seemed dizzying. When Scripture appears in hypertext format, where does "real" Scripture begin and end? What if *every* scriptural word were "hot"? Is it possible, I wondered, to read Scripture in the form of its more familiar technology (the clothbound book) as hypertext?

Just when I thought I had a firm theological foundation, I found this one as slippery as the old orthodoxies that my culture's music videos skewered. When a generation (Xers and everyone after us) grows up with access to Scripture as hypertext, what happens to the authority of Scripture, and what happens to Scripture itself? Hypertext, after all, is the most common way of navigating through documents on the Web. People usually travel on the Internet using clickable links—text leading to text leading to images leading to music leading to video leading to text leading to. . . .

After some reflection, I realized that hypertext makes us read Scripture in a new way, as a cyberBible. Reading the Bible on-line in this way disturbed my assumptions about the stability of the biblical text. When Scripture becomes hypertext, it shifts from simple inerrancy (being literally, self-evidently true) to moving errantly. When clickable Scripture leads to other Scripture, to commentaries, back to other Scriptures, to similar stories from the surrounding Middle Eastern culture, and back to Scripture, it moves *errantly.*

What does it mean to *err?* Theologian Mark C. Taylor suggests that "to err is to ramble, roam, stray, wander, like Chaucer's 'weary ghost that errest to and fro.' Such wandering inevitably leads one astray—away from one's path or line of direction. To err, therefore, is to 'fail, miss, go wrong in judgment or opinion; to make a mistake, blunder, or commit a fault; to be incorrect; to go astray morally'; even 'to sin'" (1984, pp. 11–12). It is impossible to have an inerrant text in cyberspace; a cyberBible is always wandering. It is never possible for the reader to arrive at the end—or at a conclusive, final reading.

Reading Scripture in cyberspace highlighted for me the extent to which Scripture has *always* been errant. Scripture has always needed to be interpreted by each "user" (or reader) in order to be understood—that is, it must be "clicked" mentally again and again (except that the hypertext links are in our head, not on the page). When we read Scripture, we click consciously or unconsciously on fragments of the text (we each have our favorites), clicking mentally on a sermon we heard on this text, clicking on something a friend said, clicking on our last meal with that friend, clicking back on the text with a new perspective on it, clicking onto a book we read that gave us insight into this text, clicking on the friend that loaned us the book, clicking back on another scriptural text that reminds us of this concept and helps us understand it. It seems that our clothbound Bibles are already well versed in the ways of cyberspace.

The Bible is often viewed as a collection of stories, a series of narratives about Noah's ark, Jacob and his brothers, or the parables of Jesus. But when we begin to think about Scripture as a cyberBible, its narrative structure implodes. Even as we read a clothbound Bible, we can never retrieve the beginning and end of biblical stories in their original state, because we will always enter stories as continuations of where we have just been textually. In other words, when I read the Creation story in Genesis,

I bring with me mental links to hundreds of other "texts" that help me understand the story at hand. The texts inside of me influence the way I interpret the text in front of me. For instance, will I read the Creation story (including the tale of Adam and Eve) as affirming, condemning, or remaining neutral on the issue of homosexuality? It depends on which internal texts I click on as I read the Genesis text.

In this sense, when I read the Bible, I never truly begin at the beginning. I choose where to start and decide what counts as the initial part of a story, based on all the competing texts in my past. Each word of a story I read makes sense only in relation to other texts I have encountered. No scriptural story stands on its own. My personal history, the books I have read, what I have been taught (in other words, the "text" of my life) all help me interpret every single word, phrase, sentence, and punctuation mark on the "real" page. Reading the Scriptures has always been hypertextual; cyberspace just helps us see that more clearly and might even give us new options for interpretation. The Christian Scriptures themselves (Luke 12:49) record that Jesus loved hot text: "I came to bring fire to the earth, and how I wish it were already kindled!"

When Scripture is hypertext, readers take control of the text, in effect rewriting it and becoming biblical coauthors. This makes a whole new claim on Xers of faith. I could not navigate through the cyberBible without continually selecting where I should go from among seemingly endless hypertext links. The responsibility of coauthoring sacred texts, which has always been with the reader anyway (as I have suggested), becomes more explicit in cyberspace. This possibility of Xers as biblical coauthors is perhaps the most shocking threat to old orthodoxies.

Instabilities of Space and Time

Xers' "real" lives have many instabilities, but these multiply in cyberspace with its ambiguities about location. As I suggested earlier, cyberspace has a tendency to fuse or confuse public and private, sacred and profane, individual and communal space.

Fashion trends complement this unstable space by contributing an ambiguous sense of time. The tendency toward instant nostalgia in GenX culture means that history is almost robbed of meaning. During the 1980s, we celebrated 1960s fashions. During the 1990s, we resurrected the 1970s and immediately became nostalgic (in clothing, television, and movies) for the 1980s. We make kitsch and pop culture out of yesterday almost before it is gone. I think we continually replay those years to extend an adolescence—into our thirties—that we had to leave prematurely.

The practical effect of this is to make the present moment even more precarious. It threatens to become artificial and pop-cultured in our hands before we exit it. We have an increasing sense of "frame time," looking at our lives as though they were movies, music videos, or television shows. (Tomorrow, they very well may be.) Increasingly, the network television *Monday Night Movie* is actually about the previous Monday night. When we live like this, there is less space to spread out, less of a sense that our lives won't be turned into media, less of a sense that there can be a new future.

A culture of moments has irrevocably forced us to see time in measurable chunks, in segments. We try to expand our present moment by reincorporating recent moments from our memory, to stuff the little time we have full of a past that was so incomplete that it begs to be brought forward for fulfillment. It is highly appropriate that in our computer-rich age, we experience time as fragmented and segmented, as "digital," and not as more fluid, as "analog." We imagine that we can stop the film of our lives at any frame and replay certain moments, tagged in the lower left-hand corner by precise dates and times.

Looking back on 1980s clothing reinforces this ambiguity about time. Oversized fashions, particularly tops, were popular throughout the 1980s, from too-large sweatshirts to outsized T-shirts to untucked button-down shirts, even to big hairstyles. (The shirts I retain from the mid-1980s are still much too big for me today.) Teen earrings tended to be large hoops or to have other heavy, conspicuous designs. As if the sheer sizes were not enough, fluorescent colors made a comeback. A common 1980s sight was a teen with large gold earrings and an extra large sweatshirt with neon pink lettering. Understatement was not fashionable.

I interpret our oversized clothing as an indication that we were not certain whether we were children or adults. Wearing exaggerated clothing, in sizes too big even for many adults, sent a characteristically ambivalent message from Xers—we can put on the guise of adulthood and we can also dress as infants. What is more typical of childlike curiosity than donning parental outfits? In simultaneously dressing for early childhood and middle age, we emphasized our anxiety about the current moment. Ironically, in trying to escape it through fashion, we only succeeded in highlighting it. The uncertainty of this time in our lives, of our overall sense of time, was stuffed into the ample spaces of our garments. One psychoanalyst notes that "clothing, by adding to the apparent size of the body in one way or another, gives us an increased sense of power, a sense of extension of our bodily self" (Flügel in Finkelstein, 1991, p. 143). We extended both forward into mimicked adulthood and backward into a reclamation of childhood.

This uncertainty about our position in time makes it difficult for us to feel any sense of religious stability, certainty, or confidence. On the one hand, this is a blessing because Xers are apt to pause before engaging in the triumphalistic or condescending religious behavior of some of our elders. On the other hand, our feeling that the present continually escapes us, our sense of being out(side) of time, can keep us from knowing any depth of religious experience.

God—and the mystery of our creation in God—transcends our own out-of-timeness. Being open to experiences of grace can give us a new sense of being at home in time, particularly if we can accept that our anxieties about the parameters of time stem from our own limitations, not God's. That does not make these anxieties any less real, however. It is to the experience of hesitation that I now turn; the next section explores how faith can exist even amid uncertainty.

Instabilities of the Faithless and Faithful Self

GenX pop culture explores our deep uncertainties about our self-identities. The proliferation of gender ambiguities, fractured cyber-personae, and clothing that both emphasizes and questions boundaries all feed GenX hesitations about the self. A valuable moment from one music video in particular illustrates the difficulty of naming one's own faith in the midst of such personal and cultural instability.

Deeply Resonating Surface Noise

One of the seminal moments in GenX music video combines faith with a pervasive sense of *hesitation*. In "Losing My Religion," while sitting firmly in a chair, Michael Stipe sings,

> That's me in the corner
> That's me in the spotlight
> Losing my religion
> Trying to keep up with you
> And I don't know if I can do it
> (1991)

As he sings the last line, he begins to stand up but hesitates and holds himself down. The camera validates the unrehearsed uncertainty of Stipe's movement; as Stipe begins to stand, it pans up and switches direction a moment too late, hurrying to follow him back down to his chair.

We are left to think that Stipe really could have stood up but felt too uncertain about "keeping up" with the other star of the video. This moment is a focal point of GenX music video. In the briefest of shots, in the space of a few frames, it illustrates the ambiguity and hesitation in the hearts of many Xers. They have profound moments of soul-deep hesitation and uncertainty, particularly in regard to religion. In these brief frames of the video, time skids to a crawl. We witness an unsteady moment just before or just after a deep spiritual experience. Remember that the one Stipe is trying to keep up with is himself a very unsteady messiah.

In analyzing a song by the pop group Pet Shop Boys, music critic Simon Frith observes that pop music (and I think in this case music video) excels at capturing "frozen moments in time . . . the moments just before and just after emotion" (1996a, p. 8). Stipe's movement is brief and vague; it fools many viewers into dismissing it because of its ephemerality. Again, Frith is helpful as he suggests that pop artists "know that in [pop] music it is such surface noise that resonates most deeply in our lives" (p. 8). This "surface noise," this "frozen" moment of Stipe's hesitation sent tidal waves of recognition and even sadness through me, causing me to sigh deeply when I first noticed this moment in the video.

This deeply resonating surface noise is all the more poignant for Xers because we increasingly think in fragmented images. We view time less as a continuous stretch and more as a collection of particular moments—a singular look, image, or visual moment from popular culture. Because of our deeply fragmented lives, Frith suggests, hearing music in pieces "represents experience grasped in moments" (p. 243). He notes that when we listen to popular music, we pay more attention to "sounds," which are immediate, rather than to "music," a connected structure of notes (p. 243).

I think this dynamic is operative in music video and throughout GenX pop culture. We saw this in Chapter Three, wherein the experience of the moment was paramount. Experience in moments explains MTV's rapid-fire, discontinuous cuts—a quintessential example of art's imitating (GenX) life.

When Stipe (or his persona) sits back down, he wonders if this ambiguity at his core has riddled his faith with too many holes.

> Oh, no, I've said too much
> I haven't said enough
> (1991)

Has faith crossed too deeply into doubt? Stipe describes the space where many Xers find themselves—between saying too much and not saying enough, between exposing the falsities and uncertainties of their religions and wondering whether they can say any more to redeem their religions. Xers' doubts raise the question of how much one can question institutional religion, or even a more general religiousness, before it is "lost." If we continue to plumb its lost-ness to us, will we somehow "regain" it? These lyrics are almost mystical lines in which words seemingly fail to capture the religious experience.

This area of doubt resonates deeply with many Xers. Not knowing whether they have said too much or not enough about religion, they fall into the hesitative space in between. Like some boomers, we can say too much in constructing an apology for our religiousness. Like so many of our elders who sleepwalk through their religions, however, we can say too little by not subjecting our faith to forceful critiques and being fully honest with ourselves. This is the tragic position of many Xers, signified by the spilled milk in the R.E.M. video and the hesitation about whether this spilled milk is worth crying over. What remains of faith after the milk falls onto the floor?

This hesitative space, between saying too much and not saying enough, can be mystical. When words fail, something else may take over. This is the witness of mystics, anyway. And this is why silence is a key religious "mood" for Xers, a point to which I will return in Chapter Nine.

Fashioned Identities

Paradoxical GenX clothing trends in the 1980s and 1990s illustrated this ambiguity of identity. Even as we wore oversized shirts in the 1980s, we dressed in exceedingly tight jeans—designer jeans, in particular. Blue jeans have been a staple of American culture since Levi Strauss converted his tent canvas into popular pants in the 1850s. When designer jeans arrived in Independence, Missouri, in 1982, my junior high social studies teacher interrogated a girl who was handing in an assignment. He asked how she managed to get into her unbelievably tight designer jeans. We all could have told him the answer—you lie down on your bed and pull them on and fasten them, and then you stand up.

Why these ultratight jeans, so tight that they resembled a second skin? In American culture, jeans have symbolized earthy and plainspoken qualities since they became identified with Western laborers in the late nineteenth and early twentieth centuries (Gordon, 1991, p. 32). Interestingly, one fashion observer called jeans a "virtual uniform" for artistic students at Bennington College in the 1970s (Gordon, 1991, p. 33). Certainly, Xers have also worn them as a "virtual uniform"—as an imitation of a uniform for our uniformly uniformless generation.

Bennington students wore them to symbolize Woodstock-era freedom, but jeans have represented something less idealistic for Xers—participants at the corporate-sponsored Woodstock '94. Paradoxically, Xers' tight designer jeans both liberated and constricted, revealing and concealing, conforming to the body's shape yet concealing it more securely than ever before. This style revealed something about our identity. It showed off the figure, making us transparent, but creating discomfort, immobility, and restriction. The style almost made our bodies "trans-parent" (meaning both see-through and trans-parent, "across parent"). Across the ideal of parenthood, we sacrificed our own bodies, becoming parents to ourselves by giving ourselves boundaries and restrictions (in this case, expressed as physically restrictive jeans), caring for our own well-being as premature adults or overmature adolescents. Thus was the ambiguity of our identity played out in our clothing.

Because jeans are associated with Westerns, they also symbolize for Xers a frontier mentality. The Xer Wild West is largely cyberspace, but Xers are also taming new psychological and spiritual ground in the "real" world. That we clung so tightly to blue jeans—or vice versa—reflects our "frontier," go-it-alone-if-we-must, renegade mentality. Wearing jeans with this attitude, we ironically distanced ourselves from consumer culture. Although name brand jeans were extremely popular, wearing jeans showed our rejection of the excesses of the 1980s, symbolized by more formal dress. For Xers, the meaning of jeans remained somewhat constant over time, holding the line against formality and fakery, so we embraced it in droves.

The movie *Flashdance* inspired a similar fad, sometimes called "flash-fashions." The fad involved wearing ripped or shredded clothes, especially tops, that hung off the body. Of little practical use, this fashion was almost entirely a pose. As with tight jeans, *Flashdance* fads were about being exposed. As with grunge, we put on something worn out. The fashion individualized us more (even though others were doing it, too). It covered us in a new way, being both revealing and concealing.

The implication of *Flashdance* fashions was that there was something unkempt, something ragged about us. The tops suggested activity, even aerobic life, yet concealed the ways in which we were barely breathing in the 1980s. The fashion mocked style itself; by wearing clothing that had minimal practical use and that did nothing but comment socially, we demonstrated that we could parody a culture of the image.

Torn up about our identity, we ripped our shirts. Scripture offers ample evidence of ripped clothing when identity is under attack. The apostles Paul and Barnabas rip their clothing when they are mistaken for gods in Lystra (Acts 14:14). The high priest of the Jewish Sanhedrin tears his clothes when he thinks Jesus has identified himself blasphemously as the Messiah (Matthew 26:65). When Jacob misinterprets a bloody robe as a sign that his son is dead, he rends his clothing (Genesis 37:34). In Scripture, this tearing of clothing occurs when identities are sorely confused. Likewise for Xers, our "rent" garments signified our inability to "own" ourselves completely.

Like the sleeves we tore from our shirts, the *Flashdance* fashions also symbolized how ripped off we felt as a generation. The ripped fashions signified the hard living we never had, the rough-and-tumble experiences (now frequently romanticized) like the Vietnam War that were not ours. They imply a sort of (g)ripping experience, even at the same time as they acknowledge that the whole fashion is contrived, that we cut up our clothes at home. The absence of a movement for Xers occasionally causes us to dream up evidence of having participated in one.

By the 1990s, inspired by pop performers, Xers began to display undergarments as outerwear. This fashion is almost exclusively the preserve of women, as was true for the artists who popularized it. Just today in Harvard Square, I saw an Xer wearing a negligee over a shirt. The exposure of undergarments on the outside exposes that which had previously been hidden, just as "Losing My Religion" allows doubt to surface, to be externalized. Because undergarments are associated with immediate proximity to the body, they suggest intimate disclosure, intimate association, intimate revelation.

All of these fashions witness to the uncertainty Xers feel about their identity. Collectively, these clothing trends attest to a life lived on the boundary; jeans point to a frontier that no longer exists; ripped clothes reflect a movement we never joined; inverted clothing, turned outside in and inside out, pushes the limits of propriety. I interpret this as implicit evidence of exploring a religious sensibility. Life on the margins, on the boundary, demonstrates Xers' willingness to keep their horizons open, to live unfinished lives. In this openness to the future, people can find real religious truth. In pushing boundaries and turning the inside out, Xers are implicitly preparing for (and encouraging) a religious experience, an experience of divine grace that upsets all boundaries and expectations.

To hover on the boundary is to live in anticipation of a religious revelation. To be unafraid to transcend convention is to represent a living analogy to God's boundary-crossing and propriety-flouting work in the world. Upsetting boundaries, living on the margins, and keeping the horizon open are characteristics of the prophet, a role that Xers play uncommonly well. This implicit prophethood, however, is no simple matter of self-assured truth telling. It does not mean continually rousing society and religion from its self-imposed slumber with a confident, righteous voice. Many Xers have much too slippery an identity for them to speak with such confidence.

"Which of Me Am I?"

My introduction to the Internet in 1988 was a revolution of Copernican proportions. Gaining access to electronic mail through an honors program at my university, I was immediately addicted. I whiled away hours on end in electronic conversation, sometimes with people at the terminal immediately next to mine.

My most reserved friends were suddenly gregarious, charming, or angry in their e-mail personae. I soon wanted to ask my friends if their "real" identities would please stand up! I, too, changed identities. I moved from being Tom Beaudoin to being TBEAUDOIN, a cyberentity at the University of Missouri. Under this name, I explored new facets of my personality, had franker exchanges with friends, and then had to reconcile my on-line selves with my "real-life" persona. Then it occurred to me that a "real-life" self has much in common with a cyberspace persona.

To investigate this insight, I enlisted a psychology professor's help and began an independent study of how Internet access affected my undergraduate peers' senses of identity. My small study concluded that because the anonymity of the Internet often enabled people to choose any persona they desired, it made almost everyone feel freer. At the same time, they began to have crises about which of their identities was the "real" one. "It is a good thing that most of my e-mail friends don't know me in real life," one friend wrote me. "They wouldn't recognize me off-line." Another noted, "The Internet gives me power to explore who I am, but I was surprised to find that it revealed to me new things about myself, part of me that I didn't know existed. It revealed to me, I guess, who I am *and* who I might be."

During my second year as a high school teacher, all my students had e-mail access for class projects, as well as for general conversation with me and each other. Again, some of the most reticent personalities off-line were some of the most aggressive on-line. One student who was something of a bully during class was chivalrous and tentative on e-mail. As a teacher, I had to relearn who my students "really" were. I began to receive e-mail from lots of different students who revealed a great complexity of identities to me. At the end of the school year, I asked students to evaluate my teaching and their own learning. One wrote, "Having an e-mail account gave me a place where I could stop being the class clown and actually interact with my teachers as an intellectual. I don't know how I would have been able to do this otherwise."

Through electronic mail, people take on various identities in different conversations. Being a member of an electronic "group" means that the person must maintain the identity over time, often while sustaining different identities in other e-mail communities or exchanges. Anonymity allows users to unleash a flurry of selves, with MUDs being one important site of experimentation. *MUDs* (Multi-User Dungeons) are virtual sites in which users can assume whichever identities they desire. They generally choose their own names and reveal whatever they like about their attributes. Their identities are completely self-styled. They can also design their own virtual rooms and wander throughout the dungeon, or "domain," conversing with other "people." Most MUDs allow users to manipulate objects, such as radios, chairs, and refrigerators, to make for more realistic interaction. Variants of MUDs include the "chat rooms" established on all the major Internet providers. Users can simply drop into chat rooms, mask themselves as they wish, and assume particular identities in conversations with others from around the globe.

It seems as if cyberspace unlocks the extent to which our identities have always harbored other possibilities, just waiting to get out on their own. Sometimes, of course, unstable identities pose threats to Net communities. The press reports with frequency the most appalling incidents—middle-aged men who pretend to be young girls and who lure other youngsters to secret meeting places. The mother of one of my students refused to let her daughter have access to e-mail because of this threat, which the medium's opacity makes possible.

While I was trawling in a MUD using the gender-ambiguous initial *T*, I struck up a conversation with "Debbie," who introduced "herself" to me by offering a virtual long-stemmed rose, which "she" typed out like this: @}—'—; (turn your head to the left and you will see it). After this introduction, I was surprised how quickly the discussion turned theological, especially because Debbie spent the first several minutes in sexual innuendo (I soon discovered that she had assumed "T" was male). When I began asking religious questions on a lark, "Debbie" responded with verve. Several minutes into the conversation, I received this startling message: "T., I'm not a woman. I'm a minister, and a married man. The spirit is willing but the flesh is weak." Astounded, I quickly wrote back with a series of questions. With whom had I really been corresponding? Was "she" really a male, married, and a minister? Or someone else pretending to have these identities? I received no further responses.

There were times when the cacophony of selves in cyberspace frustrated me so much that I attempted to end to my virtual life, literally. The drama of identity in cyberspace brought me great anxiety about my "real" identity. On three different occasions, I sent my acquaintances, friends, and virtual communities what a friend later called "virtual suicide notes." I wrote the first after only six months on-line, and I wrote the last after about three years on-line (coinciding with the attempt I described in Chapter One to extricate myself from all forms of popular culture). Each of the virtual suicide notes followed the same format, which went something like this:

> Dear virtual friends,
>   I can no longer tolerate life in this virtual world. I need more real forms of relationship than I can find here. It would be inappropriate to say *good-bye,* that I will never see you again, since in fact I have never seen you. That is a key reason I must end my life in cyberspace. There is something profoundly absent from our knowledge of each other in this medium. I want and need something more real.

Each of my virtual suicides was short-lived. I was usually back on-line within two weeks. (The longest I have been away from the Internet since 1988 was one month, after my last virtual suicide.) Just as I was wiping out my e-mail account—the warehouse of my virtual identities—a friend sent me a note in response to my message:

> I am sorry you are leaving this world. But I don't know why you think this is less real than RL [real life].

I could no longer maintain such an aggregation of personae. I wanted to stop and separate myself from this society of identities that all reflected me and yet did not represent me. I had let my self (selves) become too diffused throughout cyberspace. The person I thought of as Tom Beaudoin dissolved into a wide-ranging constellation of personalities that different on-line communities knew only as TBEAUDOIN. If asked, they would all have described TBEAUDOIN differently.

I could deal with this in real life, but it quickly became overwhelming in cyberspace. With each virtual suicide, I wanted to give my identity some breathing space, to collect myself (my selves) and reincorporate and reintegrate these scattered pieces of who I was. I eventually charged back into cyberspace, established new relationships, reexperienced this segmentation into different and diffuse selves, and began to feel unsteady again. My life became too virtual; I was maintaining a series of virtual selves.

When a friend told me that my first good-bye message sounded like a suicide note, I felt frightened. Later, I could see that he was right. I was trying to kill my selves in cyberspace, because they had gotten out of control. I was having trouble corralling them.

It has been five years since my last virtual suicide. Somehow I now manage to "cycle through" my selves on a regular basis, to quote psychoanalyst and computer philosopher Sherry Turkle (1995, pp. 178–179). I am now better able to imagine a plumb line running through this cycle of selves that I explore on a daily basis in cyberspace, virtual games, cybercommunities, and private e-mail.

The fluidity of identity in cyberspace enables Generation X to explore the great degree to which *all* identities are fluid. This cybercultural insight, which is increasingly becoming an *epistemology* (a way of knowing) for Xers, may be one reason Xers are more accepting of sexual diversity than our elders have been. We increasingly recognize the indeterminacy of all social identities, for instance the degree to which gender roles are socially constructed, not divinely ordained or biologically determined. Some sociologists now discuss the concept of "performing" various gender roles from situation to situation, which sounds strikingly similar to the way we present our various selves on the Internet.

For Xers, both our *experience* and our *imagination* of our selves are characterized more by incoherence than coherence, more by fragmentation than unity. In cyberspace, technology mirrors life, giving us an experimental space in which to explore our multiplicity of selves, to unleash the way our "persons" are always competing "personae," at least more than we previously admitted. For a generation that has been under as much stress as ours, this tension creeps into our identity, such that who we are never seems fixed or final. Instead, identity always seems like a series of possibilities. We seem to have many centers, each of them shifting and unstable.

As with many other aspects of GenX life, there is irony here, because we continually speak of ourselves (and interact in cyberspace) as a singular, unified "I." Even the narrator of "Losing My Religion," a video about the ambiguity of faith, speaks in the first person singular.

We are, it seems, caught in the cultural haze between modernity and postmodernity. These attitudes about the self bear a striking resemblance to postmodern theories about the self as "multiple," in contrast to "modern" assumptions about the self as stable, singular, and unified. Freud, of course, initiated our cultural conversation about a disunified self by suggesting that the unconscious unsteadied our sense of autonomy and subverted the freedom to do as we consciously desired. After Freud, some psychoanalysts and cultural theorists have speculated that rather than having one indivisible self, we have multiple "selves" with warring desires. These postmodern conceptions of the self owe much to Freud, but whereas Freud credited the unconscious for our decenteredness, later theories have cited other reasons for this condition.

In much postmodern writing, the self is not a unified entity, but is instead a mere "construct," a tentative arrangement of various personal and social expectations about selfhood. Thus, the self has many *subjectivities,* or several identities with which it views the world and can be viewed. Our identities are not singular but multiple. Cultural theorist Fredric Jameson calls our contemporary time a state of "psychic fragmentation" (1995, p. 90).

I believe it is this fragmentation that GenX pop culture explores, particularly through cyberidentities. Sometimes, it directly addresses theological aspects of this splitting, as in "Losing My Religion." GenX pop culture and postmodern theory both raise the troubling question that Michael Saunders (1996, p. 40) articulated after surfing through cyberspace: "Which of me am I?"

Seeing this psychic fragmentation in a theological context means returning to Mark 9:24, "I believe; help my unbelief!" This key Scripture passage for Xers—call it a GenX theological credo—is appropriately paradoxical, an expression of faith and doubt, belief and hesitation.

When one reads this passage from a GenX pop culture perspective, it is as if two selves share the exclamation, even though one person is ostensibly speaking! If unbelief and belief were so intermixed in the Scriptures, we can feel reassured that our situation is not new and that we can practice religiousness despite our psychic fragmentation. Perhaps we are even at a spiritual advantage over other generations; because we are more comfortable with a diffuse sense of self, we can more easily understand that a person can have faith and doubt simultaneously. Older generations, for whom a unitary, singular self was the ideal, have perhaps had more difficulty allowing doubt to take a central place in their spiritual identity. (Ambiguity, or a concurring belief *and* unbelief, cannot easily be tolerated in a singular, unified identity.)

Gendered Ambiguity

This fractured sense of self is evident in the instabilities of GenX sexual identities. A legion of 1980s pop stars intimated androgyny and sexual ambiguity through their clothing and affect, including Madonna, Boy George, Michael Jackson, Prince, Annie Lennox, Duran Duran, and George Michael. Pop culturally, the 1980s were a feast of androgyny, both encouraging and reflecting the sexual ambiguity afoot in the generation. Central to this androgynous aesthetic were 1980s "hard rock" stars.

I was a devoted fan of hard rock (or "heavy metal") in the 1980s, if a naive one. I had little clue about the ambiguous sexual messages being "performed" in the wearing of rock clothing. Notable in hard rock fashions were unapologetic, even exaggerated, applications of makeup, including lipstick and eyeliner. Even the platform shoes (which I wore for the first time in a campy parody of rock bands in a mid-1980s high school assembly) that some band members wore resembled women's high heels. Around the rock aesthetic, flowing, colored hair became stylish for men again, and by the late 1980s, long permed hair for men was quite common. Tight leather pants for both men or women were also popular. Men frequently wore accessories that were generally considered "feminine," such as bandannas, bracelets, and necklaces. Men began to wear earrings, even in both ears, which was relatively taboo in the United States before GenX. Other related trends included ponytails for men and popular unisex clothing such as jeans and T-shirts. Men even began to appear in dresses in the 1990s at mainstream concerts.

Although Xers have now eschewed some of these fashions, their formative role in Xer upbringing should not be discounted. These general adornment trends decreased rigid distinctions between the sexes. At the same time, Xers have ironized sex differences by playing up stereotypical gender expectations, as when women in rock (or punk women) wear skirts or dresses or excessive makeup.

Here we have confirmation of something hinted at in both the fashion and cyberspace experiences of ambiguity—a crisis of limits. Our willingness to establish limits provisionally and to demolish them authentically indicates a spirit that seeks to move beyond the parameters established by our culture. Some of our elders complain that the rejection of rigid gender distinctions represents a loss of boundaries and a crisis of limits. This is true—but in a very different way than they imagine.

· We seek to live with the constant threat of a loss of boundaries. This goal becomes a new boundary itself. We aim to explore, exploit, and explode old limits because of our deep-seated, religious thirst for meaning. The degree to which we have offended canons of propriety among our elders is an index of the potentially prophetic word we offer—in our very living—about the temporary nature of all boundaries.

In doing so, however, we emphasize the constant necessity of boundaries. A nihilistic attitude (which Xers are often accused of having) would wantonly destroy all limits and boundaries just for the sake of destruction. A religious attitude, on the other hand, seeks to unravel all that impedes the radical infusion of God's grace, love, and freedom. At their most prophetic, Xers seek these fruits of God's activity in the world and expect that God can make *all things new* (Revelation 21:5)—including assumptions about gender, clothing, and old concepts of identity that were never essential to faith and are no longer necessary.

Faith in Ambiguity

To practice religiosity amid such instabilities—of orthodoxy, self, and gender—is a characteristically GenX way of being "virtually religious."

Xers have a sense of self that, in its fragmentation, simulates the real, undivided self that we were assumed to have. We simulate unity by calling ourselves "I" even though we are sometimes unsure which self "I" represents. We imitate "real" faith by taking faithlike stances, but at the same time we introduce heresy and profound doubt. Pushing the boundaries of orthodoxy, we live theologian Friedrich Schleiermacher's assertion (1996, p. 99) that "it is the properly religious view of all things to seek every trace of the divine, the true and the eternal, even in what appears to us to be vulgar and base, and to worship even the most distant trace." (Xers should not, however, go so far as Schleiermacher did when he suggested, "Everything human is holy, for everything is divine" [p. 94]. Such an attitude can underestimate the sin and distortions present in culture.) Xers experiment with virtual faith, rather than having real, "complete," absolute faith. To others, Xers' religiosity frequently looks like partiality, like "virtual" faith. We invest our virtual faith in everything, from our selves to God.

That is why I boil down the religious quest of GenX pop culture to one question that begins on the most intimate level possible and in the midst of profound ambiguity. Our most fundamental question is "Will you be there for me?" We ask this of our selves, bodies, parents, friends, partners, society, religions, leaders, nation, and even God. The frailty that we perceive threatening all of these relationships continually provokes us to ask this question.

This is different from the primary question that baby boomers asked: "What is the meaning of life, of my life?" In 1967, 83 percent of college freshmen (mostly baby boomers) ranked "developing a meaningful philosophy of life" as the most popular value. With Xers in college, 1987 (the heart of Xer college years) marked a twenty-year low in choosing a "meaningful philosophy of life" as the most important goal, with only 39 percent of freshmen selecting it. That year also saw a twenty-year high in "being well-off financially" as freshmen's highest value. In addition, 1987 was the peak year for interest in majoring in business (at 27 percent). These two high points suggest that securing a future (forging one's own answer to "Will you be there for me?") had prime interest (Dunn, 1993, pp. 41, 120).

Xers start their fundamental questioning not with a grand quest for the meaning of their life but by querying those around them (including their "selves") in regard to their fidelity. Because these are *boundary questions,* informing the core of GenX identity and giving shape to the limits of how we understand ourselves (our hopes, fears, and expectations about tomorrow always shape our identities today), they are ultimately *religious questions:*

"Will you be there for me?"

"I believe; help my unbelief!"

We shout out this question and assertion from the depths of our souls across the rough and complicated textures of our lives, ultimately directing them over the horizon to our faith, to God. We ask "Will you be there for me?" of our country (Jeremy's rage against the failed promise of America; our futures mortgaged by debt), of our self (the slippage in cyberspace between a singular and multiple sense of self), of our partners and families (sex and gender anxieties, divorce, easy mobility, the flux of contemporary life), and of God (the failure of the reliable, eternal sun in "Black Hole Sun").

Frequently, we address our question of fidelity to the body. We seem at odds with our own bodies in the threat of HIV and alienated from our bodies in cyberspace, particularly with the rise of cybersex. When we ask "Will you be there for me?" of our bodies, we often answer by piercing and tattooing. These bodily incisions stay with us for the rest of our lives. They will be one certain source of continued identity amid the flux of identity in our simulational popular culture. They also create continuity over time. Piercing and tattooing are ways to weave Ariadne's thread through a series of days that could otherwise seem incoherent in a culture of moments. In a sense, these bodily incisions love our bodies (and there is a great confusion between body and self) unconditionally. They will never leave, which is blessed assurance for our abandoned generation. Paradoxically, this painful, permanent union of incision and body also symbolizes the unhappy relationships to which we cling in our fear of abandonment.

In asking our questions, in asserting this scriptural credo, Xers can call others to reconsider what faith really means. Theologian Paul Tillich suggests that faith should not be imagined as a bunker of impregnable walls around the religious person, immune to all uncertainty. He writes that "in every act of faith, there is risk, and the courage to take this risk, and the necessary doubt which distinguishes faith from mathematical or empirical evidence" (1959, p. 155). Xers remind others that faith is a house divided against itself that does not fall, because faith can be seen as "comprising itself and the doubt about itself" (p. 155). Because Xers have too

seldom heard from religious elders and institutions about the role of doubt
and uncertainty in the life of faith, we sometimes take our fragmented
lives as evidence that we cannot be people of faith. We assume that stable, unitary faith comes only from a stable, unitary person.

My claim that faith may be discovered and practiced in ambiguity does
not mean simply "tailoring" or "fashioning" the demands of faith to
Xers' situation. It doesn't follow that Xers should simply surrender faith
to culture. It especially does not imply avoiding relative certainties when
they are attainable. But it does mean seriously attending to the revelatory
significance of hesitation, ambiguity, ambivalence, and instability in the
lives (and faith experiences) of many Xers. God is revealed even in this
sensus infidelium. Xers claim a wider space for indecision in faith, opening it widely enough that it becomes a revelatory moment.

———————o———————

How can such GenX ambiguity and hesitation coincide with a faith that
is recognizable to more "traditional" people of faith? As I will suggest in
Chapter Eight, everything hinges on how one understands "tradition."

PART THREE

BEING RELIGIOUS NOW

A NEW UNDERSTANDING

8

MAKING THE VIRTUAL
LEAD SOMEWHERE

A SPIRITUAL CHALLENGE TO GENERATION X

I HAVE SKETCHED FOUR MAIN THEMES of GenX's irreverent spirituality: suspicion of institutions, personal experience, suffering, and ambiguity. If this lived theology is worthy of continued practice, how can Xers deepen and extend it beyond the horizon of the moment into the next decades? I suggest that deepening this irreverent spirituality requires an understanding of our contemporary "virtualized" culture and a reexamination of the concept of tradition.

Revisiting Religiosity

At the beginning of this book, I discussed Katherine Bergeron's analysis of chant music. There, I suggested that Generation X is a "both-and" generation, practicing both "virtual" and "real" religiousness. What I mean by this distinction is that although Xers live religiously in *real* ways (involving real faith, real practice, and a real spiritual journey), they also indulge in an imitation of religiousness. Being "virtually religious," they imitate real faith and real practice, simulating what they expect institutional religion and real religiousness to be. They enact both this real and virtual religiousness through the popular culture. Generation X, in other words, seems to want the "real" thing and an "imitation" of the real thing. Xers want the genuine *and* the posture, the authentic *and* the artificial.

For example, the crucifix is an imitation of piety and yet an authentic gesture of religiosity. Music videos imitate the use of Catholic symbols and yet genuinely appropriate them. Cyberspace imitates real community and yet also provides authentic community. That the pop culture dwells on suffering makes Xers virtually religious, and yet there is an authenticity in using biblical images of suffering to describe the generation. We pose as unified persons at the same time as we explore the genuine experience of plural selfhood.

By practicing religiosity in popular culture, Xers stake out their own space for religious practice, expression, and experimentation. It is a safe, if unlikely, environment in which to be "real." At the same time, by practicing religiosity in pop culture, Xers use the superficiality, irony, mockery, fluidity, and ephemerality of pop culture to imitate real religion. This is also a safe place to be "virtually" religious.

This is why Xers are a both-and generation. We are experts in superficiality and in posing, and we have also rediscovered authenticity. Indeed, we know that to engage in one involves us deeply in the other. Thus, we call out the ways in which other generations have also been "virtually" religious, even when they have not named it as such; no one is as authentic as they claim to be, no religious practice as "real" as anyone desires. There is always an element of imitating what is considered to be real religion in one's practice, of approximating authentic religious behavior. (Recall the example of the crucifix as a fashion accessory; wearing it as fashion underscores how those who pretend to wear it as a symbol of piety are really also wearing it as a fashion statement.)

Xers have found this gap between reality and imitation and plunged into its crevice, widening it and claiming both sides as their own. This is not heresy or heterodoxy; it is *orthopraxis,* or seeking right practice through erring and fumbling, through imitation and experimentation. I have used *religiosity* to characterize this way in which Xers both authentically and inauthentically practice religion, because it is a word of paradox, perfect for this ambivalent generation.

Generation X did not simply create "religiosity" out of nothing. Although Xers can claim credit for their uniquely virtual and real religiosity in pop culture, it would be impossible for them to see the religious as both virtual and real without the influence of our wider culture, which has been called a "culture of simulation." Our culture creates imitations and illusions to simulate a "real" experience, instead of offering the actual experience itself. (This, you may recall, was Bergeron's point about how the *Chant* CD offers an illusion of a sacred time, even though the CD itself cannot provide such time.)

Many philosophers and sociologists have offered accounts of this simulational culture that provide insight into the images, symbols, and simulations of GenX popular culture. A detour into the work of some of these thinkers can illuminate the cultural situation in which Generation X—and much of America—finds its religious practices.

Making Sense of Simulation

If GenX culture is so skilled at simulation, even to the point of celebrating a "virtual" religiosity, how did this come about, and what does it mean for spirituality today and in the future? French sociologist Jean Baudrillard helps to explore this difficult question.

According to Baudrillard, much of what we commonly used to refer to as "real" has been replaced by imitations or simulations of reality. To understand what has happened to our sense of reality, it is necessary to understand Baudrillard's concept of the simulacrum. A *simulacrum* is an odd concept—it is a copy for which no original exists. This may sound confusing, but it is strangely insightful.

Take the example of a dude ranch to which middle-class suburbanites repair for a vacation. There is no Wild West left in the United States that the ranch can represent. There are only simulations of the Wild West to which the ranch can be compared—movies and television shows with figures such as John Wayne, Clint Eastwood, and the Lone Ranger. As an original Wild West is nowhere to be found, the dude ranch is founded on simulations of other simulations of life in the Wild West. The dude ranch, therefore, is a simulacrum, a copy whose original does not exist. The "western" experience it provides can only be measured against other simulations of the Wild West, not against "reality." (Many ethnic areas of theme parks, such as Disney World, are other examples of such simulacra.)

These simulacra—pure imitations whose "real" referent has been lost— are freely at play in our culture. Baudrillard thinks we have moved beyond any certainty about knowledge of reality and can only deal in simulations. As with the dude ranch, each time we think we have found the "real" thing to which a simulation refers, we realize that we have merely discovered another simulation. Because of this, Baudrillard suggests that we live in the age not of the "real" but of the "hyperreal." Each simulation refers only to other simulations and can never come to rest on any "real," original ground.

Popular images in the media—such as the "images" of the Wild West in movies—perpetuate this culture of simulation. Baudrillard suggests that in contemporary culture, the image "bears no relation to any reality whatever: it is its own pure simulacrum" (1983, p. 11). Baudrillard thinks we have moved as far away as possible in our culture from the notion that our images have anything to do with reality. We merely have copies of what we thought reality to be, but there is no reality left against which we can measure our images or simulations.

Separating simulation from reality, unhinging the image from what it represents, makes it possible to have the free-floating religious images we have examined in music video and cyberspace (and even fashion, with crucifixes and pierced navels). When all we have are religious simulations, instead of real religiousness, the lambs, stigmata, crosses, and baptisms all begin to escape the grip of their old religious contexts and to spin a new spiritual web of associations.

This cultural situation is what Jameson has evocatively called "surrealism without the unconscious" (1995, p. 174). We live with an unsettling surreal fluidity of ever-shifting imagery, and we do not even need the concept of an unconscious to concoct or understand such images. In other words, we cannot pin our bizarre situation on the workings of our unconscious. Losing firm contact with the "real" is an unusual place in which to practice spirituality or religiosity, to say the least. But like virtual reality games or cyberspace dreamscapes, "simulations" of reality can help us imagine "the real" differently; they can give us new critical lenses.

By considering simulated, virtual religiousness, we can understand and critique "real" religiousness. If our life increasingly offers surrealism without the unconscious, then the line between the virtual and the real becomes more difficult to pinpoint. As one woman who ministers to Xers said to me, "Your generation doesn't seem to mind not being able to tell the real from the unreal." But it all depends on whether one thinks the virtual can inform the real, as I think it can. And as I will shortly suggest, a trust that we can still distinguish between the virtual and the real means that Baudrillard's effacing of reality may not be the final word on the matter.

Whether or not one completely agrees with Baudrillard, what are the implications for our spiritual lives in a culture in which there is so much simulation? As Xers adorn themselves with imitations of a religious sensibility, their "personal" sense of the religious becomes a collection of images and symbols from various religions. French religious scholar Daniele Hervieu-Leger writes that religious traditions have become "symbolic 'toolboxes' on which the men and women of today draw freely, without this necessarily meaning that they identify themselves with the comprehensive view of the world . . . that historically was part of the language of the traditions concerned" (1993, p. 141). In other words, just as our culture is driving a wedge between simulation and reality, religious symbols (doctrines, beliefs, morals, rituals, sacred texts) are also increasingly unhinged from the religious traditions to which they belong in "reality."

Cultural critic Douglas Rushkoff puts Hervieu-Leger's insights about contemporary religiousness and culture into a GenX context. Rushkoff perceptively observes that "GenX engages in the techniques of recycling, juxtaposing, and recontextualizing existing imagery, and doing so with ironic distance" (1994a, p. 8). Jameson, too, has suggested that there is a tendency in contemporary culture to "ceaselessly reshuffle the fragments of preexistent texts . . . in some new and heightened bricolage" (1995, p. 96).

This last word is very important. *Bricolage* (a term brought into prominence by French anthropologist Claude Lévi-Strauss) means an improvised, rough assemblage of whatever tools are at hand to solve a problem. Xers are frequently *bricoleurs,* piecing together religious systems from available images, symbols, doctrines, moral codes, and texts. In cyberspace, music video, and other forms of culture that feature religious imagery, pop culture borrows from various (even contradictory) religious perspectives. For example, Madonna can use Catholic symbols while keeping the institution at arm's length, Tori Amos can appropriate baptism apart from a Sunday morning church service, and Xer fashion can celebrate the navel while ignoring the religious traditions that gave meaning to the navel in the first place.

As "bricoleurs," Xers will continue to reshape both American popular culture and what is considered to be "religion." We share this impulse with many baby boomers, who borrowed from Eastern religions a few decades ago to enliven Western spiritualities. Wade Clark Roof finds that among boomers in particular, and American culture in general, "A dynamic, democratic religious culture is evolving, its many elements ever recombining, mixing and matching with one another to create new syncretisms" (1993, p. 31). According to Roof, "No quality of the contemporary religious and spiritual ferment is of more interest, or of greater significance in the long run for American religion" (p. 31). Harvey Cox has identified this bricolage as an important characteristic of the generations and cultures involved in the Pentecostal movement (1995, pp. 304–307). Immersed in pop culture, Generation X is at the heart of this "spiritual ferment."

Floating between reality and simulation, sifting through culture, and bricolating religious images to deconstruct and reconstruct religious meaning, Xers have learned that the sacred always dresses in the trappings of culture, never apart from it. Knowing this, Xers thrive in their popular culture as one way of encountering the divine.

Critics of Baudrillard and of other theorists of the image have frequently accused them of cynicism, even nihilism, in their assessments of the image's role in contemporary culture. Simply put, life seems hopelessly adrift if we have lost touch with reality. It is certainly premature for us to announce the end of "reality." The tendency of some cultural theorists to locate our postmodern culture at the end of the history of reality is a serious enough reason to hold back from embracing Baudrillardian theories of the image wholeheartedly. Nevertheless, Baudrillard and Hervieu-Leger offer incisive reflections on the nature of the culture that confronts Generation X, the first generation to grow up almost entirely in a popular culture of simulation.

The simulation in our culture holds many promises for religion and religious practice. Although people frequently voice fears that simulated religion and GenX pop culture are watering down "true religion" and leaving authentic religious practice wounded and bleeding at the roadside, the virtually religious can at times help us understand real religiousness better. I continue to make the distinction between virtual and real, even though I am often uncertain where to draw that line.

Reclaiming Tradition

To continue to "live theology," to practice a thriving irreverent spirituality, Xers can recycle and recombine not only the present pop culture and religious landscape but also the rich past of religious tradition.

In order to make the virtually religious a gateway to (or a criticism of) the "really" religious, we must understand and engage "real" religion, the way religious practice functions in the real world, even as given to us by institutions. That is, we must confront what is called "religion," as it is handed down to us, and not just in the way we experiment with it or take ironic stances toward it in the popular culture.

This means that we must reappropriate tradition, which is one of my primary challenges to Xers themselves. Virtual religiosity, an imitation of real religious practice, is not enough. If the virtual is to have significant value, it must lead somewhere, it must help clarify the real, and it must make our authentic lived practice more truly religious. As much as I revere the emerging religiosity of Xers found in the popular culture, for all its richness and irreverence, this GenX pop culture religiosity must be brought into conversation with "real" religiousness and with religious institutions. I suggest that Xers make a wholesale reconsideration of religious tradition.

A reconsideration of tradition offers a check on GenX spirituality. It keeps those beliefs from becoming too subjective and merely personal. But isn't a concern for tradition a threat to our suspicion of institutions and personal experience? After all, isn't tradition all about maintaining institutions and overruling personal experience? Despite these concerns, the future of a growing GenX spirituality depends on how Xers understand and appropriate religious tradition.

Recovering a renewed sense of religious tradition will provide Xers with the resources to continue to do the following: reintegrate the spiritual and sensual; unite religion and politics; critique the Church's Jesus; emphasize a return to community; utter prophetic and apocalyptic words; and bring theological values of anti-institutionalism, personal experience, suffering, and ambiguity to bear on religion beyond this ephemeral moment in our culture.

Tradition, Not Traditionalism

Tradition is a word with which many Xers are uncomfortable, and for good reason. People with religious authority have abused tradition as a way of excluding dissent, solidifying "orthodoxy," and protecting the "truth" from the counterattacks of the "heterodox." To many, Xers and their popular culture represent the latest in a dangerous history of atheism, heresy, and hostility to institutions. These iconoclasts have discarded the "truth" of the past, of the so-called fixed tradition, in favor of the pseudotruths of the moment, of mere fancy. When Xers complain about religious institutions, people often invoke religious tradition to dismiss their views and to stifle further discussion.

I experienced such a stifling use of tradition when I wrote a letter a few years ago to a prominent member of the Roman Catholic hierarchy. I asked for a dialogue about various issues between this official and members of our "Saving Remnant" at Harvard Divinity School. I received a reply stating that the Church's "tradition" was "clear," implying that further discussion was impossible. Indeed, the letter noted, the issues I raised could not even be called "questions," as the "tradition" had already "answered" them all.

I suggest that Xers can take a more life-giving, theologically responsible, and intellectually honest approach to the nature of "tradition." If we are to gain a wider and perhaps even more authoritative and ancient understanding of tradition, we need to open our lives and let our particular religious traditions make serious claims on our lives. No amount of ironizing or cynical mocking can brush aside this challenge.

There are many ways of interpreting the concept of tradition. My purpose is to recommend some recent work in philosophy and theology that may help Xers rediscover the value of tradition. A key insight for Xers is that the ways we struggle with particular religious traditions *already* gives us an important role in those traditions. Philosopher Alisdair MacIntyre makes that point, writing that the struggle to define exactly what makes a tradition is required for a tradition to exist in the first place. For people to struggle, argue, push, and pull within a tradition—over precisely what the tradition means or doesn't mean—is no serious cause for concern, since only traditions in their most primitive stages harbor no major disagreements. Indeed, MacIntyre suggests, a tradition grows when those in a tradition "attempt to engage in its debates and to carry its inquiries forward" (1988, p. 326). Struggling, in other words, is a fundamental part of carrying on a tradition. This is good news for Xers, many of whom seem to be passively or actively struggling with religious traditions.

A tradition can only progress, according to MacIntyre, when it encounters strife or challenges from the inside and the outside (1988, p. 12). Thus, as philosopher Georgia Warnke concludes, in order to continue to live, "A single tradition needs a plurality of interpretations of itself" (1993, p. 124). This need for diversity at the very heart of tradition makes me hopeful that Xers can tussle with their own religious traditions and reshape them in the process.

What is essential to living traditions is that they are always incomplete. Whenever religious leaders pretend that religions are complete, finished, and impervious to further difficult debate and strife, they are defending (in the words of Jaroslav Pelikan) not *tradition* but *traditionalism*. Tradition is "the living faith of the dead." Traditionalism is the "dead faith of the living," as is all too familiar to Xers (1984, p. 65).

German philosopher Hans-Georg Gadamer contributes to a dynamic understanding of tradition that is useful for Xers. Gadamer reminds all of us, perhaps especially Xers (who are often quick to try shedding their relation to the past), that we all stand in a tradition, whether we like it or not. The existence of tradition cannot be proven or disproven. "Tradition," writes Gadamer, "has a justification that lies beyond rational grounding and in large measure determines our institutions and attitudes" (1994, p. 281).

Gadamer's key insight for Xers is this: tradition does not simply restrain us (despite what some of our religious leaders may argue). Instead, it gives us the tools to liberate us, even from the way traditions have been used against us. As Gadamer writes, "To be situated within a tradition does not limit the freedom of knowledge but *makes it possible*" (p. 361, italics mine).

According to Gadamer, "Even the most genuine and pure tradition does not persist because of the inertia of what once existed. *It needs to be affirmed, embraced, cultivated*" (p. 281, italics mine). Thus, instead of being a stagnant swamp for Xers, tradition can be a living fountain. But how can that be true if, as Xers know so well, tradition preserves the past? Gadamer argues that preservation can be reasonable and conscious, not just a thoughtless passing on of ideas. "Preservation is an act of reason, though an inconspicuous one. For this reason, only innovation and planning appear to be the result of reason. But this is an illusion. Even where life changes violently, as in ages of revolution, far more of the old is preserved in the supposed transformation of everything than anyone knows, and it combines with the new to create a new value. At any rate, preservation is as much a freely chosen action as are revolution and renewal" (pp. 281–282).

Against those who try to dissuade Xers from bringing their criticisms and prophetic voices to their religious traditions, Xers can employ Gadamer's interpretation of tradition as *active preservation,* not *mindless repetition.* In this view, tradition does not trample us; rather, it engages us intimately and personally. Gadamer writes that "tradition is a genuine partner in dialogue, and we belong to it, as does the I with a Thou" (p. 358).

Insofar as Xers are embracing, struggling, or wrestling with spirituality, they are already carrying forward religious traditions—but with varying degrees of consciousness. The question is to what extent this will be a thought-out and constructive exercise. Xers must continually return to the resources of their inherited or freely chosen religious traditions, bringing them into the light of their own experiences of living in culture. They must take on their traditions, interpreting them anew for their unique culture. As theologian Terry Veling suggests, "It is in the event of interpretation that tradition itself happens. Tradition vanishes utterly when it is not interpreted" (1996, p. 39).

The Tradition of Irreverence and the Irreverence of Tradition

As an example of this reencounter with tradition from a specific religious context, Catholic theologian David Tracy argues that tradition can and should be encountered with a trustful attitude. To keep reforming religious tradition in a prophetic spirit (one which I discern among Xers) is to be faithful to the witness of the biblical communities of faith. For Tracy, these early witnesses are the foundations of Christian faith. It is therefore possible to have a fundamental "trust in the tradition for the sake of the tradition" (1991, p. 237).

This approach enables Xers to challenge radically individualistic interpretations of Christianity that ignore the claims of tradition. Just as Xers understand that the sacred is always embodied in symbols that are influenced by culture, so we are poised to see that our encounters with the sacred are mediated by religious tradition, whether we like it or not. According to Tracy, a trust in tradition makes it possible for Christians to have faith in Christ; without tradition, we would have no way of knowing "the Jesus remembered as the Christ by the tradition and its fidelity to the original apostolic witness" (1991, p. 237).

The tradition needs correction or criticism wherever it distorts the message of Jesus for us today. Paradoxically, it is the memory of Jesus bequeathed to us by the tradition that makes possible such correction and criticism! This trustworthy character of the tradition as bearer of the message of Jesus challenges Christian Xers. As I noted in Chapter Four, GenX pop culture reclaims the life (and even the death and often the resurrection) of Jesus as a criticism of the Church's modern configuration and practices. But where would this access to Jesus be if this same Church that is the object of so much criticism had not handed down the tradition of Jesus, however imperfectly?

Thus, for Christian Xers, faith in Jesus entails faith in the institutional Church. Christianity does not require blind faith, but without dignifying the Church as a trustworthy guarantor of the tradition of Jesus, it is impossible for Xers to claim Jesus against distortions or incompetencies in the Church today.

Tracy's eloquence summarizes the challenge to Christian Xers to engage the Church's tradition: "A respect for tradition grounded in the recognition of its mediation to us of . . . the memory of Jesus, its very formation of our capacity to experience that event, does call for a faith in the church. It does not call for, or even allow, the familiar distortions of that faith into ecclesiolatry [idolizing the church] and traditionalism [the dead faith of the living]" (1991, p. 323). Tracy reminds Christian Xers that Jesus is the reason we must constantly reform our religious traditions. The memory of his subversive practices inspires us today. Tracy writes: "To disown [the] reformatory impulse at the heart of the tradition is also to disown the church's apostolic memories of the message, actions and fate of Jesus. It is to disallow that subversive and dangerous memory of Jesus in the church" (1991, p. 324).

Just as in Chapter Three I noted that "timeless" Gregorian chant is really a recent development, much of what is called "tradition" today is really an innovation little older than our grandparents. When Xers hear that particular forms of worship, beliefs, or doctrines are "traditional," our first questions should be "For whom?" "Why?" and "How old is this tradition?" History helps us take an irreverent stance toward religion, but occasionally we should take an irreverent stance toward history itself! We might even want to oppose the prevailing interpretation of a religious tradition and current religious practices. As I have suggested, this irreverence and opposition, however, are made possible by the religious tradition itself.

As an example, one Xer who struggled with tradition noted, "I have been able to rediscover the fundamental and radical truths of my Catholic heritage. I have also realized that I was a poseur to hope for a transformation of the church while I turned my back on it. If we are to participate authentically in our experiences and be enriched by our faith and ideals, we must have the guts to hang in there and struggle to make it *real*" (Trinidad, 1994, p. 17, italics mine). The experience of this Xer illustrates the truth of Veling's conviction that "tradition is reformed *within* the tradition" (1996, p. 53). Tradition is our heritage, and it also allows us to critique and reform this heritage! One can often subvert the inadequacies and injustices of a religious tradition using tools from the tradition itself (for example, when pop culture recovers forgotten aspects of Christian tradition, such as sensual spirituality). This is a liberating truth for Xers.

Our challenge is to take up our traditions actively, to bring them into dialogue with the lived experience of the generation, and to carry them into the next century. We can make our skepticism, irony, cynicism, and sensitivity to hypocrisy—our irreverence—*useful* as we sustain our faith in its institutional expressions.

Giving the Gift of Theological Imagination

One of the joyous religious experiences of my twenties has been coming to believe that imagination is the touchstone of religious experience. I feel that imagination is in some way connected to the divine, linked by a sacred tether to God's creative (and sometimes irreverent) inspiration. I came to believe this when I studied postmodern biblical interpretation, which was a surprisingly sacred experience for me. As I read the imaginative, playful, transgressive, and creative work of biblical interpreters (such as Stephen Moore, whom I quoted earlier in this book), wisps of spiritual inspiration rose like incense from the page, tickling and enticing my nostrils theologically.

Many writers have cited a mysterious connection between God and the imagination. Søren Kierkegaard writes that his thoughts "go strolling in the cool of the evening" (1989, p. x), an allusion to Genesis 3:8, in which God strolled in the cool of the evening. I interpret David Porush as challenging us to worship God through our imagination when he writes that "the most portable altar of all is in your head" (1996, p. 130).

One way in which Xers can receive and reform tradition, particularly in our popular culture, is to observe the creative spirit in pop culture's religious dimension and to bring that imagination to bear on religious traditions. It is no accident that Xers have such an imaginative popular culture. First of all, they have a finite—if quite diverse—set of references with which to work and so are forced to be creative. As Rushkoff points out, we continually recycle images already in the media (we are *bricoleurs*), making and finding new meaning in older pop culture references and artifacts. Second, our popular culture is heavily image oriented and iconographic. From music video to cyberspace to fashion, image is our story as much as text was the story for past generations. The icon is the common currency of our popular culture. (Even our common text, hypertext, behaves more like a picture—or an icon—than like a printed word.)

Given this heavily iconographic culture, GenX is beginning to understand implicitly what many theologians are also coming to understand—the degree to which religious revelation does not happen directly from God to humans but is mediated through symbols. Symbolic thinking is a natural way of thinking for a generation that, as I suggested, knows that the sacred is always cloaked in cultural forms. As Catholic theologian Avery Dulles writes, "Revelation never occurs in a purely interior experience or an unmediated encounter with God" (1983, p. 131). Even through our imaginations, revelation is not a simple matter of God's speaking a word and our understanding that word as God intends it. Revelation always happens in symbols that "suggest more than [they] can clearly describe or define" (p. 131). Symbols suggest a rich overabundance of meaning, whether they come from a religion or appear on a screen or in fashion. This richness means that the viewer must have imagination. Only with imagination can the religious meaning (perhaps God's own inspiration) come alive and make a claim on the person (as I have tried to show in my interpretations of pop culture). This is why Catholic religious educator Thomas Groome suggests that "revelation comes first to meet us in our imaginations" (1991, p. 197). Imagination allows us to make and receive infinite interpretations of how symbols represent God's presence in the world. It is hardly surprising that, in an iconographic pop culture, Xers have offered imaginative religious commentary that can be interpreted many times over (as I have done in this book).

Imagination helps virtual religiosity inspire real religiosity. For example, Xers imagine new forms of community on-line, which can inspire new forms of "real" religious community. Xers imagine new relationships between the spiritual and sensual in music video, innovations which can inspire real-life sexual and religious understandings. Xers imagine new fluidities of orthodoxy, challenging "real" religious beliefs and practices. Xers imagine new sex and gender relationships and ambiguities in cyberspace, inspiring changes in "real" ways of living religiously. Xers imagine faith as being unsteady, wrought by the indeterminacy and ambiguity of GenX life and culture, and explored as a gift from God to a culture dying from its pretended certainties.

GenX's imagination about religiosity pops up in the most irreverent places. At O'Neill Library at Boston College, I saw the following inscription written on the wall of the men's bathroom:

O

L

O L D M A N

M

A

N

I wondered if this was a statement about Jesus, in keeping with the depictions of an elderly Jesus I have detailed in music video. If so, it was highly ironic. Jesus' influence at Xer-rich Boston College had stalled in a new way. Yet I had to ask myself, If this "old man" is so irrelevant, why mark out these letters in cruciform? Indeed, why take the time to scrawl them at all? Boston College is hardly a haven of traditional Catholic piety (among undergraduates, anyway), so it must not have been meant to offend. Besides, it was too cryptic for that. If nothing else, the inscription could be interpreted as suggestive of GenX attitudes about the commodeification of religion by conveying a fascination with one of its key figures.

This way of pitting Jesus against the Church is not new. A philosophical tradition skeptical of or hostile to Christianity influenced by Friedrich Nietzsche espoused this perspective before Xers did. Nietzsche wrote pointedly that it is a "misuse of words when such manifestations of decay and abortions as 'Christian church,' 'Christian faith,' and 'Christian life' label themselves with that holy name. What did Christ *deny*? Everything that is today called Christian" (1968, pp. 97–98). Thus did Nietzsche popularize pitting the teachings of Jesus against Christianity's later institutional developments.

I mention Nietzsche to note that the images of Jesus in the videos I have discussed may be seen as part of a philosophical tradition, a criticism of religious institutions that Xers are carrying forward. This is simply further evidence that Xers should take hold of the traditions in which they stand, so that they do not unthinkingly repeat the past and can consciously take the past into the future.

One Christian Xer described his religious quest, his emerging ownership of his religious tradition, in this way:

> This radical Jesus, this social gospel, this promise of liberation are always and forever in the back of my mind. I have been very fortunate to come . . . into a place where it is safe to ask questions, to be angry, to struggle openly with some of the very difficult issues of our times. I have learned there are no easy answers, that if answers are to be found at all they will come only in the context of a faith community. . . . So here I am roaming the fringes of the institutional church, becoming a stranger to my family and friends, challenging the status quo, and seeking [Helmer, 1994, p. 16].

"Roaming the fringes" may be a concise summary of the way in which GenX can relate again to religious institutions. Xers can paradoxically find a home by risking homelessness, wandering the edges of the institution.

------------ o ------------

As practitioners of an irreverent spirituality, we must decide our generation's religious future. By taking advantage of a culture of simulation, we explore real religiousness through virtual religiousness. By taking on tradition, we can see how tradition has made our irreverence possible. We can also shoulder our responsibility for ensuring that religious tradition maintains its irreverent possibilities. Taking responsibility for tradition will not compromise our irreverence; it will only fund it more deeply.

9

REDISCOVERING
HUMILITY IN MINISTRY

A SPIRITUAL CHALLENGE FROM GENERATION X

THE WORST SERMON I EVER HEARD was at a secular event. It was a university commencement and one featured speaker was a campus minister who thought it would be appropriate to preach about pop artist Joan Osborne's hit song "One of Us." The song, which is essentially about the mystery of God in human form, is a wonderful work of theology in itself. What could have been an opportunity to discuss the mystery of the incarnation in our culture, however, turned into a simple celebration of pop culture, as the speaker offered no perspective from religious tradition, no creative or ironic interpretations, and no dialogue with Scripture. In short, there was no richness in her theological interpretation.

Although her execution was lacking, she had the right instinct—while representing a religious (and secular) institution, she took GenX pop culture seriously as an expression of Xers' lived theology. Following that instinct, in this chapter I consider pop culture as a resource for rethinking ministry.

Traveling Companions

GenX popular culture can refresh the religious imagination for ministry. Imagination is central to ministry because it is indispensable to theology. As Catholic theologian Roger Haight notes, theology springs from the content of our imagination (which itself derives from what we experience through our senses). When I "do" theology, in other words, it is not a matter of taking direct dictation from God onto paper but of working with lived faith, Scripture, and tradition (certainly, I think, under divine influence), all of which are assembled and reassembled together (more or less creatively) in my imagination. What is possible theologically, then, depends on what is possible imaginatively. According to Haight, "The imagination [has] an important role in the way we construe things, even the personal, spiritual, eternal, and transcendent reality of God" (1996, p. 219).

Similarly, the limits of our ministries are the limits of our imaginations. Therefore, the range of theological imagination that pop culture displays can be a resource for ministry. In other words, ministry, pop culture, and imagination are cordial traveling companions.

One need only look at many successful baby boomer churches to see where pop culture has influenced ministry, particularly through worship. Many boomer churches—particularly evangelical Protestant—have been inspired by boomer popular culture, from popular music to television shows. The pop culture events then become the content of sermons, influence the style of music, and serve as the subject matter of Sunday school classes. Several boomer friends of mine report that in the 1970s, they watched scenes from the popular movies *Godspell* or *Jesus Christ Superstar* in church or sang the movie sound tracks as worship hymns.

When my own ministry in the 1980s was oriented around playing Christian rock music, our band found inspiration from several Christian rock bands, who themselves were imitating heavy metal bands from "secular" pop culture. Although my own band borrowed its sound from secular pop culture, we were subtly deriving our theology from Christian rock music. In other words, both "secular" and "Christian" pop culture was shaping our ministerial imaginations, giving us a ministry that was accessible to teens and young adults (whom I now look back on as young Xers).

Accessible ministry is a hallmark of the work of Paul in the Christian Scriptures. Paul himself summed up this accessibility in trying "to be all things to all people" (1 Corinthians 9:22), and a glance at his sports metaphors (as I noted in Chapter Two) sheds light on the ways in which Greek popular culture influenced Paul's own ministerial imagination. I have been in several churches that, during worship, featured slide presentations of mission trips and set them to music. In these popular innovations, movies and music video seem to have fed the ministerial imagination. This happy companionship between imagination, pop culture, and ministry, which is so evident in boomer ministries, should extend to GenX ministries; GenX popular culture should become an imaginative resource for ministry. By drawing on GenX pop culture, religious institutions will become more accessible to Generation X, while creatively carrying forward their particular religious traditions.

To sketch some imaginative implications for ministry, I will revisit the four themes that show how pop culture characterizes GenX's lived theology. Of course, these themes will have different practical implications for a Southern Baptist church than for a reform synagogue; I will ground my discussion in implications that pertain to the four themes.

Suspicion of Institutions

GenX's suspicion of institutions implies a threefold emphasis for ministry to Xers: a return to humility in ministry, a willingness to "go virtual," and a renewal of mystical practices or spiritual disciplines.

A Call to Humility

GenX's suspicion or outright derision of institutions, which includes particular attacks on the Catholic Church and a reclamation of Jesus against institutions, is a bedrock component of Xers' irreverent spirituality.

Xer religiosity squarely challenges institutions to come to terms with their relevance or irrelevance, to question whether they have become institutionalized. Because Xers have an astute understanding of institutions' limited and tentative nature, it may benefit a religious institution to respond to Xer criticisms. They can do this by incorporating their failures and limits into preaching and practice, which will make them more accessible to Xers.

For example, I once heard an extremely powerful sermon to a largely Xer audience at a Wednesday night service in a Baptist church. The sermon was about the brokenness of the Church as a model for the brokenness of our lives. The rhythm of the Church's faithfulness and faithlessness throughout history served as a metaphor for our own struggles with faith. An Xer in the pew in front of me, who responded by going forward to profess faith at the "altar call" at the end of the service, wrote me over e-mail later, "It wasn't Jesus I really had a problem with. I've simply never heard a description of the Church that I could trust until I heard that sermon."

To reach more Xers, institutions that are beholden to their own power structures, whether a parish council or governing committees, could try to loosen the grip of local bureaucracies (that have so plagued the "secular" world) and make access to institutional authority more ad hoc, more fluid. For instance, one Catholic church of which I am aware established small groups of Xers (and they were *very* small in this previously Xer-indifferent church), akin to miniature town meetings, to sound out Xer concerns on a regular basis. They gave Xers greater influence over the common liturgy and eventually their own monthly Mass.

In highlighting religious institutions' complicity with particularly demeaning, outdated, or oppressive practices, GenX pop culture offers an opportunity for religious institutions to do a critical examination of the space between the institution and the surrounding culture. As more than one Xer said to me, "If I can read pop psychology at the local bookstore, why go to church to hear about it?"

In general, GenX culture challenges Churches to preach and practice from a position of humility and weakness in the world. By shunning the trappings of privileged social status (where that still remains) and seeking to serve, not to be served, Churches will respond faithfully not only to the prophetic charge brought by GenX but, more important, to the example of Jesus.

Langdon Gilkey offers powerful advice about the type of ministry or mission to which Xers will likely listen: "A mission that dies itself, that sacrifices what it is in the world—in culture, in religion, in theological formulations, and in ecclesiastical might—in favor of the transcendent to which it seeks to witness, can be heard. . . . For that alone is the voice, and the commission, that comes to us from the cross and from beyond the tomb" (1981, p. 156). Being willing to sacrifice power and status for the sake of service to the gospel will do more for the Church's message about Jesus than any amount of rhetoric from pulpits. It will also go far in addressing Xers' suspicion of religious institutions.

A few years ago in midtown Kansas City, Missouri, I witnessed an example of this humility—a mission not dependent on success for its religious validation. A few of my high school students had gone into town on a Friday night clad in T-shirts that advertised Jesus. They intended to "evangelize" the bustling Westport area (I lived near there and met them accidentally), but somehow they became separated from their youth minister. Instead of handing out tracts on a street corner, they decided it would be more interesting to talk to a homeless man who regularly begged at a busy corner. They later confided to me the spiritual significance of their brief companionship with this man and the little monetary assistance they were able to give him. Their original "mission" had failed in a sense, but in Gilkey's words, it had failed in favor of the larger purpose to which it sought to witness.

Virtual Ministry

Xers' suspicion of institutions has a more positive side, which is GenX's embrace of the noninstitutional. Among the various opportunities for non-institutional ministry (on the part of institutions) are ventures into cyber-space. Religious communities, particularly of Xers, are beginning to thrive in virtual space. In that arena, faith and life mingle at all hours of the night—with less reservation than one finds in the coffee hour after most worship services.

The public face that institutions erect in cyberspace is crucial, however. As I was leading a class for religious educators on Catholic communities in cyberspace, I was embarrassed to come across several Church or diocesan Web sites that "welcomed" visitors by way of an imperious picture of the local hierarch. He had worded his greeting in language unintelligible or uninteresting to most Xers, particularly those seeking religious direction in cyberspace. My colleagues in the class, both Xers and boomers, could only smirk at the sites, which is certainly not the reaction that these virtual institutions desired.

Also off-putting are Catholic Web sites that force users to "venerate" triumphalistic and outdated images or icons, often by clicking them to get around on a Web site. Some sites use the keys of Saint Peter or medieval Catholic shields (or subject visitors to several minutes of "Ave Maria" played on a cheap synthesizer). As I had discussions with Xers while doing research for this book and as I led classes for teachers and religious educators on using the Web, I learned that others also found these sites less than spiritually inviting. In the name of GenX's irreverent spirituality, these sorts of Web sites beg to be parodied. They do not confront the challenges of GenX's lived theology, even though most of their visitors will be Xers. Contemporary technology does not happily marry with outdated ministry.

Several monasteries in cyberspace offer witnesses that are more appropriate to both cyberspace and the gospel. Monks volunteer to pray with or for the site's visitors; chant music is accessible, as are ancient texts of the tradition; and all have intriguing hypertext links with abundant images. Authentic witnesses to the vowed religious life are otherwise hard to come by for Xers. Cyberspace at its best can give access to the music, images, worship, sacramentality, and the general richness of a religious tradition. These are helpful examples for other religious institutions to follow, although they are not the only ones.

It may also be instructive to use the boundary-crossing nature of cyber-space to invade "real" ministries, for the sake of making institutions more accessible. As GenXers respond to a religious pluralism, institutions could highlight the different ways in which cultures around the world practice a particular Christian tradition. Rather than undermining ministry, attention to various forms of the same religious tradition highlights the significance of religious particularity, including local ministries, rituals, preaching, and liturgy. (Such an emphasis also comports well with the multiculturalism that has been so central to most Xers' upbringing and higher education.)

One youth ministry event that I attended in Kansas City illuminated the varieties of Catholic practice around the world by inviting foreign exchange students to speak on "What being Catholic means to me." My GenX peers and I were fascinated by the multiplicity of expressions of Catholicism. We also sensed that our own practices lacked the faith-filled dynamism evident in other cultures. My GenX friends and I observed both the limits of the Catholic institutional Church (in failing to keep this colorful diversity of practice in mind on an institutional level), as well as the benefits of the institutional Church (as a guarantor of the bond between Catholics worldwide).

Spirituality and Mysticism

GenX's suspicion of institutions can give Churches an opportunity to revive the spiritual or mystical tradition, to rediscover spiritual growth and religious journey. I count these as noninstitutional entities because GenX pop culture, and much Xer practice, perceives spirituality and mysticism as only loosely connected to the public face of religious institutions.

In Chapter Seven, I discussed Xers' hesitation about saying too much versus not saying enough. Our generation is often caught between keen insights into religious institutions' insufficiencies and abuses and a stubborn need for community. These experiences could be taken (and are increasingly taken by Xers) as invitations to explore "spirituality" and mystical experience. Xers occasionally need respite from the fashioned, ever-moving, image-rich life of pop culture.

My own experience is that I desire both monastic times away from and a continued engagement with the popular culture. When I taught high school in Kansas City, hunkered with my students in the trenches of popular culture, I often took a day off each month and retreated to the nearby Benedictine Monastery in Atchison, Kansas, for a day or two of almost complete silence. I was seeking a brush, however brief, with spiritual discipline. And I found it there, in regular prayer with the monks, communal and simple meals, and long periods of solitary silence in the dark and cavernous chapel. But this did not sever my ties with the popular culture; frequently, I returned from the monastery and immediately went to practice with a rock band, to meet friends at the movies or video arcade. Xers tend to live on a continuum of religious experiences; we are able to find God at the monastery or movies, in the convent or cyberspace. But we need a way to connect it all, and a ministerial gift from institutions would be to provide these links and support.

At ministry conferences in the past several years, I have been quite surprised by the number of evangelical and mainline Protestant Xers, both lay and ministers, who wanted to know what they might read for instruction in Catholic spirituality. Should they read general "spiritual discipline" or something more specific, such as centering prayer? Some have even asked outright for directions to the convent or monastery nearest their home. (Of course, I rarely can help them with this one.) One of the most common spiritual questions I have heard from Xers is "Where and how can I get away and not see anyone?" Apparently, Xers already understand the *why.* Many Xer friends and colleagues are spending time with Saints John of the Cross, Ignatius, Teresa of Avila, and others from the rich heritage of spirituality. Sometimes, I suggest neglected, somewhat obscure works such as the *Rule* of Saint Benedict for a spiritual challenge on a weekend retreat, because it is a way of life that is full of *difference,* exuding forgotten spiritual possibilities.

The revival of these forgotten spiritual possibilities can be a gift from institutions to Xers leery of getting too close. For example, I am astounded by the number of ministers—and not just Catholics—who are taking groups to monasteries or convents for practice in the spiritual life. A Methodist colleague who took his young adult group to a monastery and read mystical works with them told me that he has been hounded ever since with requests to return; he dryly compared this with the lack of requests to repeat a recent young adult worship service his church had sponsored.

It seems that in this renewed interest in spirituality and mysticism, Xers combine their suspicion of institutions with the knowledge that, as sociologist Jean Baudrillard observes, our "entire society . . . has lost the formula for stopping" (1988, p. 39).

Experience in Religious Context

The turn to experience in GenX pop culture encompasses not only personal and communal religious experience but also an emerging sensual spirituality, an experience of living faith in the world, and a desire for an encounter of the human and divine.

Sacramentality Distinguished from Seduction

One institutional response to GenX pop culture can be to broaden a sense of sacramentality in both worship and daily ministry with Xers. What this entails is attending to the "incarnational" character of our experiences, to examine the possibility of God's presence in individuals and in communities within religious institutions. A GenX Methodist minister shared with me his successes in turning his church into a coffeehouse on weekends, replete with music, "bohemian" decor, and jugs of java. On the first weekend of the coffeehouse, he gave a three-minute "sermon" between music sets about the presence of Christ among the two or three gathered at each table. "Nothing too confrontational, but hopefully invitational," he said. When I suggested "sacramental," he agreed.

In my own "ministry" of high school teaching, I realized at long last the depth of sacramentality in the mere *presence* of my (GenX) students. They continually disclosed God's grace, humor, mercy, wit, and passion to me. When I came to see this, it radicalized my own teaching, as I suddenly understood my students in an entirely new light. I had a fresh sense of what was at work in my own ministry of teaching—the presence of the living God in hundreds of daily sacramental encounters. I sketched the following personal credo on a piece of paper and taped it to my lectern: "I can be a teacher of souls, and yet blind to the gifts my students bring, if I refuse to allow them to bless my day." Such sacramentality amid my ministry of high school teaching in a "secular" setting dramatically reframed my relationships with my students. I am convinced that many ministers believe this—but also that many merely mouth it. Including Xers within the orbit of lived sacramentality would be a life-giving response to GenX pop culture, while also making institutions more accessible to Xers.

Institutions that actually learn from GenX culture may also find true moments to teach. One of the most important instructional opportunities is to help Xers sort sin from grace, real sacramentality from mere seduction in their daily lives and popular culture. Such a task will find different concrete expression across religious traditions. I have known different traditions to take successful, intelligent approaches to sacramentality through small pop culture study groups, in which the goal is both to learn from and to teach pop culture from the perspective of one's religious tradition. I learned of one such study group through an e-mail conversation with one of its participants, a young minister in California who arranged for the group to meet monthly in a local Catholic church. The group, mostly Xers, took turns presenting their favorite movies and songs, which were then discussed in light of each participant's faith, Church teaching, and even Catholic theology (courtesy of two participants who were divinity students).

Through groups such as these, both Xers and institutions can consider the emerging sensual spirituality in GenX pop culture, noting the sacramentality of human sexuality and critiquing its abuses in popular culture and practice. This will require a discerning attitude on the part of institutions. Simply denouncing (or uncritically accepting) all instances of sensuality in pop culture will not satisfy GenX religiosity. It is more effective to interpret sensuality in pop culture by correlating it with similar expressions in Christian tradition.

Experience and Liturgy

Institutions need no better excuse to revisit liturgy or worship than GenX pop culture's emphasis on personal and communal experience. *Liturgy,* after all, is where people gather to experience each other's presence and God's presence, to give thanks and to mourn, and to ritualize the experience of sensing God's presence.

Attention to the moment and to the image—key facets of pop culture—opens the door to imagining liturgy or ritual as a series of moments or images. If Xers know that changing the image is part of changing reality, as Douglas Rushkoff suggests (1996, p. 6), then ministerial attention to the images used in liturgy is vital to influencing GenX's spiritual reality.

As is true for images in GenX pop culture, images used in liturgy should be evocative, inclusive, and capable of many interpretations. One colleague who ministers to Xers in an evangelical church (a convert from Catholicism) started using the Catholic term *Eucharist* for his communion service because of its rich symbolism and sacramentality. He has also adapted some Catholic prayers and designed symbols on a cloth on the communion table to evoke deeper imagery in his church's liturgy.

The religious scholar Rudolf Otto, in his classic study *The Idea of the Holy,* notes that liturgy's religious power (what he calls "the ability to reveal the holy") partly lies in its invocation of symbols that "provide no clear meaning," including phrases such as *kyrie eleison* and *hallelujah*. To Otto, they resonate deeply and continuously because they are "wholly other," always escaping finally being grasped (1969, p. 65). The liturgies that invoke the holy are "instances of the analogy to 'the mysterious' afforded by *that which is not wholly understood* . . . and at the same time venerable through age" (p. 65, italics mine).

Not only is Otto making a plea for a return to the mysterious in worship but his words are strangely resonant with the contemporary rebirth

of Pentecostalism, which (in different ways from more traditionally liturgical traditions) provides for suggestive and ambiguous meaning. Speaking in tongues is as "wholly other" as chanting the phrase *kyrie eleison.*
This emphasis on having no clear meaning and on moments in liturgy not
wholly understood reemerges as a necessity in GenX's postmodern culture.

As I have suggested earlier in this book, pop culture protests that too
much theology (and by implication, worship) has been rendered domes-
tic and easily explainable (as with Jesus and his suffering and death). This
is an invitation for institutions to include unusual, even exotic chants or
songs in worship services. My own local (largely white) Catholic church
opens up these types of experiences by employing modern Spanish and
ancient Latin hymns for communal singing.

This emphasis on a "not wholly understood," spacious mystery can
also be evoked in worship through the experience of *silence.* As one GenX
evangelical church minister said to me, "My church does not know how
to endure silence for longer than ten seconds in our worship services, and
twenty-somethings are the ones who have been complaining to me about
it." Even Catholics have taken to filling up their entire liturgies with song,
as if silence is something to be endured and not experienced! For centuries, Catholic congregations did not make joyful enough noise at Mass;
they are now atoning for this by being unable to stop making joyful noises
at some of our more vibrant Catholic churches. If silence only reappears
for Christians during the season of Lent, as is common, ministers risk
associating silence exclusively with sorrow and repentance, which is not
a blessing for institutional accessibility to Xers.

Otto suggests that Western art has two ways of making the experience
of holiness directly accessible: silence and darkness (1969, p. 68). Regarding liturgical silence, he writes of the importance of "no mere momentary
pause, but an absolute cessation of sound long enough to 'hear the silence'
itself" (p. 70). I have yet to hear an Xer complain of too much silence or
darkness during a worship service. Liturgical silence and darkness redram-
atize some of the most intimate poverties of our lives, but frame them in
a religious picture, affording meaning to the gaps that are prevalent in
Xers' lives.

Liberation of Jesus

If GenX pop culture is at all accurate in its criticism, Christian Churches
are at great risk of domesticating their core message.

In pop culture, the crucified Christ is attacked and mocked, and Jesus
as a sacrificial lamb is ironized. Videos on these themes highlight the in-

adequacy for Christian Xers of imagining or preaching Jesus as merely the Suffering One, because the cross has become not a scandal (as it was for the earliest Christian witnesses) but a leash. Suffering for its own sake is nothing; it must be liberating and redemptive. The pop culture attention to Jesus suggests that Churches must unleash Jesus. As biblical scholar Joseph Fitzmyer writes in a commentary on Paul's letter to the Romans, "The gospel is not just a message sent from God; it is a 'power' unleashed in the world of humanity that actively accosts human beings" (1993, p. 254). Because the gospel is rooted in God, it is always and in every instance beyond what we can imagine or finally grasp, evading simple logic or domestication.

I believe the insufficiency of the Jesus portrayed in videos is not so much about the insufficiency of what Jesus truly is but about the total inadequacy of what the Church presents. Videos by Soundgarden and Tori Amos hint that Xers might claim Jesus against the Christian institution, because (or in spite) of some of its worst excesses (for Soundgarden, middle-class Christianity and media preachers, and for Amos, the sexism and abuse that the Church tolerates or causes). In this GenX Christian theological assertion, it is Jesus who bears ultimate authority about what is and is not "Christian," not the painfully fallible leaders of the Church.

Against the sweet and domesticated preaching of churches and the bottling up of God's cosmic presence in Christ, pop culture testifies that Christian Xers were too often spiritually fed like children by patronizing adults. This is surely one reason for Xers' lack of loyalty to churches and exodus from the religious scene, as well as the turn toward a host of fundamentalisms that seek to provide all the answers for people's lives.

How can Christian institutions unleash Jesus? This is an exceedingly difficult and sensitive question, because it goes to the heart of the experience of Christian faith—the encounter with Jesus. It is difficult to suggest in detail a successful unleashing of Jesus without falling into the fawning piety or offensive domestication against which GenX protests. After several years of talking with Xers and reflecting on pop culture, however, I conclude that Xers most commonly encounter a living, undomesticated Jesus through the following practices: serving others, displaying a commitment to community, building the scriptural reign of God. In short, the practice of discipleship. As religious institutions foster both an individual and a communal path of well-rounded discipleship, as laypeople share journeys of faith, political and social tasks, frequent prayer, and identification with the poor and marginalized, Jesus begins to be unleashed.

Indeed, Xers learn that Jesus was never in the institution's clutches in the first place, because Jesus as Jesus cannot be domesticated; only an idol can be chained. In fact, a god on a leash is an apt definition of idolatry (recall Soundgarden's little lamb!). It is the idolatry of a domesticated Jesus that Xers continually challenge institutions to check.

The Religious Dimension of Suffering

Anyone who wades even shallowly into GenX pop culture notices the myriad references to suffering. As I suggested in Chapter Six, suffering can be interpreted in religious terms, as suffering servanthood, prophecy, apocalypticism, and eschatology.

GenX pop culture suggests that it is not wise for religious institutions to dwell heavily on GenX's suffering, but neither should they ignore or dismiss it. Institutions learning from GenX pop culture can relate suffering to the sacred, connecting it to God's presence and mercy, not to God's absence and judgment. I have witnessed many churches that try to lead Xers from situations of suffering to wholeness, but that are in too much of a rush to wipe away the suffering. If the pop culture is any evidence of a lived theology, a generation's suffering will not be easily or quickly dismissed.

Institutions should avoid capitalizing on suffering, however; there is a real danger of exploitation here. At a GenX ministry conference, I was worshiping in a room filled with five hundred Xers. The words to one song were projected on a screen in front of us, encouraging God to break the hearts of those in attendance by awakening us to God's own "broken heart." On the one hand, this was a powerful theological message, asking God to grant us the grace to feel the pain that God "feels" when people allow sin and injustice to thrive in the world. On the other hand, I thought to myself, aren't there already enough broken hearts in this room? Wouldn't that be an interesting question to ask from the pulpit? Hasn't my generation dwelled enough on pain, insufficiency, and not measuring up, and isn't it time for some salvation and experience of resurrection? I was overcome with resentment at a worship service that would not hesitate to make Xers dwell on their own inadequacy, thinking it would make them more receptive to the message that would be preached from the pulpit. It struck me as opportunistic and even exploitative.

GenXers have witnessed enough suffering in their generation, in their own lives, and in the life of their culture. Many have lived the suffering that Churches or other religious institutions mention when they preach. Yet these institutions rarely consult Xers theologically or liturgically, often berate their popular culture, and ground little of their preaching in Xers' lived experience. Churches should view suffering—the fruit of the dysfunctions visited upon GenX—in a theological context, rather than amplifying or exploiting that pain. In Christian language, Xers have spent decades at the cross. They are ready for a taste of new life.

At the same time, appropriate preaching, reflection, and liturgy that try to give meaning to suffering speak to this generation. For example, I once attended a liberating Catholic ritual in which participants were asked to write down a cause of deep personal suffering on a slip of paper and to place the paper in a small fire, allowing the smoke and ashes to carry the suffering away to God. To ritualize suffering in this way, so that stories of suffering become part of God's story of mercy and redemption, can be an effective ministerial tool in making institutions accessible to Xers.

GenX challenges ministers to lift up the experience of the excluded, including women, but not to fetishize it. Tori Amos makes a claim on institutions by intimating that many women have scars from their involvement with the Church and need to be recognized as Christlike figures who suffer in postmodern society and at the hands of the Church. Until recently, many Churches have systematically excluded women from influencing liturgy, preaching, and governing. A great many Churches today still prevent women from performing these functions, a situation I find inconsistent with Christian Scripture, tradition, and contemporary experience.

To imagine women such as Saint Catherine of Siena, Tori Amos, and Madonna with the stigmata is to imagine Christa—Christ who suffers as a woman, a female Christ. These suffering women incarnate the suffering body of Christ in our midst. Madonna and Tori Amos challenge Christians to interpret the female body as the site where Christ suffers in the world today; Christ reemerges in the female form, because of the marginalized situation of many, if not most, women.

Institutions need to proceed with caution, however, in linking women to suffering. Institutions have used the image of the suffering servant to justify myriad forms of sexism. Now it is particularly important for institutions to emphasize that women are not just suffering servants but working, political servants. This is precisely why they do suffer, as the prophets and Jesus did.

Faith and Ambiguity

The experience of faith in profound ambiguity is perhaps the most theologically compelling theme of GenX's lived theology. A pervasive uncertainty makes orthodoxy, space, time, self, gender, and faith into ever more tentative categories for interpreting life. Perhaps the biggest challenge for institutions is to consider that GenX's ambiguity might be a gift from God and not absolutely sinful or discouraging news.

A Challenge to Orthodoxy

Xers' ambiguity about orthodoxy does not mean that institutions simply must embrace whatever they might consider heretical, even as they open a space for wider discernment about the boundaries of orthodoxy and encourage orthopraxis, right living, and searching. Instead, Xers' ambiguity about orthodoxy is an opportunity for institutions to reconsider ecumenism, a reconciliation between various Christian traditions.

Churches might, for example, celebrate the diversity of Christian beliefs and practice and the plural reality of Christian "orthodoxy." They could engage in ministerial bricolage, using several sorts of media and religious traditions when they perform ministerial tasks. For example, I once taught a church course on Jesus. Inspired by the presence of several Xers in the class, I had them read Christian Scriptures, watch Jesus in movies, listen for Jesus in music, and attend to writings about Jesus from Jewish perspectives. Friends of mine who are Protestant ministers use Gregorian chants in Presbyterian services, encourage Talmudlike (playful and even irreverent) commentary in Catholic Bible study groups, and celebrate communion across denominational lines.

Much of this is happening and should happen with artistic forms and media borrowed from popular culture. For art to be the medium of this ecumenism, institutions may have to be less attached to the environments of particular buildings and let religious experience happen in the unlikeliest of places, as well as in the institution. An institution that shows that it fears the outside world, particularly the popular culture, has forfeited its religious authority in Generation X's eyes. One Presbyterian church on the West Coast, in an effort to reach out to Xers, installed a church "outlet" in a thriving urban area. Xers (or anyone) can drop in for a snack, Internet access, or (why not?) even a free Bible or a chat with the minister on duty. Taking the institution itself beyond the institution's walls is critical.

Fragmented Selves

The theme of ambiguity calls attention to Xers' fragmented or unstable sense of self (even multiple "selves"), which demands new spiritual approaches. One implication of GenX pop culture is that the stability of once-and-for-all conversions may need to be reconsidered. Many Christians, particularly in evangelical traditions, mark the birth of their faith from a particular date, but given Xers' habits of hesitation and fractured selves, a onetime conversion may not be the sole way of conversion.

Although once-and-for-all conversion could be deemphasized, other opportunities open up. Religious institutions can reaffirm in preaching and practice that people make decisions for or against faith every day, in all of their beliefs and actions. Martin Luther and Tori Amos (an unlikely couple) remind Christians that "a Christian life is nothing else than a *daily baptism,* once begun and even continued" (Luther, 1959, p. 445, italics mine).

At the same time, there is an opportunity for a renewal of spirituality, spiritual growth, and spiritual direction. This reclamation of spirituality as a journey into faith is practical, individualized, and tied to tradition. It anchors Xers to communities and provides them with potential spiritual mentors. These communities can contribute to a continual reintegration of identity, however unstable it may be for Xers, in the context of a relationship with God.

For example, I have discovered that many campus ministers try to give Xers what I (and much of the Catholic tradition) would call "spiritual direction." That is, they attend to the life of the individual and explore ways for that individual to gain a deeper awareness of God and a deeper practice of spirituality. Although I am not aware that spiritual direction is set up especially for Xers at any churches, that would certainly be an idea worth trying. First, however, institutions and ministers would have to reacquaint themselves with the tradition of spiritual direction, spirituality, and Christian mysticism.

Ministers cannot ignore the crisis of self within the generation. Neither should they blow it out of proportion, though, viewing it as Xers' ultimate problem, as our heavily psychologistic culture is bound to do.

Dietrich Bonhoeffer offers helpful theological words on this matter. While he was imprisoned in Nazi Germany on suspicion of participating in a conspiracy against the Reich, Bonhoeffer confronted a deep dilemma about his own identity. He wrote, "I often wonder who I really am—the man who goes on squirming under these ghastly experiences in wretchedness that cries to heaven, or the man who scourges himself and pretends to others (and even to himself) that he is placid, cheerful, composed, and in control of himself, and allows people to admire him for it (i.e. *for playing the part—or is it not playing a part?)*" (1971, p. 162, italics mine). Bonhoeffer came to the spiritual conclusion that these questions should not haunt him. "In short, I know less than ever about myself, and I'm no longer attaching any importance to it. . . . There is something more at stake than self-knowledge" (p. 162). For Xer religiosity, too, there is "something more at stake" than finally determining the extent of our fragmentation, or what sort of society of selves each of us really is. In a poem entitled "Who Am I?" Bonhoeffer wrote:

> Who am I? This or the other?
> Am I one person today, and tomorrow another?
> Am I both at once? A hypocrite before others,
> and before myself a contemptible woebegone weakling?
> Or is something within me still like a beaten army,
> fleeing in disorder from victory already achieved?
> Who am I? They mock me, these lonely questions of mine.
> Whoever I am, thou knowest, O God, I am thine.
> (1971, p. 348)

Whenever institutions can encourage Xers in knowing that despite and within their crises of selfhood, they belong to God, they have rendered a positive, scriptural, and deeply needed service. How can institutions implement this insight? One GenX minister told me that he highlights Jesus' own crises about his identity. I engaged the problem of selfhood by encouraging GenX high school students with whom I was close to question, probe, and experiment in cyberspace, keeping in regular e-mail dialogue with me. I asked them to imagine a divine plumb line through their multiple e-mail identities. I sought to help them with this by providing an implicit "yes" to what I considered to be their primary question, as I highlighted in Chapter Seven: "Will you be there for me?"

○

Pop culture can be a resource for rethinking ministry and reaching Generation X, as it offers a fresh religious imagination. If religious institutions are to become more accessible to GenXers, then they will bear in mind the implications for ministry suggested by the theological themes of GenX pop culture. These themes and implications need not collide with tradition, as some institutions fear. Rather, they can collude with tradition to foster a life-giving dynamic between tradition and culture. As a result, both culture and institutions will teach and learn from each other, ministry will be pulled into the present, and Xers will be offered a hospitable place in institutions. It is the chief characteristic of GenX's theological imagination, its spiritual irreverence, to which I turn in the Conclusion of this book.

CONCLUSION

GIVING IRREVERENCE ITS DUE

THIS BOOK HAS TRAVELED the terrain of popular culture, exploring GenX's lived theology. I have evoked major themes of this theology through a theological interpretation of music video, cyberspace, and fashion. Taking examples directly from popular culture, I have sought to show how GenX culture is not a theological wasteland but instead is theologically compelling. Indeed, it is so compelling that this pop culture has implications for ministering to the generation.

A Journey Through Spiritual Irreverence

GenX's journey through spiritual irreverence has three movements. First, religion seems to be "lost" to us, because we do not practice religiousness like our elders. Second, religion seems to be "found" again when we interpret the religious character of GenX popular culture. Finally, the embrace of a renewed sense of tradition gives us the ground on which to practice our irreverence into the future.

Part One: Why Religion Still Matters

Part One of the book set Generation X, theology, and pop culture in their own contexts and in relation to each other. *Generation X* can be defined as a cohort of tens of millions, born from the early 1960s through the late 1970s, who share pop culture references that shape meaning in their lives. One of the identifying marks of Xers, then, is a deeply symbiotic relationship with popular culture. One common assumption about GenX that this book has thrown into doubt is that Xers are simply irreligious or generally indifferent toward spirituality. The popular culture of GenX alone, according to my theological interpretation, provides ample evidence to counter this assumption.

This theological framework is actually key to understanding GenX pop culture. Theology is "talk" about God, but it is not only talk. It arises from the practical human experience of God in the world, in culture. In addition, theology points the way to further practical experience of God in and through culture.

By definition, then, theology and culture always need each other. Theology draws its terms, questions, and basic material from the culture in which it finds itself, and culture's own questions, needs, desires, and depths of meaning are influenced by the theology (or theologies) that are both theorized and practiced in that particular culture. All culture therefore has a theological character, even as all theology has a strongly cultural character. (This explains why theologies can be so varied in their aims and assumptions across cultures; God is not divided, but our cultures and experiences are!)

I have further affirmed that because culture has a theological character, it can disclose the religious. That is, attention to culture can teach us something about God, faith, and religious practice. Just as the Scriptures and tradition attest that God can work in and through culture, so GenX pop culture can reveal a great deal about Xers' religious convictions.

I employed three different theological concepts to show how valuable it may be to use pop culture as an indicator of GenX's lived theology— and thus to interpret God's work amid Generation X. First, I invoked the concept of the signs of the times, noting that the content of pop culture is a sign of GenX's "times," a provocative barometer of GenX religious needs, desires, and practices.

Second, and related to this, I noted the concept of the sense of the faithful. In this regard, I suggested that GenX pop culture is one indication of what "faithful" Xers believe and how they are responding to Church teaching, preaching, and practices. This sense of the faithful, according to theologians, should influence what the Church does, as this sense is a source of revelation from God.

I found, however, that the sense of the faithful was not enough, because much of GenX culture, and many Xers themselves, might be considered "unfaithful." In response to this problem, I advanced my third idea—a suggestion that the Church attend to the sense of the unfaithful as well as the sense of the faithful. In my view, the sense of the unfaithful can and should influence religious institutions' practices. Just as some liberation theologians are looking to non-Christian peoples and sources for deeper revelations about Christ and Christianity, so it is possible for a sense of the unfaithful from GenX pop culture to make a real claim on religious institutions.

Because our culture increasingly simulates and imitates reality, I described both "virtual" and "real" forms of religiousness—or what I simply call "religiosity"—in pop culture. GenX pop culture offers "virtual" religiousness when it imitates or simulates "real" religiousness. For example, GenX has established virtual religious communities in cyberspace that mirror churches and synagogues in the "real" world. The primary value of understanding the difference between virtual and "real" religiousness is that the virtual can be a way to experiment with and criticize the "real." This occurs, for instance, when the benefits of religious cybercommunities (including frankness in faith discussions and access to on-line religious resources) are brought to bear on real religious communities.

In Part One, then, I looked at Generation X, popular culture, and theology all at once. I highlighted the need to use theology as a way of understanding Generation X's popular culture and therefore as a way to view GenX's religiousness.

Part Two: How Religion Still Matters

Part Two illustrated four primary theological themes in GenX popular culture: suspicion of institutions, experience, suffering, and ambiguity. Each chapter in Part Two cited examples of these themes from music video, cyberspace, and fashion. I chose these themes because they reflect GenX's lived theology. They also open further avenues for religious practice on the part of the generation.

The first and perhaps most common theological theme in GenX popular culture is an abiding suspicion of religious institutions. This suspicion manifests in severe criticisms of religious institutions, particularly the Catholic Church. GenX pop culture commonly exhibits this suspicion of institutions by reclaiming Jesus from the very institutions that minister in Jesus' name.

The sacred nature of experience constitutes the second theological theme. GenX pop culture celebrates lived experience in a religious context and shows a fascination with experience at the nexus of the human and divine, as well as at the intersection of the spiritual and sensual. GenXers share religious experience by flocking to cybercommunities of faith and by living their faith outside institutional walls in the rough-and-tumble of the world.

The third theological theme emphasizes the religious dimension of suffering. Popular culture is heavily invested in plumbing the myriad sufferings of Generation X, imaging them in religious context. Explicitly theological

images of suffering appear in pop culture's illustrations of suffering servanthood (in which one suffers for the sake of many), prophecy (in which
one calls out the sins of the many who cause suffering), and apocalypticism (in which one expects the radical arrival of a divine revelation to alle-
viate suffering).

Ambiguity is the fourth theological theme. The instability of many categories of GenX existence mark this theme, and all point to the ultimate
question of whether faithfulness can accommodate faithlessness. GenX
culture's theme of ambiguity highlights a hesitation to affirm religious orthodoxies, a newly slippery reading of Scripture in cyberspace, instabilities of
space and time, deep uncertainties about the self and gender, and the role
that faith (supposedly a certainty) plays amid so many ambiguities.

Part Three: Being Religious Now

In the final section of the book, Part Three, I underscored the importance
of virtual culture and religious tradition for understanding GenX as a generation practicing "religiosity." I suggested that Xers have this authentic
but imitation faith because the culture itself is so heavily invested in mimicking reality.

A central dynamic and challenge emerging for Generation X is that of
"bricolating" their own spirituality and carrying forward religious traditions. *Bricolage* means making do with the materials at hand to solve particular (in this case religious) problems and questions. This term describes
the way GenX pop culture brings together diverse religious symbols and
images, forever recombining and forming new spiritualities. GenX pop
culture does not respect the boundaries of tradition or religious dogma.

At the same time that such bricolating and reassembling become even
more widespread in GenX pop culture, Xers are challenged to renew their
own spiritualities and those of their religious traditions by giving the concept of tradition itself a fresh look. Tradition is not something Xers can
choose to embrace or reject. They already stand in various religious traditions. Indeed, those traditions have made possible the irreverent spirituality that Xers have today. Xers now have the opportunity to engage with
religious traditions and to use their irreverent and unique GenX insights
to carry forward their particular traditions. At the same time, traditions
make claims on Xers about their responsibility to the past, present, and
future as they work in their own religious communities.

Holding bricolage and tradition together is a unique task for GenX. It
is a challenge that a generation so steeped in irreverence—in revising,
dashing, and subverting expectations—is likely to meet well. This irrev-

erence gives GenX pop culture its most unique theological gift: a colorful theological imagination by which it experiments with, ironizes, and re-appropriates religious symbols and traditions, constructing its own brands of spirituality.

This theological imagination can be a tremendous font of challenges and inspiration for religious institutions; if they take GenX pop culture seriously, they can discover resources for refreshing their own ministries. By attending to the rich theological imagination of GenX pop culture, institutions have a ready-made spring from which to draw new minister-ial ideas. In this way, they can make their institutions more accessible to Xers. Thus the teaching and learning dynamic between Generation X and religious institutions may prove spiritually enriching for both Xers and institutions.

Irreverence as a Spiritual Gift

Over the course of this book, I have sought to illustrate four main claims in regard to Generation X, popular culture, and theology. First, a theo-logical interpretation of popular culture reveals a spirituality character-ized by irreverence on the part of Generation X. This irreverence is manifest in many ways, from music video's scandalous depictions of Jesus as Santa Claus or a tired old man, to the adoption of cyberspace as a place to explore spirituality, to the public meditation on suffering in gothic clothing. There are varying degrees of this irreverence among Xers, but essentially we tend to insert a large question mark after any religious idea, doctrine, or assumption that our elders have taken to be theologically cer-tain or that they approach with reverence.

Second, this lived theology can both teach religious institutions and learn from them. My entire method of interpretation reflects this assump-tion; I have used theological resources, such as Scripture and tradition (including the work of theologians), to interpret pop culture events, such as particular fashions, uses of cyberspace, and scenes in music video. For example, I use the religious scholarship of Eliade to interpret pierced navels, I refer back to Saint Bernard of Clairvaux when I examine sensual spirituality, and I invoke an ancient Christian fish symbol as an interpre-tive key to a moment in a music video. This book has shown how theol-ogy can shed light on interpreting popular culture, even as popular culture imagines new ways of illustrating, upending, and carrying forward theo-logical themes.

Starting from my assumption about how culture and institutions have much to teach each other, I have drawn very different conclusions about popular culture compared with many other cultural critics. Frequently, for example, those in religious institutions—or those who otherwise ignore the theological imagination of popular culture—deride popular culture as being full of sin and devoid of grace. In contrast, I believe that popular culture should be taken seriously from a religious perspective. For this reason, I have brought theological tools to bear on interpretations of culture. My purpose was to bear witness to a lived generational theology.

Third, Generation X is religious, in its own characteristic "religiosity." Because of this religiosity, it is possible to divine a theology by, for, and about Generation X. Regarding the generation's faith seriously affords an opportunity to take the religious pulse of a cohort steeped in popular culture, as well as to inspire further religious practice on the part of Generation X. This approach to GenX's pop culture, then, is valid and important; it illuminates practices, claims, and implications for the lived religiousness of both Generation X and institutions.

All of this brings me to the book's fourth and final claim. Religious institutions, our elders, or other skeptics should not fear irreverence and popular culture. Paradoxically, interpreting pop culture theologically— especially with an eye to its irreverence—highlights the depth of Generation X's religious practice. The more popular culture is explored, and the more irreverence is viewed as a legitimate mode of religiosity (in all its illegitimacy), the more Generation X will be shown as having a real religious contribution to make. GenX can make great strides not only toward fostering its own spirituality but also toward reinvigorating religious institutions and challenging the faith of older generations.

AFTERWORD

FOR SUCH A PRAGMATIC GENERATION as ours, it is not adequate for a book of theology to claim that it is "right" in any final sense. It must serve to provoke, challenge, poke, and stimulate readers along a religious journey, toward a deeper spiritual encounter. Although it may seem like a paradox to talk about a responsible irreverence in one's spirituality, I think that responsibility must accompany irreverence. If we let go of the notion of responsibility, we risk overreverencing irreverence. In my view, the last thing our generation should do is move from a criticism of the false gods of our religious forebears into baptizing our own false gods in the name of irreverence. This is why I stressed tradition in Chapter Eight. For a GenX lived theology to be sustainable in the future, an encounter with tradition is essential.

As I intimate in the Dedication of this book, pious reverence and outright laughter—the cackles and chortles of irreverence—can both be religious responses. Genesis 17:17 and 2 Samuel 9:6 should always be read together: "He fell on his face and did reverence" and "He fell on his face and laughed." Perhaps we are unsettled by the references to falling on one's face—a humiliating and reverent position. But even when Xers have their heads down, it is never quite clear whether they are praying or laughing. We bring to light what others try to mask—that faith is often a matter of being caught between belief and unbelief (Mark 9:24).

When I first considered writing this book almost three years ago, I imagined it as what I bombastically termed "a call to theological awareness" on the part of the generation. Now I think we do not so much need the call to awareness as we need clarification. The generation is already theological by virtue of its popular culture. Theo-logic, God-talk, is already loose in the culture. Engaging in pop culture theology is GenX's irreverent way of emerging into spiritual maturity.

As our generation lacks a theme, this irreverent pop culture religiosity may be our one big movement, which—for a generation often described as irreligious—is the final irony I will mention in this book. This irreverence might be the lasting heritage from the first decades of our generation.

APPENDIX: NOTES ON METHOD

METHODS OF INTERPRETING POPULAR CULTURE theologically are still in flux. Thus, it is important that I explain the goals as well as the methods of my interpretation.

Playful Irreverence

My goal has been to articulate, where possible, a redemptive theological reclamation of GenX popular culture. In other words, I have tried to offer an interpretation that listens for religious intonations and bounces theological concepts off the culture. The point of my interpretation is to make culture speak to the task of living religiously.

It should be noted that my initial question is not "What did the author or designer *intend?*" Neither is it "What is the *real* meaning of pop culture?" Nor even "How did the audience interpret this?" I have not intended to give the final meaning or the authoritative reading of GenX pop culture. I have offered an interpretation, which springs from my autobiography, theological training, educational work, spirituality, and religious history. I have brought all of this, the "text" of my own life, to the pop culture "texts"—to music video, cyberspace, and fashion.

I do not think an adequate or meaningful interpretation of pop culture requires an excavation of the author's intention, "knowing the authors better than they know themselves." I advocate distinguishing the meanings of a pop culture event from the intention of its "authors," whether artists, designers, or corporate executives. I want to open up the meaning of pop culture to playfulness, so that I can plumb, inquire, interrogate, associate, unleash, and generate play. I wish to look for traces of theological residue on the surfaces of these images. I attempt to interpret pop culture in light of theology and the situation of Generation X. This means that my approach is experimental, even transgressive, and draws from the array of theological resources at my disposal.

Although I have frequently referred to artists as the "authors" of music video, I am aware that the "production" of music video—the process by which it is made—is complex (see Goodwin, 1992). For me, however, this authorship convention is a helpful shorthand, given my primary interest in the finished product. I do not discount the importance of interpretations that account for the process of "authorship" or "production." This is where the uses of the particular interpretations are paramount. I am not trying primarily to untangle the politics of pop culture but rather to encounter the images that are present in a theological context. I certainly think that others could take a different, perhaps even contrary, approach.

This method of interpretation is not a form of relativism, as if I were claiming that pop culture means whatever I want it to mean. Why not? Because I must confront the "text" itself, the particular event of pop culture in front of me. I do not get to make up what happens in a video, the different pieces of fashion, or the way cyberspace functions. Description, though, is always interpretation. And interpretation always derives from a particular perspective. It always comes from someone, somewhere, in a specific time and place and with a particular history. Further protecting my interpretations from relativism are the claims I have built into this study about the *sensus infidelium*. If, upon reflection, a reader finds my interpretation inadequate for the generation (in other words, if it does not resonate, deepen spirituality, offer provocative intellectual and theological questions, make incisive theological cuts), if this is the *sensus* of the *infidelium*, then to whatever extent my interpretation is inadequate, I invite the reader to interpret pop culture along with me. That I have had the more objective goal of spiritual sustenance in mind has kept my interpretive approach away from the relativism of letting a thousand flowers bloom.

I am not, of course, the first person in Christian tradition to take on this style of playful, even irreverent interpretation. Although such theological giants as the early church fathers and Thomas Aquinas were not "postmodern," they were frequently open to various levels of meaning in a text, almost none of which had to do with the text's original context or authorial intention (or even its audience's reception). What the text (or, in our case, pop culture event) means theologically in each new moment or day may change or evolve; there may be a surplus of that meaning as it meets each new situation in which we find ourselves.

One recent, rough approximation of my interpretation strategy is *Pop-Up Video,* a show on cable music station VH-1. On this show, as popular music videos play, bubbles regularly pop up with text that comments on the video. Each bubble's content is often unconnected to previous bubbles, focusing on particular video scenes and images. The bubbles take their interpretive clues from hints in the video that the writers arrived at "intertextually." For instance, in a video by the Irish pop group the Cranberries, several bubbles address the meaning of *cranberries* in Irish culinary history and play on the word *berry*. Bubbles that appear during certain scenes in the video refer viewers to scenes in other videos; this does not occur textually but visually, as the bubbles play other videos on top of the video being showcased. Some of the interpretations are straightforward, whereas others are irreverent or ludicrous. I do not know which criteria this show's writers use for their interpretation, but below I make mine explicit.

Commitments

Theologian Paul Tillich (1959, p. 60) asks, "What is the relationship to the ultimate which is symbolized in these [cultural] symbols?" His question prompts a reflection on the method used to interpret culture theologically.

The theological observer of popular culture is struck by how little immediately self-evident religious meaning it has. This is so not only because students of popular culture would identify a wide variety of different symbols as religious but also because even those who would agree on a general catalogue of religious symbols and themes might seriously disagree on what they mean. Thus, it becomes necessary to interpret, not simply to observe.

The method I suggest is based on several commitments that I consider important to a theological interpretation of GenX popular culture. First, my method is ecumenical, employing insights from various religious traditions (even as it reflects my own Catholic standpoint). Second, I have attempted to incorporate interpretational strategies that have been identified as both modern and postmodern. I feel that this is an appropriate way to examine our culture (popular and otherwise), which in my view has not yet decided whether this is a modern or postmodern age. Third, my method is an opening framework, and to this end it is rather provisional; I do not intend it as the final word on method, and I expect that it will be revised as it enters into critical discussion with others. I understand this method more as a set of questions to ask rather than as a blueprint to follow in lockstep when interpreting popular culture theologically. Fourth, I have not used each element of this method in every form of popular culture that I interpret. To be comprehensive, I include the whole list here, but the contrast between the list's fullness and the way I have applied it makes my fifth point necessary: this method stands in judgment of my own work.

Stages of Inquiry

My method—more rigorously stated here than practiced throughout the book—is divided into three stages. The first stage concerns preliminary methodological questions (Who are the "players"?). The second stage involves ways of encountering a particular form or event in popular culture (What is being "played"?). Finally, the third stage offers a way of assessing "authentic" interpretations (Will this "play" endure?). In my discussion of each stage, I include typical questions that I have asked of pop culture.

Stage One: Who Are the "Players"?

There are two primary players in the performance of my interpretation. I will focus on these players—the text and myself—in the form of two problems: What precisely is the pop culture "text" to be interpreted? What do I bring to the text?

WHAT IS THE "TEXT" THAT I HAVE CONSIDERED IN MY INTERPRETATION? By *text* I mean any popular culture "event," from a dance to a bodily costume to a sporting event to a music video. I have considered three types of "texts" in this book. In music video, the "text" includes most fundamentally images and music, including lyrics. In cyberspace, the "text" includes the medium of cyberspace, as well as many phenomena of virtual communication, including e-mail and sites in cyberspace. When it comes to costuming and bodily adornment, the "text" includes many forms of "fashion," including clothing and hairstyles. The identification of the text is central to method, because it stands apart from the interpreter and by its very presence already sets some boundaries of interpretation.

WHAT DO I BRING TO THE TEXT? Included in this category are my own presuppositions and prejudices.

The play between these two issues—what text is to be considered and what the viewer brings to the text—is the overarching dynamic of interpretation. Play is a "to-and-fro movement that is not tied to any goal that would bring it to an end" (Gadamer, 1994, p. 103). Play is not something we enact; it is something in which we find ourselves, or rather lose ourselves, when we interpret. "All playing is a being-played," writes Gadamer (p. 106).

Stage Two: What Is Being "Played" Religiously?

To consider what is being "played" interpretively, it is necessary to highlight what the pop culture text "says" theologically, which includes an enumeration of problems in "hearing" the religious character of the text. This enumeration will itself contain a brief excursus into theological warrants for interpreting the text as playfully as I do.

As Gadamer suggests, "The text . . . if it is to be understood properly—i.e., according to the claim it makes—must be understood at every moment, in every concrete situation, in a new and different way. *Understanding here is always application*" (1994, p. 309, italics mine). In regard to this book, I take the truth of Gadamer's observation to mean that an interpretation is useful if it produces further religious meaning (including religious practice).

As I have suggested, the understanding and application divined from a popular culture "event" are not necessarily fixed for eternity. To appropriate the words of Paul Ricoeur, each religious symbol disclosed in a popular culture event may have many interpretations, a "surplus of meaning." As Ricoeur writes, "Symbols give rise to an endless exegesis" (1976, p. 57). In other words, the interpretation of a text (in our case, popular culture) may exceed the bounds of the form or manner in which the text was produced (such as the original time, place, authorship, audience, and so forth). Unlike Ricoeur, I am not certain that my interpretation of the pop culture event is "inherent" in the text; some slippage may occur and the interpretation may still be counted as a legitimate "understanding" and "application." In Stage Three, I try to build guardrails against subjectivism in theologically interpreting popular culture.

When one distills a surplus of meaning from a pop culture event and applies that interpretation to religious life, one may employ numerous concrete strategies. Several such strategies have been integral to my own method. I have listed them below in the form of suggestive questions with occasional discussion.

- What religious images or references are explicitly or implicitly present?

- Is a "negation" of religion present, such as in the form of supposed heresy, profanity, or obscenity? Might this be an indication of the presence of religious meaning?

- Can the pop culture event be understood when interpreted through other sacred "media," such as books or art?

○ Does the pop culture event have different "senses"? In the early centuries of the Christian Church, some theologians interpreted different "senses" of Scripture, only one of them literal. As Manlio Simonetti argues in a discussion of scriptural interpretation in the second through fifth centuries (1994, p. 122, italics mine), "Scriptural passages used for doctrinal ends were normally *taken out of their original context and considered in isolation,* producing results sometimes quite foreign to the sense which they would have had if interpreted within their proper context." (Compare this to some of my own interpretations in this book.)

Four "senses" that guided interpretation of Scripture were common from at least the fifth century through the Middle Ages. These senses included the *literal* (biblical facts), *allegorical* (illustrations of spirituality or doctrine), *moral* (how one should live), and *anagogical* (references to the end of times). I am not suggesting a reproduction of these categories but rather that we be inspired today by the early Church's surprising openness to the freedom of interpretation. This freedom, it should be remembered, was not for the sake of radical subjectivity but (in the words of Vatican II) "for the sake of our salvation."

In the Jewish tradition, the rich heritage of rabbinic midrash illustrates the playful character of interpretation that has inspired my own work. As Terry Veling observes, the "Talmud speaks of the great delight God takes in the interpretive play of the rabbis" (1996, p. 149). The rabbis were not interpreting for their own pleasure, of course, but for the spiritual edification of their readers, as I have tried to do.

According to one passage in the Talmud, "It was taught in the School of Rabbi Yishmael: 'Behold, My word is like fire—declares the Lord—and like a hammer that shatters rock (Jeremiah 23:29). Just as this hammer produces many sparks [when it strikes the rock], so a single verse has several meanings'" (in Veling, 1996, p. 150). In a comment relevant to my undertaking, Burton Visotzky remarks of the Talmudic tradition, "No longer can authority be construed 'as it is written'; a new source of religious authority is now found in the words '*Rabbi X [!] says*'" (1991, p. 44, italics mine). Generation X, then, can be seen as neorabbinic, interpreting God in popular culture.

Visotzky names another great inspiration for my interpretations—the great rabbinic playfulness in the forms of parables, allegories, anachronism, and puns (pp. 225–240). Biblical scholar Stephen Moore reclaims puns and jokes in his biblical interpretations. He rightly laments the "exclusion of noninferential associations from the Western intellectual tradition—the homonym, homophone, or garden-variety pun. This exclusion can be traced back to such contingencies as Aristotle's strictures against homonyms . . . and Plato's exclusion of poets from his ideal state" (1992, p. 68). Moore wants to resurrect playful interpretation, noting that as "the trope of our age," the pun runs rampant across the surfaces of popular culture. "Its irruption in academic discourse represents a fusion of popular and elite cultural forms" (p. 41). Indeed, puns threaten the distinction between popular and elite cultural forms. In my own work, I have tried to use puns to hammer out new meaning.

It is helpful to remember that what we are after in our theological interpretation of popular culture is not interpretive play for the sake of play, but application—further religious understanding. Gregory Ulmer made a useful point about Jacques Derrida's very playful writing, which Ulmer finds "productive in its own terms of knowledge and insight. . . . It is one thing to engage in wordplay, but another thing to sustain it and extend it into an epistemology" (1985, pp. xi–xii).

Still, questions about the religious character of the text are not exhausted. Further questions include the following:

○ How does the event relate to other events within popular culture?

○ How is the event popularly "used"? Where is the clothing worn? How is the video watched? What happens to a person using cybertechnology?

○ How are race and gender "produced" or shaped by the event?

○ Where might the event or its religious indications be located in the history of religious ideas?

○ How might different religious traditions interpret this event?

○ What theological associations does this event have with other popular culture events that bear some proximity to this one? That is, does the event confirm a theological movement already thought to be at work in the culture?

○ From what traditions do the explicit or implicit religious references derive? How does their use in the event create tension with their traditional meanings?

○ How does the event reflect concrete practices commonly associated with or derived from religious "values"? In what way does it affirm or critique those practices?

○ Who is included in and excluded from participating in this event?

I have applied these questions to all aspects of GenX culture. Some of my questions, however, are germane only to particular forms of popular culture. I will summarize them here.

Music Video. What is the interrelationship between the music, the words heard, the "official" lyrics, and the visual images? How do these relate to the performance of the same piece in other media, for example live or on record? What role do titles, epigrams (preludes), or epitaphs (postscripts) play in illuminating the video's meaning? How does the staging of the video, for instance its framing or lighting, influence its meaning? How does this video relate to other videos by the same artist? How does this video compare with similar videos or similar musical or film styles? What is the video's "narrative," and what is the video's relation to the musical narrative? Is there any invocation of "classical" religious images; if so, how are they used? Where are the gaps, inconsistencies, and indeterminacies in all of the above? (For a more technical discussion of some problems in interpreting music video theologically, see Beaudoin, 1997b.)

Fashion. What are the variations in how the event is worn or displayed? How do various social groups appropriate the fashion, and does this differ according to gender or race? What relationship does the fashion have to the body? How does it relate to other fashion events, especially in its genre? Did the fashion event originate from "above" or "below," from the streets or the fashion industry? How does it "work" in relation to a larger "outfit" or assembly of fashion accessories? What does it conceal and reveal?

Cyberspace. What is the medium's relation to the message? How ephemeral is the event or phenomenon under study? Is the theological issue raised in cyberspace momentary or lasting? That is, how intimately related is it to the technology that supports the event? (For further discussion on cyberspace, GenX, and religion, see Beaudoin, 1997a.)

Stage Three: Will This "Play" Endure?

If all theological interpretations of popular culture were equally valid, none at all would be convincing, and we would be lost in a swirl of relativism. Therefore, it is necessary to sketch criteria to serve as an index of more or less "authentic" interpretations. I offer the following criteria in the same provisional tone with which I offer this entire book. I propose that an authentic interpretation address the following questions:

○ Did the interpreter account for all phenomena in the event, or as many as possible?

○ Is the interpretation internally coherent and consistent?

○ Is the interpretation appropriate for the religious tradition of the community to which the interpreter is responsible?

○ Is the interpretation life-giving? That is, does it tend to deepen the religious experience? Is the interpretation adequate to the lived experience of those for whom the interpretation is given?

○ Has the interpretation accounted for the sense of the unfaithful (the *sensus infidelium*)?

○ Over time, do others find it a useful starting place for further theological interpretations of popular culture?

———— ○ ————

It could be said that I have "performed" an interpretation for the readers of this book along the guidelines sketched above. According to these criteria (see also my discussion of a proposed *sensus infidelium* in Chapter Two), my own theological interpretations of pop culture can be evaluated.

REFERENCES

Abbott, W. M. (ed.). *Documents of Vatican II.* (J. Gallagher, trans.). New York: America Press, 1966.

Amos, T. "Crucify." *Little Earthquakes.* Atlantic, 1991. Compact disc.

Barna, G. *Baby Busters: The Disillusioned Generation.* Chicago: Northfield, 1994.

Baudrillard, J. *Simulations.* (P. Foss, P. Patton, and P. Beitchman, trans.). New York: Semiotext[e], 1983.

Baudrillard, J. *America.* (C. Turner, trans.). London: Verso, 1988.

Beaudoin, T. "Generation X and the Cyberspatialization of Religion." Paper presented at the annual conference of the Society for the Scientific Study of Religion, San Diego, Nov. 1997a.

Beaudoin, T. "Looking for a Savior: Jesus and Music Video." Paper presented at the annual conference of the American Academy of Religion, San Francisco, Nov. 1997b.

Benedictine Monks of Santo Domingo de Silos. *Chant.* Angel, 1994. Compact disc.

Bergeron, K. "The Virtual Sacred." *New Republic,* 1995, *212*(9), 29–34.

Bernard of Clairvaux. *Bernard of Clairvaux: Selected Writings.* (G. R. Evans, trans.). Mahwah, N.J.: Paulist Press, 1987.

Bonhoeffer, D. *Letters and Papers from Prison.* Old Tappan, N.J.: Macmillan, 1971.

Bonhoeffer, D. *The Cost of Discipleship.* New York: Touchstone, 1995.

Carrasco, R. "A Twenty-First-Century Identity Crisis." *Sojourners,* Nov. 1994, 16.

Catechism of the Catholic Church. Liguori, Mo.: Liguori Publications, 1994.

Cohen, M. L. *The Twentysomething American Dream: A Cross-Country Quest for a Generation.* New York: Dutton, 1993.

Cooke, B. *Sacraments and Sacramentality.* Mystic, Conn.: Twenty-Third Publications, 1983.

Coupland, D. *Generation X: Tales for an Accelerated Culture.* New York: St. Martin's Press, 1991.

Coupland, D. *Shampoo Planet.* New York: Pocket Books, 1992.

Coupland, D. *Microserfs.* New York: HarperCollins, 1995.

Cox, H. *The Feast of Fools: A Theological Essay on Festivity and Fantasy.* New York: HarperCollins, 1969.

Cox, H. *Fire from Heaven: The Rise of Pentecostal Spirituality and the Reshaping of Religion in the Twenty-First Century.* Reading, Mass.: Addison-Wesley, 1995.

Crossan, J. D. *Jesus: A Revolutionary Biography.* New York: HarperCollins, 1994.

Daly, S., and Wice, N. *alt.culture: An A-to-Z Guide to the '90s (Underground, Online, and Over-the-Counter).* New York: HarperCollins, 1995.

Dostoyevsky, F. *The Brothers Karamazov.* (D. McDuff, trans.). New York: Penguin, 1993.

Dulles, A. *Models of Revelation.* Garden City, N.Y.: Doubleday, 1983.

Dunn, W. *The Baby Bust: A Generation Comes of Age.* Ithaca, N.Y.: American Demographics Books, 1993.

Eliade, M. *The Sacred and the Profane: The Nature of Religion.* Orlando, Fla.: Harcourt Brace, 1987.

Eliade, M. *Patterns in Comparative Religion.* Lincoln: University of Nebraska Press, 1996.

Finkelstein, J. *The Fashioned Self.* Philadelphia: Temple University Press, 1991.

Fiorenza, F. S. "The Crisis of Hermeneutics and Christian Theology." In S. G. Davaney (ed.), *Theology at the End of Modernity.* Philadelphia: Trinity, 1991.

Fitzmyer, J. *Romans: A New Translation with Introduction and Commentary.* Garden City, N.Y.: Doubleday, 1993.

Frend, W.H.C. *The Early Church.* Minneapolis: Augsburg Fortress, 1994.

Frith, S. *Performing Rites: On the Value of Popular Music.* Cambridge, Mass.: Harvard University Press, 1996a.

Frith, S. "Popular Culture." In M. Payne (ed.), *A Dictionary of Cultural and Critical Theory.* Cambridge, Mass.: Blackwell, 1996b.

Gadamer, H.-G. *Truth and Method.* New York: Continuum, 1994.

Gilkey, L. *Society and the Sacred.* New York: Crossroad, 1981.

Goodwin, A. *Dancing in the Distraction Factory: Music Television and Popular Culture.* Minneapolis: University of Minnesota Press, 1992.

Gordon, B. "American Denim: Blue Jeans and Their Multiple Layers of Meaning." In P. Cunningham and S. Voso Lab (eds.), *Dress and Popular Culture.* Bowling Green, Ohio: Bowling Green State University Popular Press, 1991.

Greeley, A. "Like a Catholic: Madonna's Challenge to Her Church." *America,* 1989, *160*(18), 447–449.

Groome, T. *Sharing Faith: A Comprehensive Approach to Religious Education and Pastoral Ministry: The Way of Shared Praxis.* New York: HarperCollins, 1991.

Gross, D. M., and Scott, S. "Proceeding with Caution." *Time,* July 16, 1990, 56.

Gutierrez, G. *A Theology of Liberation.* Maryknoll, N.Y.: Orbis Books, 1988.

Haight, R. "The Impact of Jesus Research on Christology." *Louvain Studies,* 1996, *21,* 216–228.

Helmer, S. "A Generation's Faith." *Sojourners,* Nov. 1994, 16.

Hervieu-Leger, D. "Present-Day Emotional Renewals: The End of Secularization or the End of Religion?" In W. H. Swatos (ed.), *A Future for Religion? New Paradigms for Social Analysis.* Thousand Oaks, Calif.: Sage, 1993.

Hoffer, E. *The True Believer.* New York: HarperCollins, 1951.

Holtz, G. *Welcome to the Jungle.* New York: St. Martin's Press, 1995.

Howe, N., and Strauss, B. *Thirteenth Gen: Abort, Retry, Ignore, Fail?* New York: Vintage Books, 1993.

Jameson, F. *Postmodernism, or the Cultural Logic of Late Capitalism.* Durham, N.C.: Duke University Press, 1995.

Jantzen, G. *Power, Gender, and Christian Mysticism.* New York: Cambridge University Press, 1995.

Kierkegaard, S. *The Concept of Irony, with Continual Reference to Socrates.* (H. Hong and E. Hong, trans.). Princeton, N.J.: Princeton University Press, 1989.

Kinney, J. "Net Worth? Religion, Cyberspace, and the Future." *Futures,* 1995, *27*(7), 763–776.

Küng, H. *Does God Exist? An Answer for Today.* New York: Vintage, 1981.

Lipsky, D., and Abrams, A. *Late Bloomers: Coming of Age in Today's America—the Right Place at the Wrong Time.* New York: Times Books, 1994.

Loeb, P. R. *Generation at the Crossroads.* New Brunswick, N.J.: Rutgers University Press, 1994.

Ludwig, R. *Reconstructing Catholicism: For a New Generation.* New York: Crossroad, 1995.

Lundbom, J. "Jeremiah." In D. N. Freedman (ed.), *The Anchor Bible Dictionary, 3.* Garden City, N.Y.: Doubleday, 1992.

Luther, M. "The Large Catechism." In T. Tappert (ed.), *The Book of Concord.* Minneapolis: Augsburg Fortress, 1959.

MacIntyre, A. *Whose Justice? Which Rationality?* Notre Dame, Ind.: University of Notre Dame Press, 1988.

MacKinnon, R. C. "Searching for the Leviathan in Usenet." In S. G. Jones (ed.), *Cybersociety.* Thousand Oaks, Calif.: Sage, 1995.

Madonna. "Like a Prayer." *Like a Prayer.* Sire, 1989. Compact disc.

Mahedy, W., and Bernardi, J. *A Generation Alone: Xers Making a Place in the World.* Downers Grove, Ill.: InterVarsity Press, 1994.

McDannell, C. *Material Christianity: Religion and Popular Culture in America.* New Haven, Conn.: Yale University Press, 1995.

Merton, T. *The Ascent to Truth*. New York: Harcourt Brace, 1981.

Metz, J. B., and Moltmann, J. *Faith and the Future: Essays on Theology, Solidarity, and Modernity*. Maryknoll, N.Y.: Orbis Books, 1995.

Moore, S. D. *Mark and Luke in Poststructuralist Perspectives: Jesus Begins to Write*. New Haven, Conn.: Yale University Press, 1992.

Mouw, R. *Consulting the Faithful: What Christian Intellectuals Can Learn from Popular Religion*. Grand Rapids, Mich.: Eerdmans, 1994.

Nelson, R., and Cowan, J. *Revolution X: A Survival Guide for Our Generation*. New York: Penguin, 1994.

Newman, J. *On Consulting the Faithful in Matters of Doctrine*. Kansas City, Mo.: Sheed and Ward, 1961.

Newman, J. *Apologia Pro Vita Sua*. New York: Image, 1989.

Nietzsche, F. *The Will to Power*. (W. Kaufmann, trans.). New York: Vintage, 1968.

Nirvana. "Heart-Shaped Box." *In Utero*. Geffen, 1993. Compact disc.

Osborne, J. "One of Us." *Relish*. Mercury, 1995.

Otto, R. *The Idea of the Holy*. New York: Oxford University Press, 1969.

Paglia, C. *Sexual Personae: Art and Decadence from Nefertiti to Emily Dickinson*. New York: Vintage Books, 1991.

Pardun, C., and McKee, K. "Strange Bedfellows: Symbols of Religion and Sexuality on MTV." *Youth and Society*, 1995, 26(4), 438–449.

Pearl Jam. "Jeremy." *Ten*. Epic, 1991. Compact disc.

Pelikan, J. *The Vindication of Tradition*. New Haven, Conn.: Yale University Press, 1984.

Pieris, A. *An Asian Theology of Liberation*. Maryknoll, N.Y.: Orbis Books, 1988.

Porush, D. "Hacking the Brainstem: Postmodern Metaphysics and Stephenson's *Snow Crash*." In R. Markley (ed.), *Virtual Realities and Their Discontents*. Baltimore: Johns Hopkins University Press, 1996.

Rahner, K. *Belief Today*. Kansas City, Mo.: Sheed and Ward, 1967.

R.E.M. "Losing My Religion." *Out of Time*. Warner, 1991. Compact disc.

Rettenmund, M. *Totally Awesome 80s*. New York: St. Martin's Press, 1996.

Ricoeur, P. *Interpretation Theory: Discourse and the Surplus of Meaning*. Fort Worth, Tex.: Texas Christian University Press, 1976.

Roberts, P. Letter to the Editor. *Wired*, 1996, 4(12), 30.

Roe, K., and Löfgren, M. "Music Video Use and Educational Achievement." *Popular Music*, 1988, 7(3), 303–314.

Roof, W. C. *A Generation of Seekers: The Spiritual Journeys of the Baby Boom Generation*. New York: HarperCollins, 1993.

Ross, A. "Tribalism in Effect." In S. Benstock and S. Ferriss (eds.), *On Fashion*. New Brunswick, N.J.: Rutgers University Press, 1994.

Rubinstein, R. "Color, Circumcision, Tattoos, and Scars." In M. Solomon (ed.), *The Psychology of Fashion*. San Francisco: New Lexington Press, 1985.

Rushkoff, D. "Introduction: Us, by Us." In D. Rushkoff (ed.), *The GenX Reader.* New York: Ballantine, 1994a.

Rushkoff, D. "Media: It's the Real Thing." *New Perspectives Quarterly,* 1994b, *11*(3), 4–15.

Rushkoff, D. *Media Virus: Hidden Agendas in Popular Culture.* New York: Ballantine, 1996.

Saunders, M. "Creatures of the Web." *Boston Globe Magazine,* June 2, 1996, 16–17, 31, 34–41.

Schleiermacher, F. *On Religion: Speeches to Its Cultured Despisers.* (R. Crouter, trans.). Cambridge, England: Cambridge University Press, 1996.

Schonfield, H. *The Passover Plot: New Light on the History of Jesus.* New York: Geis, 1966.

Schüssler Fiorenza, E. *Bread Not Stone: The Challenge of Feminist Biblical Interpretation.* Boston: Beacon Press, 1984.

Simonetti, M. *Biblical Interpretation in the Early Church.* Edinburgh, Scotland: T&T Clark, 1994.

Sobrino, J. *Jesus in Latin America.* Maryknoll, N.Y.: Orbis Books, 1988.

Sobrino, J. *Jesus the Liberator: A Historical-Theological Reading of Jesus of Nazareth.* Maryknoll, N.Y.: Orbis Books, 1993.

Soundgarden. "Black Hole Sun." *Superunknown.* A&M Records, 1994. Compact disc.

Sun, S., and Lull, J. "The Adolescent Audience for Music Videos and Why They Watch." *Journal of Communication,* 1986, *36*(1), 115–125.

Taylor, M. C. *Erring: A Postmodern A/theology.* Chicago: University of Chicago Press, 1984.

Taylor, M. C. *Nots.* Chicago: University of Chicago Press, 1993. Quoting Filippo Marinetti, "The Founding Manifesto of Futurism," *Selected Writings* (ed. R. W. Flint and Arthur A. Coppotelli), New York: Farrar, Strauss, and Giroux, 1972: 41–42.

Taylor, M. C., and Saarinen, E. *Imagologies: Media Philosophy.* New York: Routledge, 1994.

Teresa of Avila. *The Life of Saint Teresa of Avila, by Herself.* New York: Penguin, 1957.

Tillich, P. *Theology of Culture.* New York: Oxford University Press, 1959.

Tracy, D. *Blessed Rage for Order: The New Pluralism in Theology.* New York: Seabury, 1978.

Tracy, D. *The Analogical Imagination: Christian Theology and the Culture of Pluralism.* New York: Crossroad, 1991.

Tracy, D. "Theology and the Many Faces of Postmodernity." *Theology Today,* 1994, *51*(1), 104–114.

Trinidad, J. C. "A Generation's Faith." *Sojourners,* Nov. 1994, 17.

Turkle, S. *Life on the Screen: Identity in the Age of the Internet.* New York: Simon & Schuster, 1995.

Ulmer, G. *Applied Grammatology: Post(e)-Pedagogy from Jacques Derrida to Joseph Beuys.* Baltimore: Johns Hopkins University Press, 1985.

Underhill, E. *Mysticism.* Garden City, N.Y.: Doubleday, 1990. Quoting Teresa of Avila, *The Interior Castle*: translated from the autograph of St. Teresa by the Benedictines of Stanbrook Abbey. London, 1912.

Veling, T. *Living in the Margins: Intentional Communities and the Art of Interpretation.* New York: Crossroad, 1996.

Visotzky, B. *Reading the Book.* New York: Anchor Books, 1991.

Warnke, G. *Justice and Interpretation.* Cambridge, Mass.: MIT Press, 1993.

INDEX

A

Abrams, A., 97

Absence, theme of, 10

Acts: 2:23, 98; 4:28, 98; 14:14, 132

Alienation, and suffering, 100

alt.culture, 78, 117

Ambiguity: in cyberspace, 134–138; faith and, 129–139, 140–142, 171–174; in fashion, 127–128, 131–134; of gender, 138–139; Generation X theme of, 42, 121–142, 178; in hypertext Scripture, 125–127; of identity, 131–139; and ministry, 171–174; in music videos, 129–131; of orthodoxy and experimentation, 122–127, 172; of space, 57, 127; of time, 127–129

Amos, T., 45, 52–53, 71, 92, 106–108, 118, 149, 169, 171, 173. *See also* "Crucify"

Androgyny, 138–139

Apocalypticism, 42, 112–117; eschatology and, 114–117; and 1980s, 8–9; suffering prophethood and, 112–114

Aristotle, 189

Armstrong, N., 3

Asian Christian theology, 34

B

Baby boomers: meaning of life questions and, 140; mysticism and, 26; opposition to idealism of, 10–11; personal experience and, 74; popular culture in ministries of, 160; self-reliance of, 96, 109; spiritual syncretism of, 149

Baby bust, 27–28

Baptism, 108, 173

Barna, G., 23–24, 44

Baudrillard, J., 147–149, 165

Beaudoin, T., 3–20, 190

Benedictine Monastery, Atchison, Kansas, 164–165

Benedictine monks, 37–38. *See also* Gregorian chant

Bergeron, K., 37–39, 145, 146

Berlin Wall, fall of, 11, 117

Bernard of Clairvaux, Saint, 82, 83, 179

Bernardi, J., 24, 29

Bible. *See* Christian Scriptures; Hebrew Scriptures; *specific book headings*

"Black Hole Sun" (Soundgarden), 45, 141; ambiguities expressed in, 122; criticism of the Church in, 54–56, 69–71, 92; eschatology in, 114–117, 118; human-divine intersection in, 84–86; Jesus image in, 69–71, 84–86; suffering servant image in, 110–111

Blasphemy, 122–127. *See also* Ambiguity

Blended families, 8, 86

Bodily adornment. *See* Fashion

Body marking: continuity and, 46; identity and, 141; sacramentality of, 77–79, 80

Bonhoeffer, D., 35, 99, 119, 173–174

Boom boxes, 12